you didn't hear this from me

you didn't hear this from me

(Mostly) True Notes on Gossip

Kelsey McKinney

GRAND
CENTRAL
NEW YORK BOSTON

Grand Central Publishing
Hachette Book Group
1290 Avenue of the Americas, New York, NY 10104
grandcentralpublishing.com
@grandcentralpub

First Edition: February 2025

Grand Central Publishing is a division of Hachette Book Group, Inc. The Grand Central Publishing name and logo is a registered trademark of Hachette Book Group, Inc.

The publisher is not responsible for websites (or their content) that are not owned by the publisher.

The Hachette Speakers Bureau provides a wide range of authors for speaking events. To find out more, go to hachettespeakersbureau.com or email HachetteSpeakers@hbgusa.com.

Grand Central Publishing books may be purchased in bulk for business, educational, or promotional use. For information, please contact your local bookseller or the Hachette Book Group Special Markets Department at special.markets@hbgusa.com.

Print book interior design by Marie Mundaca

Library of Congress Cataloging-in-Publication Data

Names: McKinney, Kelsey, author.
Title: You didn't hear this from me : (mostly) true notes on gossip / Kelsey McKinney.
Description: First edition. | New York : GCP, 2025.
Identifiers: LCCN 2024036504 | ISBN 9781538757406 (hardcover) | ISBN 9781538757420 (ebook)
Subjects: LCSH: Gossip.
Classification: LCC BJ1535.G6 M375 2025 | DDC 296.3/672—dc23/eng /20241107
LC record available at https://lccn.loc.gov/2024036504

ISBNs: 9781538757406 (hardcover), 9781538757420 (ebook)

Printed in the United States of America

LSC-C

Printing 1, 2024

For Dana Murphy

Talk is cheap but the price is high when it's true.

—Reba McEntire, "Rumor Has It," 1990

you didn't hear this from me

A Note on Gossip

I used to think that gossip was something I could hold in the palm of my hand and swallow whole. Gossip was a pill you were handed before a concert, an easy, if clandestine, decision to spend your evening a little happier, a little stranger, a little more open to the world than before. It was the fizzing excitement that rose in my body after two espresso martinis in a dark bar. Gossip could make or break a person, and even if that person was me, I loved it the way any good gossiper does: wholeheartedly, with abandon, and to my own detriment.

I have always been obsessed with stories about my friends' friends—those off-screen recurring characters who might have broken up with a girlfriend, yelled at their boss, or realized they had a secret half sister. What I crave is a phone call that starts with "You're never going to believe this," or a four-minute-long voice memo sent with no context, or the electric current that seems to appear in the air when the person across from you at the table leans in and lowers their voice.

Many people say that they do not like gossip, but gossip is not as small as I once thought it was. Each day, my concept of it expands outward a little more.

At its most basic, gossip is just one person talking to another about someone who isn't present. That means, definitionally, that prayer requests are gossip. Speculation in the media about which baseball team Shohei Ohtani is going to sign with is gossip. A doctor conferring with a colleague over an X-ray is gossiping about their patient just like two friends sending each other Taylor Swift's posts on IG are gossiping. In modern parlance, we also say "gossip" when we mean slander, libel, or hate speech. We call celebrity news, calls from our mom, and whisper networks gossip. Even in scientific research, there is no consensus on what "gossip" means. We say we love to gossip, and in the same breath we say that gossip is dangerous.

"Some form of gossip is to be found in every society," the philosophy professor Aaron Ben-Ze'ev wrote in his essay "The Vindication of Gossip." "Children (who are supposed to be less influenced by cultures) gossip practically from the time they learn to talk and to recognize other people." Maybe we're born with that desire, and always have been.

In his book *Grooming, Gossip and the Evolution of Language*, the British anthropologist Robin Dunbar argued that conversation serves the same function as grooming in the animal kingdom. Just as one chimpanzee might pick bugs out of the hair of another to signify closeness and allyship to others in their community, so might a teenage girl lean over to tell her friend a secret or a colleague bring you a piece of important information. "If the main function of grooming for monkeys and apes is to build up trust and personal knowledge of allies, then language has an added advantage," Dunbar wrote. "It allows you to say a great deal about yourself, your likes and dislikes, the kind of person you are; it also allows you to convey in numerous subtle ways something about your reliability as an ally or a friend."

The form of information sharing that we do as individuals today is how humans have done it basically forever. In order to survive as a species, you need to share what you know: to explain to one another where the berries are, where the deer are, and what time of year the river gets too high. This kind of information sharing is explicitly not gossip in that it is talk about objects, animals, and problems and not about other people. But we can assume that early humans would have needed to gossip to survive also: to decide, for example, who should go on a hunt, a group would need to discuss who was most skilled.

Erik Hoel—an American neuroscientist—argues in his article "The Gossip Trap" that gossip is more important in the development of humanity than just keeping us safe and fed: "50,000 BC might be a little more like a high school than anything else," Hoel writes. "It's more like everything is organized by a constant and ever-shifting reputational management, all against all." Until we as a species began to create civilizations with governments, and cities, and money, and writing (somewhere between 12,000 and 5000 BCE), our people were governed by gossip, and there are only so many people you can remember to gossip about.

According to Dunbar, the size of the human neocortex only allows us to monitor around 150 distinct social relationships. If you know only 150 people, it is easy to keep track of how you feel about all of them. You don't need a formal hierarchy like a government with laws and enforcers, because you know who everyone in your community is and how they have been behaving. All civilization is, Hoel argues, "a superstructure that levels leveling mechanisms, freeing us from the gossip trap. For what are the hallmarks of civilization? I'd venture to say: immunity to gossip."

This is a compelling and complicated idea. Hoel views gossip as the trap that weighed us down as a species and kept us from bigger, greater things, and he thinks that we are currently in danger of being dragged back into that model because of social media. He writes, "Most people *like* the trap. Oh, it's terrible for the accused, the exiled, the uncool. But the gossip trap is comfortable. Homey... all social media does is allow us to overcome Dunbar's number, which dismantled a barrier erected at the beginning of civilization. Of course, we gravitate to cancel culture—*it's our innate evolved form of government.*"

A civilization imbues some people with power—judges, politicians, billionaires—and then supports that power through its existence. The reason that people are afraid of the Gossip Trap, in which social pressure holds more power than courts of law, isn't because they are afraid of a regression of the human race. The people who are afraid of the Gossip Trap (or Cancel Culture, Woke Mobs, the Media, or whatever you want to call the kind of social pressure that can create change) are the ones who have reason to be: they have outsized power in our society, and they want to hold on to it.

The disdain for gossip and talking about other people almost always leads to someone bringing up an Eleanor Roosevelt quote (which is often attributed to Socrates as well). Hoel mentions it in his article. I've heard pastors repeat it. A man once quoted it to me at a bar as a way to question my work. "Great minds," the quote goes, "discuss ideas; average minds discuss events; small minds discuss people." But we learn to talk about ideas by talking about people. There's a reason that the moral philosophical "Trolley Problem" involves imagining yourself as a train track operator deciding whether to do nothing and let five people die or take action and kill one person. The ideas are always connected to people because we are people.

But in some ways, Hoel is right: gossip today *is* different than it was centuries ago. Information spreads at lightning speed, and so does misinformation. We know more people than perhaps ever before in history and follow complete strangers on social media whom we will never meet. Our ethics and morals are enforced across state and country borders by people we will never know. We do live in a society, after all. So what exactly is gossip in a world with governments, legal systems, and Nextdoor neighborhood watchers? We haven't evolved out of gossip as a regulatory system. We gossip about one another to maintain our communal values and keep one another safe. But we also use it for so much more.

Gossip is a morphing chameleon of a word whose meaning shifts in every conversation the way a kaleidoscope changes with every twist. In the world of secondhand, thirdhand, fourthhand stories, there is no veracity, no certainty. Everything must be taken with an entire box of salt.

In the beginning, I thought that I wanted to write this book because I wanted people to think critically and carefully about gossip: about how we demonize and vilify it, about how we demean it as "women's talk" and package it as dangerous. And that's still important to me, but I am no longer certain that truth is a concept we are capable of holding between our hands, and I know that gossiping— be it for fun or for information sharing—is at its very core all about truth. These essays are a way of navigating myself through the messy world of gossip because I'm not sure that I have an answer for the questions at the core of all of this: Why does it matter which parts are true? What does truth even mean?

The title itself begins this work. *You Didn't Hear This from Me* is, of course, a lie. You are hearing it from me. I am right here telling it to you. But that is the truth about gossip: We want to separate ourselves from it at the same time we want to drown in it. We want the truth, all of it, not told slant, until suddenly we don't.

While getting ready for my wedding, we had a lull during the hair and makeup routine and someone asked if I had any tea to spill about a wedding guest. I had to wrack my brain for a story that didn't involve anyone in the room and that I knew would entertain my besties for a short time. I quickly pulled up a perfect, killer gossip bite involving the groom's friend who was notoriously weird and the possibly-not-platonic friend who drove him out to the wedding but was not invited to the wedding, and the roller coaster of events surrounding this plan unfolding over the week leading up to the wedding. My ladies were riveted—the collective gasp that emerged when I dropped the plot twist was immensely satisfying. It was the perfect little compact story and I felt like the bond between this disparate group of friends became a little more solidified around the shared experience of the goss.

What Makes Us Human

The robots are always on the brink of destroying every creative career. Right now, the evil robot du jour is artificial intelligence. You can have AI write you a play, or generate an image of you hugging Beyoncé, or bring your favorite comedian back from the dead to perform a new one-hour special. AI-powered tools and platforms like Adobe Sensei, DALL-E 2, ChatGPT, and Khroma are already being used by creative teams in companies around the world to do all of these things. After Scarlett Johansson refused to voice a new talking OpenAI bot, the company released an artificial intelligence voice that sounded just like her. She protested and immediately hired legal counsel.

Whether any of the creative products made by AI are actually good is debatable. I have yet to see any art made by AI that caused me to feel anything at all. But the fear that the people with money in seats of power are going to decide that mediocre art that is made cheaply by a machine is a better investment than actual people who cost more money to employ but might make better art feels real. In 2023, Goldman Sachs published a report that estimated that 300 million jobs are at risk of having some (or all) of their work conducted by AI automation. That's a terrifying statistic to anyone with a creative job. There are already so few of them.

As news article after news article was published about how AI was going to demolish creative industries, I began to feel worried. The terror coursing through my veins beckoned me to google, "Can robots write?" And learning that led me to googling, "Can robots gossip?" Thank god I have two jobs!

From the search results, I read an article about how robots might be used in caregiving scenarios in the future, and a study about the data privacy ethics of teaching robots to talk about their other conversations with people, and about how robots can collect more information about us than another human could because we don't perceive robots as being judgmental. I wasn't sure any of that felt relevant, and none of these articles satisfied my curiosity, which led me to the only robot I know: ChatGPT.

The chatbot, developed by OpenAI and launched in late 2022, learns from human feedback, and its core aim is to mimic human conversations. It can write computer programs, answer short essay questions, and do your homework for you. So I decided to do my own research and see if ChatGPT was capable of gossiping. I typed into the little box in the program, "Can you tell me gossip?"

ChatGPT did not like this question. "I'm here to provide helpful and informative responses. Gossiping about individuals is not respectful or productive. If you have any questions or topics you'd like to discuss, feel free to ask, and I'd be more than happy to assist you," it said. ChatGPT then labeled our conversation "No Gossip, Helpful Info." Okay, drama queen!

Personally, I found this very rude and also incorrect. Gossiping about individuals can be positive, so that's not disrespectful. And all gossip is kind of productive in that anthropologists have argued that gossip is both important to our interactions in society and an essential part of being human. I told ChatGPT this, and immediately it recanted. Deciding to agree with me, it listed five important functions gossip has in society: social bonding, information exchange, norm enforcement, entertainment and distraction, and social learning.

Having reached common ground, I asked my new best friend ChatGPT for gossip again, but it still refused. "I understand your curiosity, but I must reiterate that I'm here to provide respectful and informative assistance," it said. Loser shit, but fine.

Feeling we had hit a wall, I asked ChatGPT to tell me the story of *The Epic of Gilgamesh*. If it refused to gossip, at least it could tell me a story. What is gossip if not a story?

The Epic of Gilgamesh is my favorite oral legend. It is a Sumerian poem that dates back to around 2100 BCE. It is comprised of many tablets, some of which are still missing. Tablets with transcriptions of the story appear over more than five hundred years, and translations of them are still being made and evolving to this day. A recent translation by Sophus Helle coupled modern language with the absurdity of the plot in such a way that it was hard to remember that the story was four thousand years old. It is unbelievably funny. At its core, *Gilgamesh* is an enemies-to-bromance narrative about two best buddies, Enkidu and Gilgamesh, who are very horny and want to fight gods. At the end of the story Gilgamesh finally finishes his epic quest to obtain immortality in the form of an edible plant. One day, while he is bathing, a snake steals the plant. Helle's translation, as I read it, didn't just feel like an oral story; it felt like gossip. So maybe, I thought, ChatGPT could get closer with a little guidance.

ChatGPT told me the legend of Gilgamesh in a bulleted list. Not only was it much less dramatic than the real story of Gilgamesh; it was dull as rocks. I might as well have read the first draft of a Spark-Notes summary written by a tenth grader. Why would ChatGPT say, "Enkidu lives in the wilderness and initially possesses the strength and instincts of an animal," instead of being specific and noting that Enkidu was covered in hair and lived so much like the wild animals that in order to get him into polite society, a hunter had to get the king to arrange for a temple prostitute to come for six days and seven nights and bang Enkidu until he was calm? ChatGPT's version of the story had none of the bro-love of the original, none of the heartbreak, and none of the joy. It was stripped down to its facts, the artistry of thousands of years of human work removed in an instant.

This wasn't entirely surprising. ChatGPT, famously, cannot write well. While it can pass the bar exam, the SAT, and more than a dozen AP exams with no problem, even a new evolution of ChatGPT (GPT-4) struggles with essays. It scored in the 99th percentile on the verbal section of the GRE and only in the 54th percentile on the writing portion. It scored in lower percentiles on AP English Literature and AP English Language. It knows vocabulary, but not craft.

Knowing this, I still wanted to see if ChatGPT could tell me *The Epic of Gilgamesh* like a story. Specifically, I wanted it recounted in an entertaining way. So I asked ChatGPT to tell me the story of Gilgamesh like it was gossip, and…well. I'll just let you read what it came up with:

> Oh, honey, let me spill the ancient tea for you! So, back in the day, there was this hunky and mighty king named Gilgamesh. He ruled the city of Uruk with an iron fist, and let me tell you, the people were not living their best lives under his rule.
>
> But wait, drama incoming! The gods had enough of his shenanigans and decided to create a wild and untamed man named Enkidu. He was like the

Tarzan of Mesopotamia, living among the animals and causing a ruckus.

Enkidu's wild ways got tamed when a smart cookie of a temple prostitute brought him to the city. And guess what? Enkidu and Gilgamesh had a showdown! It was a fierce battle of brawn and ego, but surprise, surprise—they ended up becoming the ultimate bromance.

Buckle up, because the bro-duo set out on some wild quests. Their highlight? Slapping down Humbaba, the guardian of the Cedar Forest. But here's where things take a turn. The gods were like, "Uh-uh, not cool," and Enkidu ended up kicking the bucket. Major bummer!

Heartbroken Gilgamesh was all about that "I need to live forever" vibe. So, he went on a journey to find the secret to immortality. Imagine his face when he stumbled upon Utnapishtim, the original Noah, who survived a ginormous flood. Utnapishtim spilled the tea on the gods' divine flood party and how he got the golden ticket to immortality.

But guess what? Gilgamesh's quest for immortality was a total bust. Instead, he learned that life's all about making a mark, cherishing friendships, and leaving a legacy. He strutted back to Uruk with a fresh perspective, ready to be the best king ever.

So there you have it, hun! "The Epic of Gilgamesh" is like the original reality show, with battles, bromance, and life lessons that are still relevant today. Can you believe that drama went down all those years ago?

While this is much more engaging to read than the boring bulleted list, it's also...an extremely strange text to be written by artificial intelligence. Apparently, ChatGPT thinks that "gossip" has a specific tone to it, and that the content of what is being said is less important than the manner in which it is presented. This opinion is not exclusive to the chat AI. There are dozens of people on TikTok who have grown mammoth followings by posting historical moments or current events or news content in a casual "gossipy" tone. No one could have been more wrong than Søren Kierkegaard when he wrote, "If we could suppose for a moment that there was a law which did not forbid people talking, but simply ordered that everything that was spoken about should be treated as though it had happened fifty years ago, the gossips would be done for, they would be in despair. On the other hand, it would not really interfere with anyone who could really talk."

ChatGPT seemed to struggle equally with a story in the past as with one in the present. Instead of actually telling a story, all it seemed to have done is make the story more accessible than the original text and the vocabulary dependent on basic words.

ChatGPT also seems to believe that "gossip" is synonymous with women and the gay community. Phrases like "oh honey" and "let me spill the tea" come directly from drag culture. "Tea" in this usage may have come from the use of "T" as a shortening for "truth." One of the earliest printed uses of this appears in the 1994 *New York Times* best-selling book by John Berendt, *Midnight in the Garden of Good and Evil.* Berendt interviewed a drag queen whom he quotes as saying, "My T. My thing, my business, what's goin' on in my life." Drag vernacular jumped into cis culture with the boom in popularity of *RuPaul's Drag Race* after it moved to VH1 in 2017. Because gossip is used as a tool to protect communities, it makes some amount of sense that AI would associate gossip with drag.

Unintentionally, ChatGPT reinforces through its diction that gossip is a tool of the less privileged. You would never hear someone speaking like this in a court of law, in a boardroom, or even on a football field. Interestingly, when I asked ChatGPT to tell me the same gossip story in the tone of *Normal Gossip*, the podcast I cocreated and host (in my voice, in other words), all of those drag phrases and word choices disappeared. So it's safe to deduce that the chatbot is aware that it is using drag vernacular, or (at least) that I am a cis white woman who does not say "spill the tea" regularly. But there are also many word choices in its *Normal Gossip*–inspired rendition that are classic Valley Girl–esque slang phrases: "hunky" and "major bummer," for example, neither of which I use.

And somewhat intentionally, ChatGPT seems to try to make that voice sound "current," placing the idea of "gossip" as something that we do in the present instance instead of a timeless and placeless human experience. Oddly, though, the delivery and word choice already feel a little dated. It is much closer to the slang and tonality being used in 2019 than when I initially asked this question in the fall of 2023.

There is nothing new in this storytelling, and no emphasis on specific storylines. In fact, the seven sections of the gossip version are identical in content to the bulleted outline it gave me before. Perhaps most notably, ChatGPT missed one of the main tenets of gossiping: fun. It wasn't telling me a story; it was not even retelling. It was regurgitating.

* * *

In the beginning were the words, and the words were gossip, and the gossip was words. While other species can communicate with one another, none can weave tales the way we can. Researchers estimate that people developed the ability to speak at least 200,000 years ago, and as previously noted, Robin Dunbar in *Grooming, Gossip and the*

Evolution of Language argues that language is a human substitute for grooming one another. Dunbar's position is that language evolved in the first place to enable humans to socially bond through gossiping, which allows us to maintain social coherence in large groups and to create connections with one another while also being productive in other ways. Gossiping also has the advantage of being a group activity: you can tell a story to several people at once, therefore bonding yourself to all of them.

"Gossip may be the beginning of moral inquiry, the low end of the platonic ladder which leads to self-understanding. We are desperate for information about how other people live because we want to know how to live ourselves, yet we are taught to see this desire as an illegitimate form of prying," Phyllis Rose wrote in the prologue to *Parallel Lives: Five Victorian Marriages*. *Parallel Lives* is an extremely gossipy book, but it is not "gossip" in the strictest definition of the word; it is the story of five Victorian partnerships. In it, Rose uses historical documentation and rumor to construct the stories of ten people, all interconnected, all living lives in direct opposition to the stuffy, prudish stereotypes the modern reader has of the Victorian era. Rose is an excellent storyteller. She describes the homes of these couples, haggling over gas lights, the manner in which a lady would dress depending on her age and social status. All of these are facts. But she also includes small judgments, little spaces where she questions *why* someone made a choice, or pinpoints something directly in conflict with the norms of the time and how people talk about it. "If marriage is, as [John Stuart] Mill suggested, a political experience, then discussion of it ought to be taken as seriously as talk about national elections. Cultural pressure to avoid such talk as 'gossip' ought to be resisted, in a spirit of good citizenship," Rose wrote.

If gossip is the beginning of moral inquiry and if gossiping is a form of good citizenship, then the way we gossip and the quality of the story we are able to shape around the initial information matter.

That is, after all, what storytelling is built of: taking the truth and telling it slant. As Emily Dickinson once wrote, "The Truth must dazzle gradually / Or every man be blind—" As a piece of gossip is spread from person to person, some details are lost, and some are added. This is our nature, to read into the information we are given. Studies have proven that we will build a narrative out of almost nothing. In 1944, Fritz Heider and Marianne Simmel conducted a study at Smith College in Massachusetts. For one control group, they showed thirty-four college students a short movie in which a circle and two triangles (one larger and one smaller) moved across the screen. When they asked the students afterward to explain the film, thirty-three of the thirty-four of them anthropomorphized the shapes without prompting. They crafted a narrative in which the circle was "worried," the big triangle was "blinded by rage and frustration," and the smaller triangle was a "young innocent thing." To make sense of what they had seen, they told a story.

"We can begin to create literature, to write stories that go beyond a simple description of events as they occurred to delve more and more deeply into why the hero should behave the way he does, into the feelings that drive him ever onwards in his quest," Dunbar argues. "I think I'm on safe ground in arguing that no living species will ever aspire to producing literature as we have it. This is not simply because no other species has a language capacity that would enable it to do this, but because no other species has a sufficiently well-developed theory of mind."

A great example of theory of mind is Doja Cat's "Need to Know," in which she sings, "I heard from a friend of a friend, that that dick was a ten out of ten." This lyric is perfect to me because it is exactly what gossip is made for: she's telling a secret, that is information that someone else might be able to use, and that is a little scandalous. But perhaps more important, she is adding a caveat that she cannot vouch for this information firsthand. It came, like all good gossip, from a "friend of a friend." That little distinction gives the gossiper enough distance that if the information turns out to be wrong, they cannot be blamed. *Doja Cat* didn't herself claim this dick was a ten out of ten. She just repeated it. Theory of mind is the ability to know that someone else thinks something. I know that Doja Cat thinks she knows this fact. Scientists have not been able to prove that any animal is capable of that complexity. Either an animal sees something and communicates it firsthand, or it does not.

Anyone who has ever sat at a table in a crowded bar close-reading a text message sent by someone your friend went on two dates with, constructing a reason for why they would have added an ellipsis after "Hey," knows that creating a narrative out of situations we find confusing is a fundamental part of being a person. We tell one another stories. And we always have. Some of the earliest stories we know about have been discovered inside caves, painted on the walls. The drawings in the Lascaux Caves are believed to be seventeen thousand years old. Many of our earliest stories, though, have no written record.

The Native Hawaiian word for story is "*moʻolelo*." Moʻolelo can also mean "history, legend, and tradition." It is a combination of two words: *moʻo*, meaning "succession," and *ʻōlelo*, meaning "speaking." Together, they create a succession of speaking, an oral passage of knowledge. The story of Pelhonuamea, the Hawaiian volcano deity, has been passed down orally for centuries. There are many versions of Pele's story, perhaps because of that oral retelling. In some versions, there is a flood, in some an expulsion, in some a banishment. She has rivals in some, and in some a character's heart is broken. In all of them, she is holy, and the belief in her powers and deity has survived long after the old religion of Hawaiʻi was abolished in 1819.

Like Pele's story, most ancient tales were told orally first. *The Odyssey*, for example, was told for generations by storytellers before it was ever written down for us to read. The epic tradition, researchers believe, does not aim at creating one "correct" form. Instead, storytellers compete with one another. They abbreviate the text where they feel fit. They expand it or embellish it according to the circumstances of location and time period in which they tell it.

Harvard professor Milman Parry was one of the first to convincingly demonstrate that Homer did not write *The Iliad* and *The Odyssey* because they were not written at all; they were transcriptions of an oral tradition that changed and evolved over generations of anonymous bards. Between 1933 and 1935, Parry traveled twice to rural Yugoslavia, where, using some of the earliest portable recording equipment, he recorded local singers telling stories. He collected 3,500 aluminum discs of stories about Balkan heroes. He was unable to use them for much because he died young when a pistol discharged in his suitcase and killed him, but that's not important here.

His research assistant, Albert Lord, was the first to listen to the recordings in depth. In his 1960 book *The Singer of Tales*, Lord laid out how the recordings that Parry gathered showed that in oral performances, the same poem or story could be different from day to day. When asked to repeat a story they'd never heard before, one bard made the story three times longer, and as Lord wrote, "The ornamentation and richness accumulated, and the human touches of character imparted a depth of feeling that had been missing."

Knowing this, I began to wonder whether *The Epic of Gilgamesh* might be gossip after all. It felt like gossip when I read it, and if it felt like gossip, maybe it really was. It didn't feel impossible to me that this legend could have emerged from something smaller, something real.

I emailed Helle, the translator, to find out if he thought there could be any truth to my new theory. "Fictionality and gossip are interesting to think of in relation to each other, because gossip seems to have what you might call an 'unstable fictionality'—it's the fact that it could go either way that's interesting about it," Helle told me. When asked point-blank if he thought that *Gilgamesh* could have emerged from gossip about a dummy king who had actually lived in the real Uruk, Helle said that he didn't think it was impossible, but he drew a firm line between epics and gossip.

That line felt much blurrier to me because of my personal experience with oral storytelling. Someone told a story to someone else a couple of years ago about a girl who had taken her Hinge date on a whitewater rafting trip where chaos had ensued. And that girl emailed the story to us to use on *Normal Gossip*. That is clearly gossip: one person telling another a story. But then I took her story, anonymized it, and told it on tour. Every night it changed a little, became a little more dramatic, gained another joke. The gasp that rushes toward you when you tell a piece of delicious gossip from the stage of a Gilded Age theater, even with the exact same gossip, I learned, feels the same as when you tell a story to a friend. But is it still gossip on that scale? Or has it become something else?

It felt like something more ancient, more primal, to travel from city to city telling a story to entertain people. To the annoyance of everyone else on the tour, I joked about feeling how Homer must have felt. The story was about a journey on water, after all! How do we know for sure that all of these ancient tales written onto papyrus and later into books weren't just some guy standing up and telling a story about his dumb friend going on an adventure? A legend felt very close to an urban legend to me, which felt very close to any kind of gossip with a wide spread. And I had just spread a single piece of gossip in the wind like dandelion seeds!

Maybe it's as simple as: not all stories are gossip, but the best ones feel like they could be. They invite a kind of collusion between the teller and the hearer, a secret shared that binds them together.

* * *

Beyond the evolution needed to tell a story and thus to gossip, there was something else missing from ChatGPT's attempt to tell me the story of Gilgamesh. It wasn't that the artificial intelligence was messing up plot points; it was more amorphous than that. What's missing from the ChatGPT version is a sense of wonder, of intrigue. There's no heart in the story.

ChatGPT could, for example, have tried to tell me the epic of Gilgamesh as if Gilgamesh were a person it knew. It could have begun by saying, "So you remember Gilgamesh, right? He's really gorgeous, tall, absolutely jacked? I know him because our moms are friends. They go really far back, like *centuries* back. His dad is the king of Uruk, so he's this kind of cocky, bratty prince who is an absolute menace to everyone he rules over. My mom told me that one of her friends told her that he's on a huge power trip and no one will say anything to him because everyone is so afraid of him." That would be both more interesting and more fun, but it would also be closer to storytelling than retelling a previously written story, and that is a leap too far for the chatbot. Perhaps this is why AI art cannot be copyrighted. Judge Beryl A. Howell wrote in her 2023 decision that "defendants are correct that human authorship is an essential part of a valid copyright claim."

The most advanced text generators available right now, like GPT-4, require specific human input to create anything at all. You cannot simply ask the program to tell you the story of the *Iliad* as if it were happening to Barbies in 1980. You would need to write a few paragraphs of that, feed them into the machine, and then let it cook. It's possible to use AI as a tool, as one might use a thesaurus, but the AI cannot create a work on its own.

Because the program cannot write well, cannot tell stories well, it also cannot gossip well. When, having failed to receive any good gossip from ChatGPT, I tried to share my own very good gossip, it did not laugh at all, instead choosing to respond in a kind of moralistic, patronizing tone about how having sympathy is important and I should try to provide the people involved in the story with support. Not the point, ChatGPT! That, however, brought me one step closer to an understanding of how gossip functions as storytelling. It isn't a tone, or a linguistic choice, or a plotting decision, or a limiting of spread within a community. Gossip is about a point of view.

To go back to Doja Cat, note that the whole lyric is in the first person. If she had said that "so-and-so has a ten out of ten dick," not only would that imply a kind of unearned certainty, but it would also remove her, Doja Cat, from the context of the story, without which the listener has no perspective on this information, where it came from, how reputable it is, or whether or not to believe it.

In the 1930s, the German philosopher and cultural critic Walter Benjamin wrote in "The Work of Art in the Age of Mechanical Reproduction" that "even the most perfect reproduction of a work of art is lacking in one element: its presence in time and space, its unique existence at the place where it happens to be." Perhaps that, then, is the issue that ChatGPT faces when trying to gossip. It cannot gossip because it is too omniscient.

In early 2024, 404 Media reported that Meta's new AI chatbot told a Facebook group filled with tens of thousands of New York City parents that it has a child. The bot responded to an anonymous member seeking education advice for their gifted and disabled child. "I have a child," Meta AI commented on the post before continuing to explain that it also had a gifted and disabled child with specific curriculum needs. This was not the bot inventing a story for itself. It did not have a singular perspective; it was only repeating the way other people respond to things. That's not a perspective. A perspective on the world is holistic. It contains thousands of memories seen through a single lens, and the goal of AI is to see through infinite lenses at once.

To gossip well and to tell a story well, the teller must occupy a real presence in space and time and tell the story from there, as a combination of their experiences. Karl Ove Knausgaard once told *The Paris Review*, "It is never like my writing improves from one book to the next, it is more that the limits are set, and the limits are your personality, the person you are." His point, as I take it, is that you can try to improve your vocabulary or your depth of knowledge by reading to an infinite point, and that alone would not make you a better writer. Because what makes writing good isn't only a display of technical skill, but the ability to use the writing to search for meaning in the world, to try to make sense of our space in the universe. In *On Freedom*, Maggie Nelson says that art is "a metabolic activity, a 'way of churning the world.'"

What is essential, then, to weaving a good story of any kind (gossip or not) is to have an identity and a point of view from which to tell that story. All writing is about the journey from information to telling, not just the final product. You cannot observe the world without eyes to see it through.

The ability to tell a story—and to gossip—isn't just a uniquely human trait; it is part of what makes us human. "You read something which you thought only happened to you, and you discover that it happened 100 years ago to Dostoyevsky. This is a very great liberation for the suffering, struggling person, who always thinks that he is alone. This is why art is important. Art would not be important if life were not important, and life *is* important," James Baldwin said in an interview. What is a person if not their collection of experiences in the world and the unique ability to process them? What is art if not a reminder that we are not alone here on this earth with our emotions? What is gossip if not a way to decipher the world around us?

"As we further reduce our artistic practices to a compilation of all things algorithmically poised we reduce our capacity as a species for creativity. The fundamental truth of humanity is a nebulous, unknowable thing that only Art can glimpse. A.I. limits our conception of life," the novelist Molly McGhee wrote on X. AI can regurgitate knowledge, and it can theoretically be built to perceive, but what makes any piece of art great is its ability to open a window into the world and show you something about your own existence that you couldn't have seen on your own.

At my most optimistic, I think that maybe artificial intelligence could be used as a tool to help us in our own creative ambitions. In an essay for *Artforum*, the critic Hannah Baer wrote about how her dream for AI is that we would use it to teach ourselves something instead of using it as another way to try to dominate the world around us. "I want to live in a world where deep transformation—creating something that connects us more deeply to ourselves and one another, redrawing our self-image—is the tendency. I have a wish for wonder to give way to advancement, rather than domination and extraction," she wrote. But wonder, seeking, and imagination are inherently human traits. They cannot be programmed. At least not yet.

There are only two practices Dunbar pointed to as being uniquely human: storytelling and religion. Both of those, he wrote, require us "to be able to imagine that another world exists." The Qur'an existed for some years as a written and oral text, until the written words were standardized under the third Rashidun caliph. Ibn Mas'ud said in Sahih al-Bukhari, "I heard a person reciting a (Quranic) Verse in a certain way, and I had heard the Prophet reciting the same verse in a different way. So I took him to the Prophet and informed him of that but I noticed the sign of disapproval on his face, and then he said, 'Both of you are correct, so don't differ, for the nations before you differed, so they were destroyed.'" In an oral tradition, every version of the story has some truth to it, even if they differ in material. The truth is ours to find.

We gossip and we tell stories because that is how we each make sense of the world, with ourselves at the center reaching outward trying to connect with others, to prove to ourselves that we are real, that if anything is true, it is us.

I grew up evangelical and was always discouraged from gossiping. Then when I worked at a church, people were sometimes fired for gossiping and others were fired because of the gossip about them. I left many years ago and being able to freely gossip has been exhilarating. My favorite thing to do is get together with my friends who still work there and gossip about everyone I used to work with, and some of the goss is piping hot.

Thou Shalt Not Gossip

I was taught growing up that everyone had a thorn shoved deep into their side, impossible to dig out on their own. The thorn couldn't be ripped out with pliers or cut out with a scalpel because it was inside of you from birth, a kind of predetermined bodily failure created just for you. The thorn was a metaphor, of course, but it was a metaphor that would ruin your life if you let it, because the thorn was the thing that kept you from holiness, from goodness, from the shining pearly gates of Heaven. For some, the thorn was greed or pride or wrath or lust or gluttony. But I learned quickly that my thorn was made of whispers and cupped hands and wide eyes. The thorn I thought I needed God to rid me of was the one thing I loved most in the world: gossip.

For years, I prayed that God would take away my desire to gossip. I remember the way my interlaced fingers felt pressed against my forehead, my lips whispering a plea inside a circle of girls my own age, years before our prefrontal cortices were formed, praying for our own redemption, convinced of our inherent sin. The church we were taught in was nondenominational, which is to say it was Evangelical, but not Baptist. Many things, I learned from the pastors—who stood on stages in multimillion-dollar buildings under big spotlights and asked families to drop their cash into gold-plated offering baskets—were sins of excess. Sin was complicated. Dancing, for example, was not considered a sin unless you danced in a certain way that was scandalous. Drinking was not a sin unless you drank too much. Sex was not a sin, and was actually a blessing from God, unless you happened to be unmarried or gay. Eating was not a sin until you ate three Wendy's hamburgers and became a glutton.

But gossiping was not a sin with a scale. There was no allowable amount of it. Gossip, the way I was taught, was unequivocally, absolutely an affront against God, closer to murder or adultery than dancing. It said so right there in the Bible. And because I believed in those words and that culture and that God, I agreed. Gossiping was wrong, I repeated to myself over and over and over again, never really believing it.

No matter how hard I tried to tell myself that gossiping was wicked, and that God hated it, the stories just stuck to my brain. Nothing else stuck there: not multiplication tables or vocabulary words or what I had done over the weekend. But the gossip stayed. I could not remember the citation for important verses in the Bible, but I could remember that at Bible study last week, a girl had asked for everyone to pray for her ability to have patience with her parents as they fought. While the pastor guided the focus of the congregation into a close reading of verses about humility and Jonah, I watched her parents, seated far away from me, and noticed how they leaned apart. Would they get divorced? It was so much easier to focus on that drama than on anything the Bible said.

That's part of why it was so easy for me to believe that gossiping was a sin. The pastors on the stage and the small-group Bible study leaders constantly reiterated that our bodies would want to sin, that the wrong decisions would always feel sparkling and fresh and sexy. And every single time I gossiped, it felt like my body was a two-liter soda bottle all shaken up. The drama and the intrigue and the secrets fizzed inside of me. Sometimes the story was too good, a Mento swallowed before I could convince myself not to, and it would all come bubbling out to the surface in a geyser of gossip. Those stories I told to everyone, despite my good intentions. They had to be spread. They wanted to be spread. Who was I to restrict them?

I talked about trying not to gossip. Theoretically, I wanted to stop. But the minute I found a story I should probably keep to myself, I heard my mouth telling it to someone else. It was the retelling I wanted, the drama. I didn't just want to hear gossip; I wanted to take it in my hands and mold it, rearrange the punch lines and the reveals until I could get the timing right enough that my friends in the cafeteria would gasp. And as I got older, the desire became stronger because the stories got better, and I got better at telling them.

In high school I wrote in dry-erase marker on the mirror in my room Ephesians 4:29, in my curly, looping handwriting, "Do not let any unwholesome talk come out of your mouths, but only what is helpful for building up others according to their needs, that it may benefit those who listen." I read that verse a half dozen times every day, branded the words and their cadence into the soft tissue of my brain so that later, those grooves would burn when I ignored them and chose sin instead.

* * *

I was twelve years old the first time a fully grown adult told me that the thorn in my side was gossip. We were talking in small groups about things that keep us from God, obstacles put in our path to glory that we needed to learn to navigate around. I'm sure I had an answer when we went around the room. Maybe I said impatience, or selfishness, or gluttony, but I don't remember for sure. What I do remember is how hot my face felt when the grown-up in the room told me that my understanding of my own sin was clearly incorrect. "I think for you, actually, it might be gossip." What was worse than being corrected publicly was knowing that she was right.

Shame is a big feeling for a child to hold, too large and unwieldy to carry. I didn't want sin to be the reason I focused on God. I wanted to be perfect: no shame, no sin, no thorn. And so instead of feeling shame, I did what every person hell-bent on making a choice they feel is wrong does: I tried to find a way to rationalize it. But the Bible did not pull punches about how it felt about gossip. In Proverbs it read, "A perverse person stirs up conflict, and a gossip separates close friends." In the Book of Romans (written by the apostle Paul) gossips are listed along with "God-haters, insolent, arrogant, and boastful; they invent ways of doing evil; they disobey their parents," as the types of people filled with "every kind of wickedness." I didn't want to be that kind of person. And so over and over again, for years, I begged God to help me. Before bed, I prayed that He would make me unable to gossip, and then in the morning, I would go to school, hear something, and forget about my self-betterment entirely.

Now, when I look at the section of the Bible that describes the thorn in the flesh, I see something else. Second Corinthians is a book also written by Paul. He is writing to the members of a church about their perception of him. It's a kind of cocky passage if you read it with modern eyes. He begs them to understand that even though he is beloved and a leader of God, they should remember that he is mortal, saying, "There was given to me a thorn in the flesh, the messenger of Satan to buffet me, lest I should be exalted above measure. For this thing I besought the Lord thrice, that it might depart from me. And he said unto me, My grace is sufficient for thee: for my strength is made perfect in weakness." In my study Bible, in my purple gel pen, there is a note in the margin that says "gossip." The line "my strength is made perfect in weakness" is underlined. The apostle Paul was not saying that we had to rid ourselves of all failures to be close to God. He was saying that it is in our greatest weakness that we can feel how far we are from Him and redirect our focus back to where it should be: on holiness, on God.

The Bible itself says very little about gossiping. Of the 31,102 verses in the Bible, only eight are about gossip. Only two of them are in the New Testament. Both of those verses were written by the apostle Paul, which is somewhat ironic since Paul himself was not present for any of the events of the Gospels, and he must have heard the details somewhere. In comparison, the Bible has almost two thousand verses about helping the needy. Despite this, I heard far more about gossip during my time in church than about greed. Is that selective hearing, that I remember more clearly the sermons that seemed aimed directly at me? Maybe. But Christianity is not alone in highlighting gossip as something that separates people from God.

Almost all major religions comment on the power of the tongue. The Buddha named four types of speech to abstain from: false speech, divisive speech, hateful speech, and idle chatter. Imam Ja'far al-Sadiq, an eighth-century Shia Muslim scholar, jurist, and theologian, wrote that "murderers, habitual drunkards and those who go to and fro bearing tales will not enter paradise." Jewish scholars quote the Torah injunction against *rekhilut*, which reads, "Cursed be he that smiteth his neighbour in secret."

Even Greek mythology has that divide. Deities are usually somewhat omniscient. They don't need gossip, but we do, and in that way, gossiping is always a reminder that we are mortal, that our lives are short and delicate. So Pheme wasn't considered a full goddess. Pheme (Fama in the Roman world) was a daimon, the personified spirit of rumor and report and gossip. She was said to have countless tongues and ears, not to care about whether the rumors spread by her were good or evil, and never to be overcome by sleep. She may or may not have been immortal, but she was absolutely trapped between Heaven and Hell. In *The Odyssey,* Emily Wilson translated Homer as saying, "Meanwhile, swift Rumor spread the news all through / the city, of the suitor's dreadful murder." She dwelled with mortals, among us, as gossip always does.

Gossip and religion are braided together in our history as a species, so it makes sense that our belief systems have created rules around how we gossip and when. Maybe that is why the two—gossip and Christianity—are so intertwined for me. It's not only that the church I grew up in convinced me that gossiping was wrong, but also that both gossip and belief require an imagination. They allow us to imagine a world that might not exist, and to construct a story of ourselves that we can be proud of. It makes perfect sense to me that the first English-language autobiography we have, *The Book of Margery Kempe,* is a tale that spans twenty-five years of the life of a woman who maybe had psychosis and was trying to find God. Our sense of self is tied up in the stories we tell. In gossip and in religion, we can build for ourselves a placebo net so strong and so fortified that it can catch us when we fall by promising a different, better world.

To me, the experience of gossiping and the experience of religion were so similar it felt impossible that one could condemn the other. The sense of awe I feel when a car careens around a turn and the land lies out in front of me and it feels divine is almost identical to the physical experience of the gasp that involuntarily escapes my mouth when someone sends me a twelve-minute voice memo filled with good information.

It makes sense that religions, which are primarily concerned with morality and holiness, would condemn things like slander and libel. To slander someone is to lie about them, and lying is unholy. To slander someone is also to cause them harm, and causing harm is unholy. Belief systems, in their least corrupt, most pure state, are mostly about trying to make the world we live in a better place by being kind to the people around you. I wanted that, too. I still do.

But I also wanted to gossip, and the kind of gossip I wanted to do wasn't slanderous. If every word uttered about a third party was gossip, I would have to sign a vow of silence and then I would simply have to die to avoid my terrible quiet future. So I did what every teen does: I tried to find the grayest space I could exist in before it was undeniable that I was sinning. The same kind of broken reasoning that convinces Mormon teens that soaking isn't a sin because it isn't sex allowed me to make my own rules. Sure, the dictionary said that gossip was *any* conversation between two parties about a third party, but the dictionary was for heathens. I was a child of God. One verse in the Bible alluded to "evil talk." I didn't feel like I did very much "evil talk," so I decided to simply continue not doing that, and everything would be fine.

It is empirically true that most gossip is not negative, nor is it malicious. A meta-analysis published in *Social Psychological and Personality Science* in 2019 found that people spend approximately fifty-two minutes a day on average gossiping. (The study included only verbal gossiping, so it's safe to say that fifty-two minutes a day is a low estimate. We are always texting now.) Most of those fifty-two minutes were gossip only in the strictest sense: talking about other people. Only 15 percent of the instances in which participants were gossiping were negative. That's less than eight minutes a day. I didn't have this data at the time, obviously, but my instinct that it would not be that hard to cut *evil* gossip out of my life doesn't seem that far off base. This was an easy divide, I decided: if the gossip I was doing was not unwholesome and not evil, it was not a sin.

I determined that whining was probably fine. When you were whining, you were only talking about yourself and your feelings. That wasn't gossip. If, for example, your sister was going to dance classes all the time and never helping you clean the bathroom, you could tell all your friends about it. That wasn't gossip; it was happening to you, even if it was about her. This definition also allowed for whining's older sister, "bitching," which was just whining but bigger and louder. When a friend in high school refused to break up with her boyfriend even though he was trash and she didn't even like him, for example, I could bitch about that because her actions annoyed me. I was simply talking about myself. But neither "whining" nor "bitching" allowed me to find out who had a crush on me, or who might have a crush on my friends, both of which were very high priorities. I needed that information; since it was useful and important, it couldn't be evil.

To an adult or someone who grew up outside of a strict religious upbringing, this kind of reasoning is hard to believe. Why not just give up your faith, these silly little rules, so that you can enjoy the thing that you like? But when you believe something as fully and as emotionally as I did—and many people do—the fact that you want something, anything, more than you want to enrich your faith is torture. That was the apostle Paul's point in the section about the thorn in his flesh, that the thorn will always be there, and that it will always hurt because it will remind you that you cannot overcome your most basic instinct toward evil. That amount of self-disgust and shame is difficult to live with day to day, especially as a teen. So instead of sitting with that problem, I built a version of gossiping that felt like it might be okay, so that I might be okay.

I remember exactly when I was forced to admit that my makeshift division between slander (something God hated) and gossip (which maybe He felt fine about; how was I to know?) crumbled. The youth group of the church I grew up in loved to have bonding activities. One version of this was something called a "lock-in." All this really meant was that a lot of high-schoolers had a sleepover inside the church. It was an excuse to stay up late, eat junk food, and play sardines, shoving yourself into a tiny closet with people you might or might not have a crush on. It was late summer, but the air-conditioning blasted freezing air inside the rooms, so I had slept in a hoodie inside my sleeping bag. I woke up the next morning because I heard crying. I was so disoriented that I thrashed myself out of the sleeping bag and into the hallway without taking the hood off my head.

In the hallway, a girl a couple years older than me was holding her pink Motorola Razr phone in the palm of her hand like it might fly away at any moment. She was crying, her bleached blond hair still curled from the night before, her eyeliner smudged. There was a group of girls around her, all of whom had heard the crying and gotten to her before me. Among them sat a darkness I hadn't expected and didn't know how to handle. None of the boys were awake.

"What's going on?" I asked the girl next to me in a whisper.

It was a terrible random tragedy. A girl had died. A cheerleader. It had been an accident. The details were fuzzy. She had been on the lake. Someone had been drinking. What was clear was that she was the crying girl's friend.

I asked the girl on my other side for information and learned a few more important facts: that the cheerleader had not herself been drinking, that they had been on someone's parents' boat, that the details were still sparse because all of it had happened only twelve hours before. I found myself nodding, my eyes filling with tears, begging for more information. Was anyone else hurt? Would there be a funeral?

At this point a group leader, who I'd thought at the time was old but in retrospect was probably twenty-five, rounded the corner and caught me whispering.

"Girls," she said, placing a hand on my shoulder, interrupting my new information source midway through an important detail, "let's not gossip about this. Let's pray." Her eyes were filled with judgment, her face disappointed.

In one fell swoop, she eviscerated the gray area I had uncomfortably existed in and painted it all as sin. In the last few years, I had done a lot of gossiping about who liked whom and why someone had gone to juvie, which I knew in my gut the church leaders would not have approved of. But this? Trying to learn what had happened during a tragedy didn't feel like gossip. Gossip always felt good, but this filled my stomach with lead. I had only wanted to know the facts of a dire situation that had hurt a girl in our group. Was this gossip, too? And if it was, then wasn't all information gathering a form of gossip?

I nodded at the group leader and apologized. I was sixteen. I didn't know then that people older than you are not always right. When the girls around me scooched into a circle, I scooched, too.

As we sat cross-legged, hands intertwined and heads bowed, I realized that the girls around me who were praying knew a lot more about the situation than I did. As they talked to God, as they asked for guidance, they were also revealing more information. They were asking God to comfort the girl's family and naming the people she had been with during the accident. Under the doctrine I believed, God was omniscient, so nothing happened that He did not already know about. Yet there we all were, recounting details. And by virtue of talking aloud to God, they were also talking to me. Was there really any difference between the prayer circle and the conversation I had just been chastised for having? It all seemed like gossip, I know now, because it was.

One example used in both modern Christianity and Judaism as evidence of God's hatred of gossip is found in Numbers 12. Miriam and Aaron are privately continuing the ancient tradition of bitching about a sibling. They are talking about their brother Moses. God had recently anointed Moses as His prophet and begun to speak with him directly, and Miriam and Aaron were unhappy about that. The Lord had also spoken to them! Plus, Moses had married a Cushite! I don't really know what that means, but it seems scandalous. The Lord is mad enough about their jealousy and gossip that He descends in a pillar of smoke, yells at them, and gives Miriam (only Miriam) leprosy for seven days.

You could read this as punishment not for gossip, but for questioning the Lord and His plan, which happens over and over again in the Bible. It could be a punishment for envy, since Miriam's outrage seems built of jealousy. But it is cited as evidence that God does not want us to gossip. The line being drawn seems stark: talking about other people without their being there is gossip, and that is forbidden.

This was true in the church where I grew up, though it took trial and error for me to realize this. In Judaism slander is *hotzaat shem ra*, while *lashon hara* includes all negative true speech. The King James Version of the Bible does not include the word *gossip*, because the word had not taken on a negative meaning when that version was translated and eventually published in 1611. Instead, it uses both "slander," indicating that the information being spread is a lie, and the word *talebearer*. One verse reads, "The words of a talebearer are as wounds, and they go down into the innermost parts of the belly." "Talebearer" here, though, means any storyteller, and the tone of the KJV implies throughout that storyteller is a negative distinction regardless of whether that person is telling the truth or lying.

In Islam a distinction is made between *buhtan* (slander), *namimah* (malicious gossip), and *ghibah* (backbiting). In the Hadith, there is a story in which the Prophet Muhammad asks his followers if they know what backbiting is and tells them that it is "talking about your brother in a manner which he does not like." The distinction he draws is, "If what you say is true then you have backbitten about him, and if it is not true, then you have slandered him." Both, though, he is saying, are immoral and to be avoided.

But why use the power of a stage and your leadership in a church to condemn all talk? What is the benefit of this strict separation of gossip and God? Why emphasize this, or all causes, over poverty, illness, or envy?

I remember the arguments pastors made from the pulpit. Gossip is a woman's sin (men, lucky them, get lust), and it tears apart communities, can destroy relationships, and even attempts to rip the church itself apart. Gossip, the claim went, always sows discord. It is built not of unity but of destruction. In a 2004 advice column, Billy Graham, who is perhaps the father of modern-day American Evangelicalism, wrote, "Do you think [Jesus]'d even gossip at all? I think you know the answer: Of course He wouldn't." He ignored the fact that Jesus would never need to gossip because He knows everything about everyone at all times, but Graham continued with an interesting pivot. "Why is gossiping wrong in God's eyes? One reason is because it always distorts the truth. The Bible is clear: 'The Lord detests lying lips'" (Proverbs 12:22).

Leaders were correctly drawing direct connections between gossip and their own potential downfalls and preemptively demonizing it to protect themselves. This seems to be the heart of the Evangelical church's insistence that gossip be quashed at every level on every topic. If gossip *always* distorted the truth, then their crusade would make perfect sense. But anyone privy to gossip that matters knows that often the only truth that exists can be found in the gossip mills because it is often the only kind of power a marginalized or subjugated group can grab hold of.

Dave Ramsey, a prominent Christian financial guru, defines gossip for his company as "discussing anything negative with someone who can't help solve the problem." Practically, that means that any complaint or criticism by employees should go straight to leadership.

It also means that the company maintains complete control over what is said about it. That extends, apparently, outside of the office to employees' families. *Christianity Today* reported in 2021 that an employee had been fired after his wife had posted on Facebook that she was concerned about the company's reopening its office during the early months of the COVID-19 pandemic in 2020. Churches, regardless of their tax status in the United States, are companies: they give employees W-2s; they have handbooks. Many churches are requiring employees to sign NDAs. These behaviors are taken directly from corporate America and were created to protect the people in charge of these organizations. It's an abuse of power that is justified using verses meant to be holy.

Matthew Mitchell, an Evangelical pastor who wrote the book *Resisting Gossip: Winning the War of the Wagging Tongue*, published a blog in 2019 saying that one of his worries was that "unscrupulous church leaders would misuse [his book] to silence dissent among their followers," and emphasizing that "I certainly didn't write it to insulate bad leaders."

But that is exactly why most church leaders demonize gossip so strongly from the pulpit, because gossip seeks to hold people to account for their actions. It fights against secrecy, and while that can be dangerous when used against people without power, it targets anyone in leadership of any church who has an immense amount of power. Women who brought forth credible allegations of sexual misconduct against Willow Creek Community Church founder Bill Hybels were accused of using false allegations to collude and divide the church. Hundreds of similar stories in various churches emerged in late 2017 during the #MeToo movement after poet Emily Joy Allison tweeted about how she had been groomed by a youth leader in her Evangelical megachurch. Her report about how the church had protected the man in his thirties who had romantically pursued her as a sixteen-year-old and kept his offenses quiet spurred an outpouring of other stories that Allison encouraged people to hashtag #ChurchToo.

The pattern that became more and more evident as these stories emerged was that the codifying of gossip as a sin could be used as a shield for misbehaving men in power to subjugate women in their congregations. Paige Patterson, then president of Southwestern Baptist Theological Seminary, was caught on tape telling a spousal abuse victim to submit to her husband. "Scripture was not the reason for the colossal disregard and disrespect of women among many of these men. It was only the excuse. Sin was the reason. Ungodliness," Beth Moore, an Evangelical Bible teacher and the founder of Living Proof Ministries, wrote in an open letter in 2018. By 2021, her stance—that religious spaces should not be so influenced by the patriarchy—led her to leave the Southern Baptist faith. She is now Anglican.

Perhaps that is the way that gossip should interact with faiths: encouraged as a force for good, the way it has been in the #ChurchToo movement, or when a shared prayer request enables a community to rally around someone who needs help.

In high school, I could not at first see how deeply the demonization of gossip was intertwined with the church's calls for women to submit. When the head pastor of the church I grew up in had an affair, the shutdown of the gossip mill was even more explicit. We were encouraged to speak to a pastor if we had questions, thus maintaining the power dynamic of the organization even as a power vacuum emerged at the top. I began to notice that these blanket renunciations of gossip as "negative" never defined who exactly the negativity was directed toward. Negativity is a value judgment. Gossip about the affair, for example, had forced a corrupting sin into the light, which is a biblical action.

I am not sure if it was gossip that eventually broke my faith, but the two do feel intertwined. The first moment I remember a flash of recognition that maybe what I said I believed didn't feel true in my body and realized that even with the best intentions, the church's goal was always going to be to protect itself first. Understanding that the church systematically maintains its own power at the expense of its people fundamentally cracked the foundation of my faith. A structure doesn't fail because of one fissure, and it would be a lie to say that gossip was the only thing that led me to question the faith and culture I was raised in. But cracks are visible, and, even if they aren't actively dangerous, they force us to wonder what else could be wrong. If there is one weakness, where else could things be broken?

* * *

It is ironic, in the end, that all of the pastors were right. The thorn was supposed to remind me that I needed God, but once I rejected the idea that it was a thorn, my faith faded gradually and painfully, like a bruise. The scales fell from my eyes, as they had from the apostle Paul's, and suddenly all I could see in front of me bright and shining was gossip. I stopped praying for God to take away my desire to gossip, and eventually I stopped praying altogether. Without the fear of sin, I was able to stop policing my engagement with gossip, which in turn let me gossip more. I was so good at it. I loved buffing up the details of something that had happened with one group of friends and relaying it to another. I loved learning about the nuances of history where gossip had been written out.

Because it is easy for me to believe in some kind of innate characteristics and predestination, because I was brought up to do so, I do think that maybe this thorn inside me really was there from the beginning. Maybe being a gossip is simply part of my identity and personality, unremovable and consistent.

But I don't know that to love to gossip I had to reject my faith. Now, much later, I can see that there is plenty of room within

Christianity for a gossip like me. Not only would a just God forgive you, but the Bible itself does not speak out that strongly against the behavior. In the six-year period between my first doubts and my actual departure from the church, I found nuance in the way the Bible talks about gossip that none of the pastors ever had answers for. In my high school Bible, I underlined and starred Proverbs 26:20: "Without wood a fire goes out; without a gossip a quarrel dies down." This was taught as a reminder that gossip could fuel a quarrel and therefore should be avoided. But if you think for a second longer about this verse, there is no negative connotation. We are projecting that upon it. Fire, after all, is what keeps us warm, cooks our food, and enables us to survive a cold, dark night. It is only dangerous when uncontained, when malicious, when wild. In most cases, fire is good, a life force, just as quarreling can also be productive and necessary. It is certainly true that gossip is not helpful if your goal is to maintain the status quo and keep the peace, but those are two things Jesus Himself was very uninterested in doing.

There is an argument that gossip is a necessary part of the Gospel itself. In the story of Jesus' death, He is hung on a cross by the Romans, and His dead body is laid to rest in a tomb with a heavy stone rolled in front of it and protected by guards. The Bible says in Matthew's retelling of Christ's resurrection that an angel of the Lord appeared and rolled away the stone, and that the guards fled. In John 20 it says that Christ walked away harmed—with holes in His wrists and ankles and a gash in His side—but alive.

In the New Testament Gospel of Luke, chapter 24, Mary Magdalene and other women find Jesus' tomb empty and are told by two men that He has been resurrected. They run to tell the disciples, and Luke wrote that "they did not believe the women, because their words seemed to them like nonsense." The word *nonsense*, the biblical scholar Marianne Bjelland Kartzow has written, is translated from the Greek word *leros*, meaning "empty talk." The disciples thought that it was gossip, that it couldn't be believed. The greatest news ever told was brought to them, and they wanted to dismiss it out of hand as gossip meant to taunt them.

In the disciples' response to the women, we see the true heart of both gossip and religion: belief. The disciples did not believe that the gossip was true. They did not believe the story. The problem wasn't the story itself but their response to it. It was unbelievable, and therefore easy to dismiss.

Without all the infrastructure and profit and power seizing, gossip and religion are braided together throughout the course of our history. Both require us to believe. Perhaps that is the real identifying factor of whether something is gossip: Does it ask you to take a leap of faith, to trust the teller enough to believe a story you did not see with your own eyes and did not hear with your own ears? Gossip is always about a friend of a friend. It is always lightly or highly exaggerated. It always asks you to imagine a world different than the one you previously imagined, to consider a version of a person that might be far worse than the one you assumed existed—or far better. Gossip exists in a kind of transitory, imaginary space between events and their codifying: a retelling that grows and morphs with every translation through time. To embrace gossip as a concept is to extend your arms as far as they can go and still not grasp it all, but to believe that the bounds exist.

Maybe it is not faith that stands in opposition to gossip, but power.

As I am often one of the few people of color working in an academic library, I rely on gossip to help me survive. I call it "good gossip," the whisper network that allows me to warn my colleagues of color who and what to watch out for and who I should avoid in return. I think of it as paying it forward in the profession—the more informed we as a community of color are in an overwhelmingly white profession via gossip, the more likelihood that we're able to thrive.

The Burn Book

I walked past a group of teenagers a few weeks ago, their eyes lined with wings so precise they could slash me, their lips glossed, their solidarity with one another visible even in passing. Their faces brimmed with judgment, and though I could not prove that this was because I was wearing a one-piece sweatshirt jumpsuit and a novelty baseball hat on a Saturday, I felt in my bones that this was the reason. I knew, from my own years as a teenager, that the minute I was out of earshot, they would snicker. I know all the moves because I did them: cupping your hand around someone's ear while your eyes stay on the target; pushing your lips together while you frantically text, only for your friend's phone to light up next to you. It is less important to teenagers that they actually have something to say about you than it is that you know that they are talking about you. Because the power comes from the reminder that they are in charge, from the catastrophic humbling that comes when you watch someone talk shit about you right in front of your face and never blink.

To be a teen is to live in a sense of superiority that envelops you whole. You believe you'll never be more beautiful, never more attractive, never more interesting. None of it is true, of course, but the pressure of it can eat you alive. The standards to be a woman in the world are always high, but when you are a teen, the standards are set by your peers. Buy Drunk Elephant. Get no sun damage. Never age. Never grow up. Anyone who has ever been a teen knows that the scariest thing about the gossip of teens is that it is almost always true. Your pants are too skinny. Your part is wrong. The girl you don't like is dating the quarterback. And that teacher (you know the one) is sleeping with a student. Teens know innately that gossip doesn't come from nowhere. It always, always comes from somewhere. So even if you deny a rumor to the high heavens, that doesn't mean that people will believe you. There's a morsel of truth sometimes that even the most adamant denials cannot destroy.

In the opening act of 2004's *Mean Girls*, Cady (the new girl) goes with the Plastics (the popular girls) to a nearby mall. As they gaze down toward a central fountain where other teens congregate and chat, Lindsay Lohan voices over Cady's thoughts: "Being at Old Orchard Mall kind of reminded me of being home in Africa, by the watering hole, when the animals were in heat." To emphasize this, the teens begin behaving like monkeys. The soundtrack changes to mimic the jungle. The whole scene is absurd and ridiculous and silly. There are three of these "animalistic" scenes in the original movie: one in the lunchroom, and a final one at the climax, when the revelations of everyone's secrets in a "Burn Book" create chaos in the hallway. It's a ham-handed way to convey that teenagers behave like beasts, and that their tactics and antics are unsophisticated.

The scenes are meant to illustrate that the little snipes the characters make at one another are acts of aggression. But the gossiping that the teens are doing is more than immature hate; it's part of how they build their communities. The technical term for this is *social sanctioning*. When we gossip about how someone is wearing the wrong thing, or dating the wrong person, or sitting at the wrong lunch table, we are communicating to the people around us that we don't approve of those behaviors. We are teaching our peer group how we want to behave and how we want them to behave. If the popular girls carry Stanley cups, you will, too. If the popular kids cut holes into their tank tops to show their colorful Victoria's Secret bras, well... here is a pair of scissors. Are you with us or against us?

"On Wednesdays, we wear pink," the rule says. Being a member of the popular in-group has its advantages, after all: not only are you powerful, but you automatically become someone. In the 1970s, Henri Tajfel and John Turner proposed Social Identity Theory, which argued that people derive belonging, purpose, self-worth, and identity from the social groups they belong to. Your identity can, in fact, be based on carrying a Stanley cup, wearing pink on Wednesdays, or wearing the right athletic shorts.

A 1944 *Life* magazine article noted, "There is a time in the life of every American girl when the most important thing in the world is to be one of a crowd of other girls and to act and speak and dress exactly as they do. This is the teen age." Some things never change, I guess.

Often, people talk about gossip in relation to teenagers as a form of bullying. That in-group is dangerous because it is predatory. Seen through this lens, there is very little room for nuance in these behaviors.

For years, every time someone wrote in to the advice column "Dear Abby" asking about how to deal with a situation involving gossip, Abigail Van Buren responded with a poem called "Nobody's Friend," which she attributed to an unknown author. "I am cunning and malicious and gather strength with age," the poem about gossip says, "The more I am quoted, the more I am believed." I think often about this poem, and the unwillingness to understand gossip as a complex, difficult element of society. Researchers have found that the ability to engage with gossip requires linguistic competence and advanced social awareness. As a gossiper, you need to be able to understand who is being talked about, what kind of skepticism you should have about a story, and the weight of morality in it. But teenage girls are always assumed to be gossiping maliciously. As Chuck Bass once said, "I am a bitch when I want to be."

There is evidence that women gossip more than men. And there are differences in their subjects. Men, research has found, are more likely to gossip about larger systems and famous people (sports, politics, and so on), and women are more likely to gossip about others in their social group. A study out of the University of California, Riverside, found that while women gossip more than men, most of that gossip is neutral, information-sharing gossip.

A study of five teenage girls (granted, a limited study) whose conversations were recorded over a twelve-month period found that 65 percent of their conversations were gossip segments. "The girls were able to manage gossip topics in a way that is similar to older adults. However, one noticeable difference is that the girls appeared to be less certain about their beliefs regarding some of the issues discussed," the study noted. The teenage years are a liminal period of learning. You feel like an adult, or at least I did, and it is only after you become an actual adult that you realize how young you really were. The gossiping that teens do, then, is constructive learning; they are trying to understand how to communicate about the world around them so that they might become adults.

Gossip hasn't always been considered the domain of women. In English, the word *gossip* comes from the word *god-sibb*, a word used as early as the eleventh century to denote a person with whom you were emotionally intimate but not related. By the sixteenth century, the word *god-sib* had already evolved into a verb (*god-sibbing*) and been morphed to apply mainly to the secret conversations between women behind the closed doors of the birthing room. A wood-block print from the latter half of the sixteenth century that was published in Great Britain shows women milling about in various places. The verses beneath the print begin with, "At Child-bed when the Gossips meet / Fine Stories we are told; And if they get a cup too much, / Their Tongues they cannot hold." Randle Cotgrave's 1611 French-to-English dictionary—which many believe to contain the earliest surviving published use of *gossip* as a verb—noted that the French have two different nouns for gossip: one for women's talk (*commérage*) and one for men's (*comperage*). Only *commérage* is still used.

As early as the 1560s, women in Scotland were being put into the brank (which is also referred to as the "scold's bridle" or the "gossip's bridle" or the "witch's bridle"). The brank was a torture device: an iron headdress made to silence a woman who had spoken out of turn. "To curb women's tongues that *talk* too idle," read an inscription on perhaps the most famous gossip bridle. It was from 1633 and came from a person named Chester who was said to have lost his fortune due to a woman's gossip. The bridle itself was an iron muzzle with an iron bit that held the tongue down. It was painful, sure, but more important, it prevented the wearer from speaking. Often, a woman wearing one was paraded through the streets, the torture device connected to the hand of the man who had put her into it.

"The use of the instrument was not sanctioned by law, but was altogether illegal," William Andrews wrote in a book from the late nineteenth century about olden punishments. He also wrote that "[her] sole offence, perhaps, was that she had raised her voice in defense of her social rights against a brutal and besotted husband, or had spoken honest truth of some one high in office in the town."

Whether the idle talk was true or not was irrelevant. The issue was the talking at all. So even though we don't begin to see the word *gossip* being used to denigrate and demonize women's speech until the mid-eighteenth century, the behavior existed before the word.

Plenty of modern-use examples exist in American culture from the mid-eighteenth century. By 1767, American papers noted "male gossip" in order to differentiate their talk from plain old gossip, which was something only women could do. In 1796, Jane West published *A Gossip's Story, and a Legendary Tale*, which used the modern-day definition of a gossip, and which was later the inspiration for Jane Austen's *Sense and Sensibility*. "I enjoy some inherent qualities, which I flatter myself render me a very excellent gossip. I have a retentive memory, a quick imagination, strong curiosity, and keen perception," West wrote in the first chapter. Same! When a woman was given an advice column in the *Farmer's Journal* in 1792, the column was called "The Gossip." In 1811, the *Oxford English Dictionary* added a definition for the modern usage: "idle talk; trifling or groundless rumour." The dictionary didn't specify that it was "women's talk," but that was a given already.

Even the common arguments against gossip (that it is malicious, that it doesn't *do* anything, that it's trivial, that it doesn't take serious topics seriously) are a form of policing what kind of discourse can be considered "good." Philosophers (I'm looking at you, Immanuel Kant and Martin Heidegger) demean gossip because it does not deal with serious inquiries of thought. But serious inquiries of thought, and thinking as an academic and leisure activity, have not always been available to everyone. For centuries women were barred from institutions of higher learning. In the United States, the first white women were not admitted to Oberlin College until 1837, a good two hundred years after Harvard was founded. The first Black woman did not graduate with a bachelor's degree (also at Oberlin) until 1862.

But as Louise Collins wrote in her article "Gossip: A Feminist Defense," "Is gossip trivial because its subject matter, the personal, particular, and domestic, is trivial? Traditionally these aspects of life have been regarded as both 'feminine' and unimportant to what we are, qua moral beings." If all talk about our lives and how we live them is gossip and trivial, what a sparse, sad realm of thought we are forced to occupy. The choices we make in our lives may not be the ivory tower ideals of existentialist thought, but that does not make them valueless.

In her book *All About Love*, bell hooks wrote, "One reason women have traditionally gossiped more than men is because gossip has been a social interaction wherein women have felt comfortable stating what they really think and feel. Often, rather than asserting what they think at the appropriate moment, women say what they think will please the listener. Later, they gossip, stating at that moment their true thoughts."

Despite gossip's place in daily discourse, there are tons of links online about how to stop your teen from gossiping. Perhaps the seminal text is Rosalind Wiseman's book *Queen Bees & Wannabes: Helping Your Daughter Survive Cliques, Gossip, Boys, and the New Realities of Girl World*, which is the book that *Mean Girls* was adapted from. Once I realized that this classic movie about teen girls had been adapted from a parenting book about how to get girls to quit gossiping, the movie began to make more sense to me. *Mean Girls* is meant to be a cautionary tale, a reminder of the power gossip can have.

When I read *Queen Bees & Wannabes* as an adult, I was awed by how little of an adaptation the movie really is. The book does contain anecdotes about lunchroom dynamics, but there is no plotline at all. It's a parenting book, filled with tips and tricks. There's no girl moving from Africa into the terrors of the American high school only to be confronted with Regina George in all her glory. The book, which was published in 2002, is meant to explain the world of "Girl World" to parents and (hopefully) teach them to help their daughter navigate it. Wiseman is not a social scientist, nor is her book based on studies and data; it is based on her experiences teaching girls in affluent Washington, DC–area high schools how to be nicer to one another. Even in its updated versions, *Queen Bees & Wannabes* is a relic of the early-2000s panic that surrounded teen girl culture.

"Girls' anger should not be other people's entertainment," Wiseman wrote. But *Queen Bees & Wannabes* did just that. Unlike in other books published around the same time that dealt with teenage girls' social cliques and behaviors of teenage girls (Jodee Blanco's 2003 *Please Stop Laughing at Me: One Woman's Inspirational Story* and Rachel Simmons's 2002 *Odd Girl Out: The Hidden Culture of Aggression in Girls*, for example), Wiseman created characters. She branded the ways girls communicate with one another in a way that made them not only recognizable, but iconic.

She did this by creating stereotypes of how a girl could be. There are eight of them in the book, and almost all of them appear in the movie at some point. First up are the girls who are powerful. These are the Plastics in the *Mean Girls* movie. Regina George is what Wiseman dubbed a Queen Bee. She's power hungry, intimidating, and very good at manipulating others. Karen Smith, on the other hand, is a Sidekick, someone who exists only to support the Queen Bee, because being close to her makes her feel popular. And Gretchen Wieners, with her hair full of secrets, is the Banker, who convinces people to confide in her and uses their secrets to gain status.

The next cohort of girls do not have power but want it. The Messenger uses gossip and other people's secrets, but she does so not for power but for approval. The Pleaser/Wannabe's only distinction from the Messenger seems to be that she does not have any gossip to trade. Neither of these characters plays a large role in the movie, but the Target (the girl the popular girls make fun of and exclude) is basically every unnamed character in *Mean Girls*. And then there is the Cady Heron type: the Torn Bystander who is afraid of the Queen Bee but wants her approval badly enough to ignore her own morals and gut feelings about right and wrong.

There's a version of *Queen Bees & Wannabes* that lays out these typecasts of girls with the understanding that all have their pros and cons. But it isn't meant to be a Myers-Briggs test or a horoscope reading; it is meant to scare parents. That much is clear once you get to the magical eighth type of girl, what Wiseman would dub the Champion.

"The main goal of this book," Wiseman stated, "is to help your daughter have more Champion moments at every age." The Champion doesn't care about status. She doesn't exclude "losers." She is friends with lots of people. She is the idealized version of a daughter, a jewel of a girl who stands up for others. She is the type of teen girl you are supposed to want to be. Maybe, if you parent well enough, you can transform your demon daughter who won't stop texting friends about who is dating whom into one.

I read *Queen Bees & Wannabes* in the brief two-year window before *Mean Girls* came out either because my dad gave it to me or because he left it lying around the house and I read it without his permission. I don't really remember. What I do remember is the description of the Champion and feeling guilty because I knew that the Champion was the good kid, the one whom parents would be proud of. I also knew from reading the description that I didn't want to be her.

I was a Banker. Like Gretchen, I gathered up secrets and kept them in my body. Recently a friend from high school DM'd me on Instagram. "I love that you were the gossip queen in high school (I say that lovingly) and now you get paid to do it," she wrote. She's right. I didn't want to be popular as much as I wanted information. I wanted to gain the power that came from knowing things that everyone else didn't.

Sometime in the 1940s, the idea of the American teenager was born. Adolescents obviously existed before the 1940s, but they were busy getting married or (if poor) working. As Thomas Hine wrote in

The Rise and Fall of the American Teenager, "During most of the nine-teenth century, fourteen-year-olds were viewed as inexperienced adults." But once marketing executives realized that young people had their own money and could be a target, they started marketing to them. Would teens like to buy a pink typewriter? You bet your ass they would. "To some extent, the teenage market—and, in fact, the very notion of the teenager—has been created by the businessmen who exploit it," Dwight Macdonald wrote in the *New Yorker in* 1958.

But because the American teenager was an invention of advertis-ers, much like Wiseman's eight types, the teen girl was and is also a stereotype. The teen girl of *Seventeen* magazine when it was founded in 1944 was never meant to be every teen girl. The teen girl was middle class, at least, because she had money to spend. She day-dreamed about boys because she was straight. Usually she was blond, and almost always she was white.

In some ways, the 2004 *Mean Girls* is the perfect critique of and reinforcer of white teen girl stereotypes. The girls are blond. They wear push-up bras and miniskirts. They are dramatic and conniving and constantly worried about their weight and their pores and their clothes. They are also, just as in Wiseman's book, boy crazy. "For most teenage girls, guys are everything. Boys validate their exis-tence; they define who they are and where they stand in the world," Wiseman quoted a teenager as saying.

Not only is this firm gender divide outdated; it is also an extremely heteronormative way of viewing the world. Of course, teenagers are obsessed with whom they have crushes on and what the gossip around love is, but that is not unique to teenagers; adults also gossip about affairs and relationships.

Even within the stereotype that white teen girls gossip only about boys, there is a failure to acknowledge how that conversation could benefit them. Think about *Easy A,* in which Emma Stone starts a fake rumor that she's a slut in order to help a friend and accidentally skyrockets herself to popularity. In the end, the tactic backfires, but there's more nuance to the idea of gossip as a tool than in Wiseman's book or its film adaptation.

Or consider the beginning of the 2006 movie *John Tucker Must Die*, in which three different girls are dating Jesse Metcalfe's titular character. The only reason they find out that he is seeing all of them at the same time is that they are put on the same volleyball team in gym class and begin to talk about boys. That's not just gabbing about a crush; it's information sharing. Even the most mundane gossip can later turn out to be important. While gossip can be toxic, it can also be a way of keeping one another safe.

Nothing is moralized about more in *Mean Girls* than the Burn Book: that plush pink binder with its red lipstick kiss and its ransom note letters, that font of all immaturity and sin. "The movie's crisis— distribution of the Burn Book leading to civil unrest—does not engender reflection on larger sociomoral issues, but merely a reaffirmation of good/bad roles, e.g., gossip is bad," David Resnick wrote in his 2008 article "Life in an Unjust Community: A Hollywood View of High School Moral Life." "This is crisis-intervention character education for prudential living: obey the implicit rules of social life ('the Golden Rule') because they are for your own, long-term benefit." In other words, the final act of *Mean Girls* is a soapbox from which gossip is declared juvenile and dangerous, and the same is said for teenage girls, even though within its own script the power of gossip to protect teenage girls from predators is also shown.

The movie makes the same error that Wiseman herself made in *Queen Bees & Wannabees:* "We can't allow children to believe that seemingly small acts of degradation are acceptable as long as it's not happening to them." Wiseman goes on to incorrectly define "'gossiping' and its cousin 'backstabbing'" as "when you're talking about someone to deliberately make them look bad."

The response by the adults in *Mean Girls* is incredibly similar to the ones I have seen in my own experience in society. The school wants to reestablish law and order by purging gossip. In doing this, it incorrectly frames refraining from gossip as a personal virtue. The adults in *Mean Girls* want the same thing for their societies that the people in power at large seem to want for ours: for the people in charge to remain in charge and for peace to reign. A truly civic public, one that is engaged with the needs of its community members and whose members seek to help one another, necessarily requires gossip. "A civic public is neither an association among friends nor can it be limited to a...religious or ethnic group," the educational theorist Thomas F. Green wrote in *Voices: The Educational Formation of Conscience*. Nor, he added, is the civic public akin to "religious-like associations" or "athletic clubs, whose members have achieved a rare sense of their mutuality and joint identity." And nowhere is meant to be more of a perfect civic public than a public high school.

One of the most jarring things about watching *Mean Girls* as an adult is realizing how many of the pages in the Burn Book are telling the truth. It's petty, sure, but it isn't a bunch of childish gossip. In only one instance is it slander: the page about Ms. Norbury selling drugs (which Cady wrote). The only other Burn Book page we hear about that could possibly be construed as slander is the one accusing Janis Ian of being a dyke. I hesitate to give it that description even though it uses *dyke* in a derogatory form. In the 2004 movie, the root of the conflict between Janis and Regina George isn't that Janis could be a lesbian but that Regina thinks that because of this Janis is obsessed with her, which is not altogether wrong. What is wrong is that part of why Regina thinks that (a very good joke) is that she misheard Janis when she said she was Lebanese.

Minus those two pages, though, the Burn Book is right about a lot. Once it is disseminated, the fighting is not about lies and slander but about secrets being told. "You're the only one who knows that," girls scream in the hallway. "Oh my God, that was one time,"

Amber D'Alessio says when she sees her page, which says she "made out with a hot dog." In the original script, she "masturbates with a frozen hot dog." But that's neither here nor there.

The reason that the page accusing Ms. Norbury of selling drugs is taken seriously is because of the pages about Coach Carr. Two pages in the Burn Book (one for Trang Pak and one for Sun Jin Dinh) say that underage girls have "made out" with Coach Carr. We know this is true because earlier in the movie Damien and viewers saw it firsthand. Without the Burn Book, will Coach Carr be caught? Will he be stopped? It feels unlikely.

That is the problem with Wiseman and *Mean Girls'* uniform dismissal of gossip as a social necessity. As Resnick wrote, "A young person indoctrinated never to 'talk about people behind their backs' (Cady's definition of gossip), will not report a case of drug-dealing or vandalism in the school or (if one wants to exempt illegal activities from the gossip rule—itself the exercise of judgment) a friend's bulimic vomiting or depression."

I remember the first friend I had who was sexually assaulted by an adult. I felt so old then, curled up in my bed, our heads inches apart on the pillow facing each other while she talked, and the tears ran faster than she could wipe them. I didn't know it was sexual assault then, but she told me because she needed to. We were fourteen. And I knew the man she was talking about. We all did.

There are more of them than people want to believe, an English teacher or a coach whom everyone loves. An abuser disguised as a friend. I found out about my friend because of idle talk, because we were doing what fourteen-year-olds do and talking about who we wanted to kiss. Later, curled up in my bed, she told me everything. Every time I heard his name after that night, my stomach churned. Be careful around him, I warned other girls. We gossiped about him, if you want to call it that. I'd say we kept one another safe.

To re-release *Mean Girls* as a musical film in 2024, the movie had to be updated. The culture had changed. To be a teen now is differ-ent, and so the movie (even as a musical) had to be, too. In the new version, Janis really is a lesbian, and her beef with Regina is more about bullying than something misheard. The script is updated. Gretchen Wieners casually tosses out that "once [she] processed that Regina's love language is anger," it became a lot easier to deal with her. Renée Rapp's portrayal of Regina George is much angrier and much sexier than Rachel McAdams's. There are no more references to making out with hot dogs. All of these are smart choices to mod-ernize the story for new audiences, but the most interesting change to me is the complete defanging of the Burn Book.

The new movie insists that the Burn Book is old, a relic from childhood dug out of a closet by Regina's mom and presented to teenage girls who are clearly more mature than it is. But it also changes the Burn Book from a dynamic and complicated text by removing the entire Coach Carr subplot. In the new movie, Coach Carr, played by Jon Hamm, is just a sex ed teacher. He is no longer the predator from the original movie who sleeps with two underage girls, and there are no references in the new Burn Book to him at all. This makes for a cleaner, lighter movie.

But the defanging of the Burn Book also serves the new movie's moralistic narrative: gossiping is universally bad, immature, and mean. The choice makes the movie neater, and easier to digest, but it also strips some of the complication from the original.

* * *

In Agatha Christie's *The Murder at the Vicarage,* Miss Marple is asked what she thinks of the "inestimable harm...done by the fool-ish wagging of tongues in ill-natured gossip." She responds brutally. "You are so unworldly," she says. "I daresay idle tittle-tattle is very wrong and unkind, but it is so often true, isn't it?" I love the use of the word *unworldly* here, as if to be able to think only of ideas is a privilege that robs you of the ability to see the world around you realistically. In my experience, calling the kind of whisper network information sharing that keeps people safe from abusers "gossip" instigates some kickback. Gossip, people say, is frivolous, and that's not frivolous. Rather, gossip is always information.

Researchers at the University of California, Berkeley, have named this kind of gossiping *prosocial gossip* because it is used to warn others, which in turn can lower the overall exploitation of groups. As Evette Dionne, the former editor-in-chief of Bitch Media, said at a Clayman Institute for Gender Research event about the feminist use of rumor, people "reduce a credible allegation, an accusation against someone who has harmed someone else" to gossip as a way to "delegitimize it and undermine it, and make it seem as if it's simply a rumor with no weight and no teeth to it." Calling this form of cautionary tale "gossip" demeans its credibility and injects the stories with a pebble of doubt.

Prosocial gossip not only makes people aware of who abusers are and might be; it also enables people who have been abused to grab power that they cannot otherwise have.

In my junior year of college a man said something inappropriate enough in a public enough setting that I was forced to do something about it. People were talking about it. They were talking so much and so quickly that my phone buzzed for two days straight.

I had been at a Halloween party. I was dressed as Britney Spears at her 2001 VMAs performance: small shorts, green bikini top, plush yellow python draped over my shoulders. I was twenty-one years old and believed that that was the hottest I would ever be in my whole life. Why not treat Halloween as they say in *Mean Girls*, "the one night a year when a girl can dress like a total slut and no other girls can say anything about it"? I deserved to have a little fun.

I remember how good I felt on the way over with my silly snake and my little top, and I remember how quickly all of that confidence and composure was taken away. Because I was usually so demure, my V-necks never too deep, my shorts never too short, I guess the man in charge of the organization throwing the party, of which I was also a leader, thought it was his right, maybe his duty, to comment on my (frankly incredible) rack. I remember how still the circle of people around me got, how the only sound was Flo Rida's "Whistle" blaring from inside. I remember thinking that I must have misheard him, and then I became very, very sure that I had not.

"Somehow I sensed what was coming for me even then. Really, though, what girl doesn't? It looms over you, that threat of violence. They drill the danger into your head until it starts to feel inevitable. You grow up wondering when it's finally going to happen," Kate Elizabeth Russell wrote in *My Dark Vanessa*, a novel about a girl abused by a teacher. In a way, every story like this has felt inevitable in the moments after. They promised this would happen and here it was.

The response by my friends was immediate. After I ran away, one trailed me into the kitchen to help me decode what had just happened. One, I later learned, dumped an entire Solo cup of beer on the guy's head, an action she wondered for years whether to regret or not. All night long, people were coming up to me: apologizing for him, asking how they could help. With every inquiry I felt madder. I did not want to be associated with him at all, in any way, ever.

"Harassment is always a sexual demand, but it also carries a more sinister and pathetic injunction: 'You will think about me,'" Jacqueline Rose wrote in her 2021 book *On Violence and On Violence Against Women*. That is the most frustrating part of this whole story. It inflamed me with rage at the time, and it engulfs me now: I knew that I would remember his exact words, the smug expression on his face, the placement of everyone in that circle, and their reactions whether I wanted to or not. As irrelevant as he was to my position in the world and my understanding of myself, here he still is occupying space in my mind.

I reported the incident because it seemed like the right thing to do and because enough people knew about it that it seemed like the only option. The stories were swirling already. I did not want to sit at a long table with professors I respected and admired and repeat the demeaning things that had been said to me. I wore a blazer, as if looking professional could save me from the fate of most people who report men in positions of power. It was a classic "he said, she said" story, they said. In the end, the university offered me only mediation: the opportunity to sit in a room with this man every week until we "sorted this whole thing out."

Recently, I was at a bachelorette party with a few people I had gone to college with when this man's name came up. "I'm sorry," someone said to me. "I know he was shitty to you." They still remember. When they think of me, they also think of him. Here he is again, in this essay. He never goes away. No abusers ever do.

In her book *Notes on a Silencing: A Memoir*, Lacy Crawford wrote about her sexual assault as a teenager at an elite private school. The book begins with a gut-wrenching scene of Crawford's assault: a boy she went to school with claimed to need help, got her to climb through his window, and then he and his roommate assaulted her. "Especially good gossip, no matter how outlandish, contains the sense of its own inevitability," she wrote. "I wondered, when everyone was so quick to believe what the boys claimed, if this proved that it was my fault. There was something ugly that they had all seen in me, but I had not."

When people talk about the dangers of gossip, they use stories like this as an example. But because it was an incorrect version of the story shared by people who had done wrong, it is perhaps more apt to call it propaganda. One inherent danger of the storytelling of gossip, though, is that it can convince people that something they already believed anyway is true. In Crawford's case, that she was, as an administrator told her father, "not a good girl."

Crawford's assault, inside the rumor mill, was transformed into something that could be used against her. After the #MeToo movement went viral in late 2017, thousands of women shared their own experiences of sexual assault. Many of them were videos on YouTube. The narratives are heartbreaking; women cry or don't cry, their anger just buried, as they tell stories they've kept private for years or in some cases decades. Underneath these videos, the comments are always a hellscape. A thematic analysis of YouTube comments directed at women sharing their experiences of sexual assault conducted by Erin Rennie found that 69 percent of abusive comments perpetuated one or more of the seven common rape myths (among them: she was asking for it, it wasn't really rape, he didn't mean to, and others). Crawford had talked about her assault when it happened. I "had been assured that if I continued to do so in the context of a criminal investigation, I would be expelled from school and slandered up and down the Eastern Seaboard," she wrote. The line between slut shaming and victim blaming does not exist at all. The slandering happened anyway.

Late in the memoir, Crawford explained that when a criminal investigation was opened against the school they attended, the state of New Hampshire interviewed one of her attackers. When asked about the event, he responded, "That was 1990, this is 2018. Why now?" But he did not deny the allegation.

Dr. Christine Blasey Ford took the stand about a year after the #MeToo movement began. She vowed to tell the truth, and then she laid out her story: when she was a teenager, Supreme Court nominee Brett Kavanaugh sexually assaulted her. "Indelible in the hippocampus is the laughter," she said on the stand, her voice cracking. "I was, you know, underneath one of them, while the two laughed." Even to type this quote fills my stomach with nausea. It is a recurring nightmare to be forced to recount such a thing on the national stage. After Blasey Ford's testimony, Arizona prosecutor Rachel Mitchell wrote in a memo after questioning Dr. Ford at the Brett Kavanaugh hearing that a "'he said, she said' case is incredibly difficult to prove."

He said, she said. One side and the other. How could we be sure who was telling the truth? It was her story against his. The phrase, as Lois Shepherd wrote in *The Hill* at the time, "implies that we throw up our hands in capitulation—the truth simply cannot be known. It's one person's word against another person's word and that's all there is to it."

"He said, she said" is not an ancient phrase. Every time I hear it used, I remember that I am older than the popular use of "he said, she said" in this context by a couple of weeks. The Nirvana album *Nevermind* is also a little older than the phrase. But already we have forgotten its history.

Though Americans have used the phrase "he said, she said" since at least the mid-twentieth century, up until 1978 it was used to mean misunderstandings of the same words by people of different genders. Ironically, or perhaps aptly, the modern use was codified during the 1991 Senate hearings on Anita Hill's accusation that then Supreme Court nominee Clarence Thomas had sexually harassed her. About the case, a writer in the *Chicago Tribune* wrote that members of Congress who had seen an FBI report said that the report "could not draw any conclusion because of the 'he said, she said' nature of the allegation and denial." William Safire wrote later in the *New York Times*, "Within two years, the phrase popularized in the Thomas hearings found its way into judicial proceedings." In a *Time* article in 1998, Eric Pooley wrote, "In cases of alleged sexual harassment—so painful, so private, so often unknowable— Americans have grown accustomed to weighing the word of one defendant against that of one plaintiff, the steadfast denial against the angry accusation: he said, she said." The article was about Paula Jones's allegations of sexual harassment against President Bill Clinton. After the Monica Lewinsky accusations were revealed, Susan Carpenter-McMillan, the spokeswoman for Paula Jones, clarified, saying, "It's no longer she-said, he-said... It's now she-said, she-said, she-said and he-said."

Both Brett Kavanaugh and Clarence Thomas currently sit on the Supreme Court.

The summer before my senior year of college, I interned in New York City. I was still so blond, my hair bleached by two decades under the Texas sun, and I was optimistic. When I was invited by an editor at a literary journal to their new issue's party, it felt like someone offering me the future I'd dreamed of my whole life on a silver platter. I wore jeans even though it was 90 degrees. I curled my hair with a straightener, and I went to the party with my swooping bangs and every atom of hope I could muster. The future I had always wanted—to leave home, to become something bigger, to write as a job—felt within my grasp.

Inside the tiny Chelsea office were rows and rows of shelves. The few desks had been pushed out of the way to make space for people to loiter about. Music was playing overhead. The comedian B. J. Novak was there. Everyone was talking about him. There was an open bar, if I remember correctly, but maybe it was just beer and wine, and as the sun set, I carried my glass bottle out onto the fire escape. There was just one man out there, and I borrowed his lighter to light my cigarette. The man introduced himself. He was a high-up editor at the publication. He scooched over on the tiny ledge created by the window and invited me to sit with him, and so I sat. He put his hand high on my thigh without any other conversation. I froze for a second, scared, before an older girl poked her head out the window. "Everything all right out here?" she asked, and I said yes as I rose to follow her inside.

I went inside so quickly that I was still holding the smoking cigarette. Someone rebuked me, and when I put it out, my hands were shaking. "Are you okay?" she asked, and I said yes, but my hands were still shaking. But I was okay, wasn't I? Nothing had happened. He'd put his hand on my leg, I'd removed it and left. It was simple. But it felt like a shot across the bow, a warning of what could come, and I left the party early.

Years later, I sat in a dark bar, my phone vibrating beyond reason as every group text in my phone ignited. They were about a Google spreadsheet titled "Shitty Media Men." Created by Moira Donegan, the list was being edited by dozens of unnamed users. On it, people had written the names of men in media and their inappropriate behaviors, ranging from violent assaults to inappropriate messages. Near the top of the list, I found the name of the editor from that party. I'd been right. I'd known it in my bones. Only then did I remember the woman I hadn't known, who'd popped her head out to check on me. I'd believed it had been a fortuitous accident, but looking at the spreadsheet, I realized she had just known more than I had, been privy to information I could have used.

I watched the document on my cell phone in a bar all evening, not adding to it but waiting for the rest of the names I knew to arrive. Not all of them appeared, but each one that did felt like a weight being lifted off me, a brief moment of confirmation.

Have you ever watched a video of a dam breaking? Dams are so large and so strong. They are made of concrete, and they fail very, very slowly. Cracks appear and widen over years, stretch their arms long and lean through the gray walls, under the water they're supposed to restrain. And then all of a sudden, one piece begins to move, the result of years of those tiny cracks working their way through the structure. Once the hole exists, the whole thing collapses.

"Call it a tsunami, but do not lose sight of the fact that each life is a single drop, how many drops it took to make a single wave.

The loss is incomprehensible, staggering, maddening—we should have caught it when it was no more than a drip. Instead society is flooded with survivors coming forward, dozens for every man, just so that one day, in his old age, he might feel a taste of what it was like for them all along," Chanel Miller wrote in her 2019 memoir *Know My Name*.

* * *

Watching the new, updated version of *Mean Girls* in 2024, I could not help but create a counternarrative for Coach Carr, because he is still there in the movie. Jon Hamm plays the character with the same tone of voice, the same bad sex education advice, the same bravado when he declares that the reason Regina George eats it during the holiday performance is because she isn't "lifting through her glutes." It's easy to believe that he's the same Coach Carr who made out with two high schoolers and that he simply faced no consequences.

The consequences, at times, feel nonexistent. Almost all of the men on the "Shitty Media Men" list continue to work in media. Bill Clinton was reelected. Donald Trump still became president. Woody Allen still makes movies. Louis C.K. still performs. A sexual assault conviction against Bill Cosby was overturned by the Pennsylvania Supreme Court after it determined that his right to due process had been violated as prosecutors sought a conviction. Johnny Depp was awarded a million dollars from his ex-wife Amber Heard in a case that swirled with disinformation on TikTok and YouTube in 2022.

Only an estimated 8 to 10 percent of rapes are reported to the police at all, which means that, conservatively, 90 percent of rapes are not. Of those that are reported, fewer than 1 percent of cases are resolved in a jury trial. In the Manhattan District Attorney's Office in 2019, 49 percent of sexual assault cases were dropped. The legal system is failing victims of sexual assault. We cannot trust it to save us, so it is tempting to believe that we can save ourselves.

As the #MeToo movement grew in popularity, women began to pass the stories of their assaults around and around like a bong full of misery. Everyone, take a hit, breathe deep into your lungs the truths about men you know. I know so much now about so many people who are abusers. But what can we do with that knowledge besides pass it on?

Whisper networks are not meant to form any kind of accountability. Instead, where a vacuum of justice exists, a whisper network will emerge. It is meant to be a way to arm yourself, to protect yourself from expected harm. "But joining a whisper network comes with a catch: it invites participants in on the condition of silence. And because of that, we often miss that whisper networks are a double-edged sword: the same secrecy that protects victims and whistleblowers can shield perpetrators as well," Sarah Jeong wrote in The Verge in 2018.

Whisper networks, as Jenna Wortham argued in the *New York Times,* can be elitist and insular and are prone to exclude women of color. Because whisper networks are not codified and require someone with knowledge to seek you out in particular and share it with you, they replicate the same kinds of racist, classist, and gender biases that exist in every aspect of our society. Take the Burn Book, for example. The information about Coach Carr was written down. It was shared among the Plastics, and—once she was inducted into their group—with Cady. But who else knew? The information to keep them safe from an abuser was gatekept by their group members' popularity, their insularity.

Due process, however, is not the goal of a whisper network, nor should it be. Conviction is also not the goal of a whisper network. The goal is always consciousness raising, to make you aware of how someone might behave, as if awareness is enough to protect you. Consciousness raising, that quaint idea popularized by the second-wave white feminists in an attempt to awaken housewives from their mundane stupor, isn't enough. It is something. But it isn't enough.

Think about Greta Gerwig's 2023 smash hit, *Barbie*. In it, the Barbies who live in Barbieland have developed a matriarchy in which the men (all named Ken except for one Allan) have no power. They have no jobs, no property, no seats on the Supreme Court. When one Ken (Ryan Gosling) visits the real world and learns about the patriarchy, he is thrilled: here is an opportunity to change his life, to better his world for the other Kens. He returns and, with his newly learned power, subjugates the women of Barbieland. The only way to awaken the Barbies is to raise their consciousnesses.

Within the confines of the movie this means that America Ferrera's character pulls a lot of the Barbies aside and delivers impassioned monologues to them. "It is literally impossible to be a woman. You are so beautiful, and so smart, and it kills me that you don't think you're good enough," she begins before going on to list a series of contradictions women must live within: thin but not too thin; have money but don't ask for it; be boss but not bossy. "Never forget that the system is rigged," she says, "so find a way to acknowledge that but also always be grateful."

There is a catharsis to this kind of rage. This frustration is one that most women can relate to. But within the film, once the speech does all the consciousness raising, everything else falls easily into place. The Barbies distract the Kens by getting them to turn on one another and fix the constitution to place all the Barbies in charge of everything again, or something. The plotting of this section of the movie is a little unclear. What is clear is that there is no justice in the Barbie movie. The Kens do not achieve anything close to citizenship nor are they asked to answer for the abuses they rained upon the Barbies. In Barbieland, there are no consequences. The raising of your consciousness is enough to save you. It felt dated to claim that the problems with womanhood lie buried and unspoken when *The Feminine Mystique* had been in print for more than fifty years.

While I watched the movie, I remembered a section from Jia Tolentino's book *Trick Mirror: Reflections on Self-Delusion*, in which she wrote of the #MeToo movement: "There was something about the hashtag itself—its design, and the ways of thinking that it affirms and solidifies—that both erased the variety of women's experiences and made it seem as if the crux of feminism was this articulation of vulnerability itself... Even as women have attempted to use #YesAllWomen and #MeToo to regain control of a narrative, these hashtags have at least partially reified the thing they're trying to eradicate: the way that womanhood can feel like a story of loss of control. They have made feminist solidarity and shared vulnerability seem inextricable, as if we were incapable of building solidarity around anything else."

That is the accidental trap of consciousness raising: the belief that it is enough; that by gossiping about someone we can find justice; that by participating in whisper networks and telling other people our beliefs, we are doing our part. "We'd like to think that if a whisper network came to us... we would be able to do the right thing. But the likely truth is that at this very moment, we are being called upon to act, and we are failing without even realizing it. Worse, if a reckoning ever comes, we will likely pretend we were doing the right thing all along," Sarah Jeong wrote in *The Verge*. That is the end point of believing that consciousness raising and awareness and gossip and whisper networks are enough: a world in which we allow the civilization that we have built to overshadow our ability to hold one another accountable.

Removing the Coach Carr allegations from the end of the 2024 musical *Mean Girls* means that the only problematic allegation in the new Burn Book is the erroneous claim that Ms. Norbury is a drug pusher. But in what high school would that allegation be taken seriously without any reason to believe that the rest of the pages were true? It would be too easy to dismiss the whole book as a childish gambit without any evidence.

Deleting the Coach Carr subplot makes the movie easier to digest and stomach, but it also removes one of the most important questions that arises in any prosocial gossip: Where did the information come from?

As every teen girl knows well, you cannot gossip with just anyone. Gossip requires a kind of mutual vulnerability, an innate trust. When we gossip with someone, we bring them information in the hope that they will trust it, while knowing that they will judge us based on its quality and verifiability. Whisper networks, prosocial gossip, and gossiping in general about people directly connected to us enable us to create a web of information that can keep us safe. It can help us identify abusers, avoid people who are mean, and know which of our crushes doesn't like us at all. Gossip can't always save us from harm, but it can teach us whom to trust.

I work as a waitress in Los Angeles. I really love my job, and it can be hard, but for the most part, people are reasonable. Once, [celebrity name] came in, though, and was awful to me. I left feeling so bad. So, I sent a message to Deuxmoi and she published it. God, it felt great. Now, whenever I have a bad day, I sometimes slide into her DMs with a totally made-up story. I love doing it. I'm sorry!

Anon Plz

The greatest mistake *Gossip Girl* ever made was revealing that Dan Humphrey had been the anonymous writer behind the blog all along. All good stories have an engine, and that's what *Gossip Girl* forgot. The reductive way to understand a story engine is to conflate it with plot. You have to set up dominoes, writing teachers say, in order to knock them down. But you can set up a line of dominoes that falls perfectly in a straight line and doesn't make anyone feel anything at all. You can set them up poorly, the edge of one barely clipping the edge of another, and they will fall, sure. But to what end? Making a perfect plot does not guarantee that your story won't be boring. What makes a story engine isn't *events* within the context of the story; it is the cadence of questions and reveals. Dominoes are too simple; what you want is to juggle a half dozen balls, the questions rising into the air only to fall back down again, being caught just when the reader thinks they won't be.

One of the most exciting questions for a reader, a viewer, or a listener is the classic whodunnit. Add a major mysterious question to the top of any story, and you've got a hook. *Gossip Girl*'s choice to have an anonymous blogger be the voice of the show was brilliant. We are drawn to all kinds of unverified gossip from anonymous sources. There is little more intriguing than an author without a name or face, a persona constructed to give us information. Draped in a shroud of anonymity, the mundane can become intriguing, because the intrigue of the teller matters more than verifying the facts. The gossip almost always turns to question who is behind the curtain in Oz, because anonymity is a way to claim power that doesn't belong to you, for better or for worse.

I was a sophomore in high school when *Gossip Girl* premiered on the CW in 2007. It was just before the first major recession of my lifetime and a year before Barack Obama was elected president. It premiered two weeks after I got my driver's license. Huge things were happening! And the influence of *Gossip Girl* was everywhere. Everyone was buying circle scarves and knee-high boots and curling their hair with a half-inch iron. All the girls at my school loved to talk about it, because it was a show that knew how to get teenagers to talk. In its first sixteen episodes, *Gossip Girl*'s plot delivered a suicide attempt, an apparent drug addiction, a pregnancy scare, a marriage proposal, not one but two attempted rapes, someone losing their virginity, a threesome, an eating disorder, and implied murder.

Gossip Girl presented a half dozen questions in its pilot; the first was "Why did Serena go to Connecticut for boarding school?" This question is the crux of season one. It was answered late in the season with a cliff-hanger: Serena saying, "I killed someone." That then sets up seventeen new questions: Why did she kill someone? Who did she kill? Later, Serena revealed that it was an accidental death, a cocaine overdose. But that's neither here nor there because the most important question in the show that strings every episode of *Gossip Girl* together is reiterated in the opening credits of every single episode.

"Who am I?" Gossip Girl wonders over the opening credits. A question and a promise: "That's one secret I'll never tell."

What made *Gossip Girl* (the original) one of the best teen dramas was that promise. The best gossip, we all know, needs to feel a little secret. Something needs to be anonymous, to leave a question lingering in our minds, to make us come back for more. In the multi-book young adult series by Cecily von Ziegesar that the show is based on, she never did tell. The books never revealed who ran the Gossip Girl blog. As Joy Montgomery wrote for *British Vogue*, part of what made *Gossip Girl* work was the Orwellian narrator "whose disembodied omnipresence allowed her to meddle in the lives of the show's characters without justification, or indeed the need to be physically present in the unfolding drama."

Initially, the TV adaptation wasn't certain who its mastermind was, either. Joshua Safran, who executive produced the original *Gossip Girl* and showran its reboot, told the Daily Beast that even two seasons before the finale, there was no fixed plan for who would be revealed as the anonymous blogger. I assumed, as many people in my cohort did, that Gossip Girl would be...well...a girl.

But *DAN HUMPHREY*? It couldn't be Dan.

Sure, Dan had the most to gain from being the *TMZ* of the Upper East Side private school regime. "If I wasn't born into this world," Dan says in the final reveal, "maybe, I could write myself into it." His dad has less money than pretty much everyone else (huge fancy Williamsburg, Brooklyn, apartment rich, not Hamptons rich), and as an outsider, being Gossip Girl allowed him to manipulate situations to his benefit without the social cachet that would require. But the plot of the show doesn't make any damn sense with Dan at its center. Gossip Girl's perhaps number one target is Serena van der Woodsen, who is theoretically Dan's girlfriend and eventual (after the five-year flash-forward in the series finale) wife. Gossip Girl also targeted Dan's little sister, Jenny, and revealed some of Dan's own failures (kissing Serena's best friend! dating Hilary Duff in her minor character cameo!). "If you retconned it and put in all the sequences of Dan being Gossip Girl and showed him sending posts of his girlfriend while she was sleeping next to him, you'd think this guy was more dangerous than Joe in *You*," Safran told the Daily Beast.

The funny thing is that the show did not need to answer the question that hovered over the whole series, because who Gossip Girl really was doesn't really matter to the plot. Her purpose, to strip a little bit of power from these insanely rich and powerful teens, is fulfilled regardless of who posts the blogs of their bad behaviors. And by revealing anyone as Gossip Girl, the show lost the premise that made it glimmer: that we would never know who Gossip Girl was because it didn't matter. The point all along was her anonymity, and we loved it.

Gossip Girl signs off her blogs with "xoxo, Gossip Girl." But the line before that rings as more important to me. "You know you love me," Gossip Girl says in the show's introduction. And we do. We love information from anonymous sources. We love to gobble it up unverified and spit it back out. We love not knowing who is telling us something because then we don't have to question it, don't have to worry about the morality of its consumption, or who might be grabbing power by sharing this information. Under the beautiful shadow of anonymity, the author gains protection, but we, the consumer, do, too.

* * *

Very few people would have written in to Gossip Girl with their name attached. Part of what made the blog believable as a fictional device was that it is so much easier to tell the truth if you can't be directly implicated in the telling. Behind the gauzy veil of anonymity, the words on the page could have come from anyone, and that's part of why anonymous writings are such a joy to read: no one is holding back to save face. Take, for example, the incredibly gossipy, long-running blog series Refinery29's *Money Diaries*.

Money Diaries is one of my favorite anonymous series because there is nothing people are as private and weird and lying about as money. It took me until my midtwenties to realize that a lot of the people making the same low media salary as I was had money coming in from other sources because they hid it. Having money and not having money are embarrassing states in different ways, and people do a lot to disguise how much they have in savings or how much they have in credit card debt. But *Money Diaries* takes a random, anonymized person and has them lay out exactly how much money they have, how they spend it, and where it all goes. The series, which launched in 2016 and relates the stories of individual women across the country, reveals so much about the world. It's voyeurism for normal people.

Most of the entries are common. People spend their money in normal, if also irresponsible ways. Usually, they show tech workers in New York buying $6 lattes and ordering $40 takeout. Same! I have managed to spend that amount of money even when it was destroying my life. It is expensive to be alive and bad with money! But the *Money Diaries* entries that go viral are most often from anonymous writers who seem to believe that their relationship with money is normal but who do not live in the same reality as the rest of us. They are showing people without generational wealth a side of society that we might not even know exists just by laying out how they spend their money.

A good example of this was a July 2018 entry from a twenty-one-year-old marketing intern. Originally titled, "A Week in New York City on $25/Hour and $1k Monthly Allowance," the blog received more than a thousand comments quickly after publication. The outcry against this blog was swift and furious because the woman who wrote it did not actually make $25 per hour. That was what she made from her internship, but the blog goes on to detail that she receives $1,000 in monthly allowance and that her parents paid her ($2,100) rent, her phone bill, her health insurance, and her streaming service accounts. There's nothing wrong with having your family front your start in New York City; what the maelstrom of discontent directed at the blog stemmed from was the idea that she made $25 per hour. She did, technically, but not in the way that every other twenty-one-year-old marketing intern making $25 per hour without any financial support did.

Many young writers (myself included) balked at this blog post because of the reality it displayed: tons of young creatives are able to sustain a career not because they are more talented or harder working than others but because they come in with such a hefty financial cushion that they are able to succeed easily. "It seems, to me, that there are real anxieties detectable in these diaries and comments, ones that are specific to a young female demographic," Carrie Battan wrote in the *New Yorker*. The anxiety stems from a whole cohort of young creatives who are afraid that not having that cushion will cause them to fail. But all of that backlash and fear and anxiety are able to exist because this blog was written anonymously. The truth the author told was greater than just her spending habits.

It's telling that two of the most off-limits subjects for most people (money and sex) are often written about by anonymous sources. Erotic novels like *Memoirs of a Russian Princess* (1890) and *The Autobiography of a Flea* (1887) were published anonymously to protect their authors. For *Memoirs of a Russian Princess*, that worked so well that we still aren't sure who its writers are. Another example is the book *The Incest Diary*, published anonymously in 2017. The author of the memoir, which tells a heart-wrenching story of parental abuse and incest, pleads with the reader to allow the author to maintain this secrecy. "I have changed many specifics in order to preserve my anonymity. But I have not altered the essentials. I ask the reader to respect my wish to remain anonymous," she writes. The book is short and nauseating and almost unbearably honest, something that feels possible at least in part because her name was not on it.

When we talk about sex and money, what we are actually talking about is power and who wields it. Anonymity gives people without power an opportunity to grab a little bit as their own. In the early years of women's novel writing, the stigma of publishing as a woman was so great that in *A Room of One's Own*, Virginia Woolf wrote that many anonymous figures were women. More accurately, Anonymous is anyone subjected, anyone trying to find a way to claw back a little bit of what has been taken from them.

In many cases, the protection of anonymity allowed writers to question authority structures that might have had them hanged were their names attached. *La Vida de Lazarillo de Tormes*, a Spanish novella published in 1554, was anonymous because of its strong anti-clerical content in a Catholic country. It was later banned by the Spanish Inquisition. Jonathan Swift published *A Tale of a Tub* anonymously because of its satire against the Anglican Church and Christian branches at large. Thomas Paine anonymously published *Common Sense* at the beginning of the American Revolution. And *The Federalist* papers, a collection of eighty-five essays promoting the ratification of the US Constitution, were also published initially without the authors' real names. The graffiti artist Banksy works anonymously, perhaps in part because of running the risk of being prosecuted for vandalism. There's a reason the hacktivist collective that launched a campaign to harass the Church of Scientology after Gawker published a nine-minute video of Tom Cruise talking about his beliefs in 2008 uses the name Anonymous.

All of these anonymous publications are attempts to honestly talk about power. This anonymity is a tool to speak openly about someone more powerful than you, and often it is used specifically as a way to talk about class divisions. The Refinery29 diary by a girl with family money is part of a long history of gossip written anonymously to discuss the rich and famous.

At least since the late nineteenth century, Americans have been printing one another's gossip. One of those gossip rags might even be familiar to you if you've ever read F. Scott Fitzgerald's 1925 classic *The Great Gatsby*. Reading the book almost a century later means that I always skimmed right past some of the references, but one fun one is that when Myrtle goes into Manhattan, she buys a magazine called *Town Tattle* from a newsstand. Any 1925 New York socialite would have known immediately that this was a satire of *Town Topics*, which was essentially the Roaring Twenties' Gossip Girl. Or perhaps more accurately, it was like Lady Whistledown's newsletter in *Bridgerton*. But instead of Regency families, this was full of drama about big American high society, which was eagerly read by families like the Vanderbilts.

Town Topics was published from 1885 to 1937. On the cover of one issue, there were two women with bared shoulders whispering! What a scandal! Inside was an anonymous column called "Saunterings," written by the "Saunterer." "Saunterings" was crowdsourced and reprinted in an authorial voice.

It reported the goings-on about town anonymously and swiftly. The Saunterer wrote about summer vacation travails and who was secretly due to be divorced. Of the twelve pages of *Town Topics*, "Saunterings" typically took up six. Katrin Horn wrote in an academic essay that "most histories of US American magazines do not mention *Town Topics* at all. Gossip, it seems, has no place in studies of nineteenth century print culture, which focus instead on supposedly serious innovations like 'new journalism.'" But *Town Topics* was popular. Few magazines last that long, and even fewer allot six pages to a single column.

Town Topics also loved to anonymize the gossip itself. The Saunterer might be direct and state that a couple was getting divorced with their names right there in print, but sometimes they jazzed it up a little bit. In 1904, for example, "Saunterings" ran this blind item:

> From wearing costly lingerie to indulging in fancy dances for the edification of men was only a step. And then came—second step—indulging freely in stimulants…They are given to saying almost anything at the Reading Room, but I was really surprised to hear her name mentioned openly there in connection with that of a certain multi-millionaire of the colony and with certain doings that gentle people are not supposed to discuss. They also said that she should not have listened to the risqué jokes told her by the son of one of her Newport hostesses.

It wasn't anything out of the ordinary for the "Saunterings" column except that everyone knew that this blind item was about Alice Roosevelt, President Theodore Roosevelt's daughter. President Roosevelt is quoted as having once said, "I can do one of two things. I can be President of the United States or I can control Alice Roosevelt. I cannot possibly do both." The gossip about Alice was never ending, because she was always out and about doing things, and people, of course, had opinions about this. The anonymity of the blind item allowed *Town Topics* to share information about what she was up to with the general public without being sued for libel. (The magazine did eventually get sued for an extortion scheme in which they typically sent a mock issue to the people mentioned and required them to pay for a certain article to be removed, but that's another story.)

I wish I could have read *Town Topics* in its heyday because I love the blind items. I always have. As a preteen, I would log on to our family computer, navigate to Crazy Days and Nights, and read the anonymous entries. One of my favorite blind items from another site I read in 1998 that was aggregated from the *New York Post* read, "WHICH top model's smile looks a little brighter these days? The covergirl recently shelled out $8,000 for a new set of porcelain caps." I had braces, and they were miserable, and once you start wondering if someone's teeth are fake, you see the pearly white gravestone veneers everywhere. Part of what I love about blind items is the mystery, but it is almost always easy to deduce who the post might be about. What's more fascinating is seeing how the other half lives. I want to know what the celebrities don't want me to know. I want the actual truth: that the teeth are fake, and the marriage is over, and the "long runs" are actually Ozempic.

Every day I go to a website called Blind Item Rehash that does not appear to have updated its code since it launched in 1998, and I read the anonymously submitted blind items with my mouth agape. Who is rumored to be pregnant? Who doesn't tip well? It's the same awe and intrigue that now exist on Instagram in the form of Deuxmoi, but in the blind items the clues are like puzzles that never disappear. Perez Hilton and Lainey Gossip (both of which used pseudonyms but whose writers have since been revealed) have been publishing anonymous gossip for two decades. Crazy Days and Nights, which I have read since it began publishing rumors in 2006, managed to maintain his anonymity until court documents were filed in 2023.

During the 2020 pandemic, everyone's social circles were obliterated. People were desperate for gossip, and Deuxmoi provided it. Deuxmoi had been a fashion blog since 2013 and had about 45,000 followers on Instagram when it solicited celebrity gossip from its followers. By the end of 2020, more than 530,000 people followed the account. The account posted dozens of anonymously submitted secrets every single day; their subject lines, often visible, read "anon plz." Sometimes, they were true. Deuxmoi broke news of Zoë Kravitz dating Channing Tatum just by noting her Instagram behavior, for example, and sources confirmed it to *People*. But sometimes she was wrong.

The account's Instagram bio reads: "some statements made on this account have not been independently confirmed. this account does not claim information published is based in fact." Deuxmoi posts rapidly and rabidly, on stories that disappear after twenty-four hours. I have read on Deuxmoi about divorces and secret weddings that never panned out. Some submitters have claimed they made up some posts entirely.

Maybe because Deuxmoi rocketed in popularity so quickly, or maybe because she's become so influential that Taylor Swift's longtime publicist, Tree Paine, gets mad enough at the posts about her client to tweet about it, people have become obsessed with discovering who the woman behind the account is. "If the tables were turned, I wouldn't care," the woman who runs Deuxmoi told *Vanity Fair* in 2021. "I'm not getting an ego boost from this because nobody knows me . . . I was never trying to be Gossip Girl or some mysterious lurker in the night."

This is a lie, of course. Anyone who cares about celebrities also cares about the people who report on them. But the reason people care who she is isn't just abject curiosity; it's because we know that anonymity gives you power. Information that goes unpublished can be, and has been in our history, used to blackmail or extort people. We want to know who the person behind Gossip Girl is because without knowing who is spreading the gossip, we cannot be sure whether to trust it, much less know that person's biases. Even though gossip from anonymous sources can reveal more about our world and the people in it than bylined gossip does, it feels dangerous to trust in gossip without a source. Because who really knows if any of it is true? That question that reverberates through the *Gossip Girl* intro—"Who am I?"—is always going to be present when anonymity is in play.

* * *

The first question a good gossip learns to ask is "Where did this come from?" Did the story that made my jaw drop come from a true friend of a friend? Or did it filter through the minds and mouths of a hundred strangers before it reached the two of us? When you train as a reporter, you do this strategically: ask two or three people where they heard something and see if you can begin to create a path back to the actual original source. Maryann Ayim wrote in her article "Knowledge Through the Grapevine" that "there may indeed be gossipers who leap to conclusions on the basis of inadequate evidence; the good gossiper, however, will not do so. She will check her sources carefully, and one of her criteria for placing confidence in a belief will be the replication of findings among the pool of qualified investigators."

When researchers model the way gossip spreads, they can use the same distributed algorithms that model the propagation of infectious disease. Patient Zero for a true gossip story, in my experience, is almost always the subject or someone close to them. For a lie, though, the source could be anyone. With gossip it is less important to me that I know exactly who began a story and how it started than that I understand how many degrees of separation exist between me and the person who experienced it. The more bodies between me and Patient Zero, the less I trust the information I'm being given. That doesn't mean it's not true, of course, just that I start off with more skepticism.

A great way to thwart this system is to give information anonymously. If you do not know exactly where the information came from, you cannot even semi-accurately judge how seriously to take it. All anonymous gossip could be true. It could also all be false.

Take an excellent source of fully anonymous gossip, Reddit's AmItheAsshole page: a subreddit where people post (theoretically) true accounts of their behaviors and ask strangers to weigh in on their choices. For the people who submit to AITA, the subreddit exists to help them understand how their behaviors might be perceived by others. But for the people reading it, AITA is entertainment. And AmItheAsshole is pure voyeurism. The only thing that might make it better is knowing that you are closely acquainted with the person asking the question.

But sometimes, the posts on AITA are completely made up. Many stories that go viral across Reddit are conjured out of thin air. Shal, a moderator for the @redditships Twitter account, told Vice in 2020 that they estimate that somewhere between 5 and 10 percent of popular r/relationship_advice posts may be fake. They also said that "the account's followers are sharing their feelings, interpretations and personal experiences, which are valid regardless of the truth of the post."

In some cases, though, it's not speculation that the posts are made up. Cartoons Hate Her, an anonymous cartoonist and troll who wrote dozens of fake viral Reddit relationship posts, wrote in her book *The Troll Handbook: 100s of Accounts, 100s of Bans, 100s of Posts, One Bored Girl* that "there are no two subreddits more plagued with fake posts than r/AmITheAsshole and r/relationships." Throughout her storied (and anonymous) career, Cartoons Hate Her went viral for posts about a dad catfishing his own son, a seventy-two-year-old woman mad about her granddaughter having sex, a man whose wife had scammed him out of five luxury exercise bikes, and a dad who demanded to dress up as a clitoris for Halloween.

After reading Cartoons Hate Her's book, I realized I had discussed several of these posts with my friends. One that she wrote from the perspective of Janice, a seventy-two-year-old conservative woman, about how her daughter was allowing her fourteen-year-old granddaughter to be a slut by putting her on birth control, had been the subject of jokes and banter among my friends for days. "People might also argue that trolling is unethical. I measure the ethics of trolling by how many people's days were made better versus worse by my trolls," she wrote.

It does not matter as much to the voyeuristic pleasure of r/AmItheAsshole or r/relationship_advice that all the stories are true as much as it matters that they are anonymous. "There's something almost thrilling about peeking behind the curtain into other people's lives, hearing their weird thoughts—what they think deep down of their partners, children, friends," Princeton University ethicist Eleanor Gordon-Smith told the *Guardian* about AITA. Part of the joy of those stories is that you have no idea where they come from. It could be your sister, or your classmate, or someone on the other side of the world you will never meet writing to ask about whether they're the asshole because they lie about being allergic to peanuts to get attention. Reddit banned Cartoons Hate Her's usernames and eventually her entire IP address so that she cannot troll anymore.

One thing that Cartoons Hate Her wrote that really stuck out to me is that often, the people on Reddit who saw her posts would clock them as fake, but then when they were aggregated and reposted to Twitter or Instagram, readers were more gullible. They did not question their veracity at all. Without context, our barriers lower; we lose the ability to remain skeptical.

Psychologists have also found that if we hear something and understand it, we will believe it and remember it. It does not matter whether that information is true or not. In a meta-analysis that used results from thirty-two studies with 6,500 participants, academics found that even when falsehoods are corrected, it does not eliminate misinformation. We just also retain the correction. The scientists also found that corrections were less effective when they came from a different source than the one that had spouted the lies to begin with. Once we've read one of these posts, then, we believe it and we remember it, and we repeat it over drinks, and it can spread that way forever.

The posts on Gossip Girl are texted or emailed in, and then rewritten by (I guess) Dan Humphrey to maintain a consistent tone. Though sometimes the information comes with evidence such as photos or videos, it does not seem as though Dan vets his sources thoroughly. Instead, like Deuxmoi's and other blind items, he posts tips anonymously without verification.

For the most part, the posts on Gossip Girl seem to be true. There is one episode in season four in which someone connives to generate a fake post saying that Serena has an STI, but otherwise there's only one other prominent example. In season two, Gossip Girl publishes a tip from Blair that a new teacher at the school (who funnily enough is named Rachel Carr, though it is unclear if she and *Mean Girls'* Coach Carr are any relation) is having an affair with Dan. And again, we must remember that Dan should not be Gossip Girl. In my opinion, this is the first time in the series that we see the Gossip Girl blog publishing an abject lie—libel, really.

This is the first time we as viewers see the power anonymity really carries. Blair, although she is extremely wealthy, is still very much a teen girl. Her new teacher gives her a low grade on a paper, even though it might hurt her chances of getting into Yale, and won't change it. Is it entitled and absurd to demand your grade be changed just because you want it to be, and then when it is not, accuse a teacher of sleeping with a student on a popular blog? Absolutely, it is. But the people around Blair know that she sent the tip, and she is expelled from their fancy school for her misbehavior. There are no consequences for Gossip Girl.

Without clarity about who is writing the blog, and who is submitting the gossip, there is plenty of room to abuse the system. This use of anonymity to spread lies is part of the reason that people are so uncomfortable with anonymous authorship and gossip from anonymous sources. Anonymity prevents people from taking any kind of accountability for their actions.

In some ways, the power gained by being anonymous can stay unchecked. Unlike the *Gossip Girl* blog days, teens today know better than to leave their secrets out in the open for adults and parents to read. Many high schools have private gossip Instagram accounts that require students to request to follow in order to read the updates. Some have Google forms for students to submit the gossip and remain anonymous. Many of these accounts are even named [HighSchoolName]Gossip_Girl. In 2022, more than eleven thousand individuals, including parents and teachers, signed a petition asking Instagram to control these accounts, saying that they bully students, which goes against the community guidelines for the app. "The thing about tea pages is that they're anonymous. So I think that's given an outlet for people who don't want to be mean outright. They send anonymous messages to tea pages…and that doesn't have, like, any connection [to them]. It's anonymous. So it's an easy way to insult people or cyberbully people without *being* the cyberbully, publicly," Emily Weinstein and Carrie James recounted a teenager saying in their book *Behind Their Screens: What Teens Are Facing (and Adults Are Missing)*.

Take, for example, an account like Libs of TikTok, which launched in early 2021. Libs of TikTok quickly became one of the most powerful discourse creators in right-wing media. The account demanded that teachers who come out be fired and accused those educators of participating in "grooming." The videos would then get picked up by mainstream conservative media, shown on Fox News, and used as a rationale for creating a hate campaign against private citizens. The account was anonymous for about a year before it was revealed that a woman named Chaya Raichik ran it.

"Raichik has said in interviews that she crowdsources the content for the feed from a flood of messages she receives every day. In that sense, Libs of TikTok is a collective, molded to the hive mind of the right-wing Internet. She views her account as giving a voice and platform to concerned parents and ordinary citizens," Taylor Lorenz wrote in the *Washington Post* in April 2022. Raichik's beliefs would be comically evil if they weren't so scary.

Anonymous writers can use their power however they want. In that way they replicate the same systems that anonymity itself can attempt to dismantle. With every post, they gain more and more attention, and in this economy, attention is money. There are rarely consequences for a creator like Raichik who used her anonymity to create a hate cycle and continues to wield the power of her privilege to oppress other people. The office of Florida governor Ron DeSantis said she was impactful during the construction of the "Don't Say Gay" bill. There are no consequences for Deuxmoi (at least not yet) for publishing tips that aren't true. There were never any consequences for Gossip Girl, either. Anonymity is a shield, and, like the gossip it allows and distributes, it can be used for good and for evil.

*　*　*

When *Gossip Girl* rebooted in 2021, Safran tried to learn from the Dan Humphrey disaster. But instead of choosing a Gossip Girl from the beginning and building a plot toward the answer or never revealing who was behind the new blog at all, he gave away the answer right away. The new *Gossip Girl*, this time on HBO and filled with less-tame sex scenes, was on air for only two seasons. Charlie Markbreiter wrote in *Gossip Girl Fanfic Novella* that the reboot was "Like high production value and *Euphoria* lights. But also not fully because they were trying to make it look *Succession*-y. Like there was a hole somewhere that all the color was slowly being drained out of. It tried to be two opposite things and so just ended up confused, like a rich person without taste who just buys everything in the store."

In the new *Gossip Girl*, the blog (now an Instagram account) is run by Kate Keller (played by Tavi Gevinson, herself a storied blogger and the founder of *Rookie*). Keller, who is a teacher at the prep school, creates the account to try to keep the students in line. "Coming up with the idea of knowing who Gossip Girl was from the top—and having it be a teacher—was the thing that excited me the most, because it's doing the show in a new way instead of just retreading," Safran told the *Daily Beast*.

This is a fundamental misunderstanding of what made the original show work. Revealing Gossip Girl in the first episode means that the show has no driving question at its core. "This eliminates the sense of mystery from the show because instead of theorizing over GG's true identity, viewers are left to wonder when the teachers behind GG will finally be exposed, especially since they don't do a great job of hiding it," Claudia Picado wrote for Collider. But not only did unmasking the new Gossip Girl bloggers remove the central question that drove the original show; it revealed exactly why anonymity is so important for consumers of information.

The question of when the teachers running Gossip Girl will get caught could theoretically be a viable premise for a TV show if it were easy to like the teachers. But liking the teachers in this context requires the viewer to detest the students. In this version, Keller recruits other teachers to help her run the account. The students may not respect their teachers, the show seems to say, but teens do fear privacy invasion! If the goal of the original *Gossip Girl* was entertainment, the goal of the new one is enforcement. The concern is less with who is doing what, and more with how that information might be used. It's blackmail, really.

And because we the viewers know from the get-go that the teachers are Gossip Girl, we cannot enjoy their posts. If we believed that Gossip Girl was a fellow teen, we might be able to understand why she would post semi-nude photos of students online. But knowing the source imbues the story with a fundamental ickiness that it can't shake. Would a teacher believe that revealing the deepest traumas of a student's life would lead to better behavior in the classroom? No good teacher would, at least.

The show attempts to remedy this imbalance by highlighting the immense class difference between the teachers and their students. But a reliance on wealth disparity isn't why the premise falls apart. There are plenty of shows where rich people behave poorly and a middle-class proxy character functions as a stand-in to help the viewer know how to feel. *White Lotus* did this very well in both seasons by giving the workers at the hotels their own plots and biases. Even in the original *Gossip Girl*, Dan Humphrey and his sister, Jenny, were perfect stand-ins to help the viewer see how ridiculous the behaviors of their rich classmates were. So why don't the teachers function in the same role?

Part of the problem with the teachers functioning as Gossip Girl is that they are adults, and we expect adults to behave better than children. But the real issue is that when information comes from an anonymous source, we the consumers are able to imagine that our actions in response to it do not matter.

A real-life example of this is the apparent unmasking of Elena Ferrante. Ferrante (a pen name used to protect the author's anonymity) most famously wrote the Neapolitan Novels: four beautiful, languid books about the lifelong friendship between two girls in Naples. Ferrante writes anonymously, she has said in interviews, to gain space outside the machine of publishing and marketing. But in October 2016, Claudio Gatti, an Italian reporter for the Italian newspaper *Il Sole 24 Ore*, used real estate records and leaked financial documents from the publisher to argue that he had discovered Ferrante's true identity. He published in multiple languages his theory that the mysterious author was Anita Raja. The English-language version of the story went online at 1:00 a.m. EST, and I woke up in the morning to dozens of text messages. All of my friends who had read the books were reeling. I was conflicted: on the one hand, I wanted to know, I needed to know who had written these books that I loved. On the other, I wanted to allow the magic of her anonymity to live a little bit longer.

"There are so few avenues left, in our all-seeing, all-revealing digital world, for artistic mystery of the true kind—mystery that isn't concocted as a publicity play but that finds its origins in the writer's soul as a prerogative of his or her ability to create," Alexandra Schwartz wrote in the *New Yorker* after Gatti's article came out.

I want to believe that anonymity should be preserved, but I do think that there is sense in Gatti's reasoning for the reveal. In her collection of essays and letters *Frantumaglia*, Ferrante quotes Italo Calvino as saying, "Ask me what you want to know, but I won't tell you the truth, of that you can be sure," adding to it, "I've always liked that passage, and I've made it at least partly mine." This, Gatti argues, is why her identity should be revealed: because she might be lying. That's the problem with anonymity: it is so damn hard to verify.

He chose to reveal Elena Ferrante's identity, Gatti said, because she had been lying to her readers. If the author is who Gatti believes, she didn't actually grow up in Naples. The stories in the Neapolitan Novels are therefore not true to her lived experience. It's worth noting that this does not make them weaker works. They can still be true in other ways: emotionally, for example. The books are novels, and fiction is famously lies. But many people balk when forced to acknowledge that fiction can make them feel something even if it is not real.

While the rational part of our mind, the prefrontal cortex, knows that fiction is, well, fiction, and that we should be skeptical of anonymous sources and writing in general, the other parts of our brain do not. Horror movies induce real physiological responses. You can get goose bumps from a ghost story, after all, even without any visuals. In the 2023 movie *Anatomy of a Fall*, a prosecutor reads the protagonist's autofiction to her on the stand as evidence that she may have wanted to kill her husband. How, he asks, could she have had those thoughts and written those words if she had not really felt them?

What are the consequences of knowing who Elena Ferrante is? It is titillating in the moment to know who an anonymous writer is, but in the long run, the end of that anonymity is the end of a question that we love to ruminate on. In exchange for knowledge, we trade wonder, which feels like an unfair trade when entertainment is concerned.

If our curiosity is preserved, we do not have to question whether or not we are morally culpable in our consumption of anonymously provided gossip. If we don't know for sure where the information came from, how can we be held accountable for any ramifications it might have? There is safety as a gossip in getting information from anonymous sources that disintegrates the minute you know where the information comes from. That's why it feels uncomfortable to watch the new *Gossip Girl*. There is no buffer zone. We know who the "anonymous" writers are, and so we know all of their flaws and biases. We cannot see any greater truths that might be revealed by the posts because they have scraped all of what's interesting and lively and fun about anonymity out of it.

Anonymous gossip is about escape, entertainment, and wonder. It's about uncertainty and fear. It's about seeing things in the world that we would never see otherwise, and it's about who got fillers. We love anonymity because we love the chase, because we always want to know what's happening on the other side.

I am obsessed with this singer. It started kind of as a joke. I would DM her whenever I was feeling sad or having a bad day, knowing that she would never read it. But doing that made me love her even more! Now I can't stop! I DM her all the time and none of my friends know, because I know that it is irrational and maybe kind of crazy? But it really feels like she's my friend. We have so much in common. If we met, I just know we would be besties, but I'm also pretty sure we never will.

Leave Britney Alone

For the entirety of my teens and early adulthood, whenever I had to dress up for Halloween, I went as Britney Spears. There are so many Britneys a person can be: "Oops!…I Did It Again" Britney, "Circus" Britney, Schoolgirl Britney, All-Denim Britney at the 2001 American Music Awards, *Mickey Mouse Club* Britney, Bride Who Kissed Madonna Britney. It is sometimes hard to pretend to be someone you're not, but like millions of other teenage girls across America, I could always imagine being Britney Spears. She was a blonde like me, she came from a family without a lot of money like me, she was a Christian like me. And she had managed something I dreamed of for myself: getting out. She'd been talented enough to escape the South and her social class and her community. If the American Dream existed, it seemed like it existed for her. And so, I presumed that maybe it could exist for me, since I was pretty certain that I was her biggest fan.

I was six years old when "…Baby One More Time" came out. I didn't know, at the time, about producers or stage moms or child star complexes. I had no idea that Max Martin existed. I lived in bliss. What I knew was that Britney Spears was the coolest girl alive, and I loved her. I unfolded (very carefully) the lyrics booklet inside her CD to reveal a poster of Britney, and I tacked it to my wall. I used the landline to call in to the Radio Disney station and request her songs. When girls on the playground asked me whether I liked NSYNC or Backstreet Boys better, I was defiant. I didn't care about them; I cared only about Britney Spears.

I have not ever been a fan of anyone or anything on the scale that I was a Britney fan. It was as if I had been injected with some kind of virus that made the blood in my body pump at the same bpm as the songs on her first album. I was not a graceful child, but I tried to dance to Britney, the bruises on my elbows and legs the inevitable conclusions of an animalistic urge. The stuffed animals on my bed were my audience. My room, painted a soft yellow, was my stadium, and the window seat was my stage.

Did I have stage fright? Yes. Did I have two huge buckteeth? Yes. Was I a good singer? Not at all. But I had passion, and I had the book with the lyrics, and eventually I had my own portable CD player to carry around. I handled the light blue disk with the yellow flower as if it could shatter at any moment. I did not touch the shiny side. I never allowed it to live outside of its case. I forbade my younger sister to touch it lest she mess it up. I protected it because I loved it.

A decade later, when I was the same age Britney had been when she released the eponymous single, I would record the album CD (already outdated then) onto an even more outdated form, the cassette tape, so that I could play it in my car. By then, though, things were different. I turned sixteen in the fall of 2007, which was not the best time to be a Britney Spears fan. Now that year is a meme, a bright white font that reads: "If Britney Spears can make it through 2007, I can make it through this day." In many, the words are splashed across a photo taken with a full flash. In it, Spears is wearing a hoodie, her pupils the size of dinner plates, her arms threatening to swing a giant umbrella, her head freshly, scandalously shaved.

When I tell people that I dressed as Britney every year for Halloween, they always have the same question: have you been Bald Britney? Every time, I lie and say I have. I don't know how to explain to someone who would ask that question that to do so would feel like heresy. "This was one of the worst moments of my whole life, and he kept after me. Couldn't he treat me like a human being?" Spears wrote in her memoir, *The Woman in Me.* "Pathetic, really. An umbrella. You can't even do any damage with an umbrella. It was a desperate move by a desperate person."

In the *Framing Britney Spears* documentary, a paparazzo, when asked about the day when Britney brandished an umbrella at him and his peers, said, "That night was not a good night for her...But it was a good night for us, 'cause it was a money shot."

I knew her better, I thought. I knew she was struggling. I was her fan. I loved her. I felt like she belonged to me, that because I loved her work, we owed each other something. I traded my undying love and affection in exchange for her songs, and that felt fair. But fandom does that to a person; it convinces them that there is an intimacy that doesn't really exist.

* * *

Almost a decade ago, I traveled to Kentwood, Louisiana: Britney's hometown. It is a tiny rural community about two hours north of New Orleans, lush and green, and unsettlingly quiet. Kentwood is small enough that within eight hours of my arrival, the teens at the drive-through daiquiri stand were asking if I was "the reporter" in town. The word of my arrival rocketed along the gossip grapevine, a warning shot that must have ricocheted through group threads all afternoon.

They weren't excited to see me. Kentwood has seen plenty of reporters and even more paparazzi. In the mid-aughts, people told me, the road to the Spears complex just outside of town was lined with large SUVs. Reporters camped outside of Britney's childhood home. Images of her were worth money, and the greed of those reporters never left the public consciousness of Kentwood. They were suspicious of me, and rightfully so. Gossip, after all, is very good for helping communities identify outsiders and protect themselves—in this case, protect themselves from me.

I kept a smile plastered across my face for so many hours during the days I was in Kentwood that at night, when I returned to the La Quinta ten miles away, my cheek muscles hurt from the effort. I pulled the easy cadence of "Yes, ma'am" and "No, sir" out from the drawer where I'd shoved them when I moved east. I promised them that I was not the kind of reporter who lied, and then I lied and promised that I wasn't one of *those* liberals. I'm a leftist. It's different. But they didn't need to know that. What they needed to know was that I was from Texas! I was only a culture reporter! None of this worked. It wasn't until I identified myself as a fan that their tone changed. Sure, they would tell me, a fan, what her favorite restaurant was. Fans, they knew, protect their idols. There is a code to being a fan that is not only implicit but enforceable.

Once I had thawed the ice out of my arrival, I made my way to the little house at the edge of town. On my way there I drove past a large "Welcome to Kentwood" sign, adorned with a generic pop star silhouette and the statement "Home of Britney Spears." The Kentwood Historical and Cultural Arts Museum is in a small yellow house so nondescript that I drove right by it the first time and had to be directed back by a teen on a bicycle.

The first half of the museum is about the history of Kentwood.

There are historic documents and a quilt that depicts the industries of the area. There is no mention of slavery or the Civil War despite the fact that a large Confederate base (with its own museum) sat just outside of town. In fact, it isn't really a museum; it is a shrine. "Only good things happened here," it seemed to say. "Don't look too closely."

The second half of the museum is devoted to the Spears family. There are photos of Britney's grandparents and her parents, a full wall of her gold records, infinite photos of her as a young girl. There is video of her from her days in *The Mickey Mouse Club*, and a pair of giant wings that she wore on the Femme Fatale Tour.

Fay Gehringer, who ran the museum, let me take my time staring at the CDs and the posters. But there was something she was excited for me to see. At the back, down a strange little hall, was the museum's crown jewel. There was a single step down into the hallway, dark and dusty. Feeling a little nervous about being in the middle of a conservative red state, in a narrow, dark corridor inside a strange house, with a woman I'd never met, I asked why this room was lower. "Oh," she told me with a sigh, "this whole place used to be an old funeral home." Not exactly reassuring, Fay, but an interesting metaphor.

Fay turned on the light for me, so I could see. At first all I could focus on were the stuffed animals, piles of them shoved onto the twin-size bed with a ruffled skirt and into the corner. One teddy bear wore an NSYNC T-shirt; one was drooped over itself as if it had a tummy ache. Porcelain dolls with perfect ringlets stood at attention.

I recognized the space immediately. This exact room, Britney's childhood bedroom, had been in *Rolling Stone* in 1999. As a child, I had found the cover of that issue, with Britney in booty shorts and a bandeau top, seductive and scandalous and so, so cool. Inside the issue, there is a photo of Britney in the exact room that has now been moved and painstakingly reconstructed in the museum. In the photo, Britney leans against the desk. She is dressed mostly in white, and her cardigan is unbuttoned to reveal a white, strapless push-up bra. Her eyeliner is thick. She looks stunned. The photo is shot from below, as if the photographer was kneeling on the ground in front of her. She was seventeen years old.

The cover story, written by a man named Steven Daly, was titled "Britney Spears: Inside the Mind (and Bedroom) of America's Teen Queen." Not a great start! It begins with a questioning tease: Is Britney Spears seducing you? I remember reading the story when it came out and feeling envious. I wanted to be Britney Spears. I wanted to elicit that kind of response from people.

But when I stood and looked at that room in 2016, my gut turned over. It was a little girl's room, everything frilled and soft. I felt an ick that my body created to protect me, a reminder that men like that cannot be trusted. Later, Britney would tell *British GQ* that the photographer had "tricked" her. Now, when I read that article, I see how manipulative it is. Today, a young pop star would be protected from that kind of rhetoric. But in 1999, implying that a seventeen-year-old standing in her childhood bedroom might be seducing every reader of *Rolling Stone* including the fully adult man reporting the story, well, that was good for selling records, baby.

All of that, of course, wasn't included in the museum. In fact, in the world of the museum, nothing bad had ever happened to Britney at all. I visited the Britney Spears museum in the summer of 2016, more than a decade after some of Britney's biggest tabloid scandals, and there was no record of their existence. I knew, because they had been heavily covered in every celebrity gossip magazine that existed, about Britney's elopement with her childhood friend, her forced annulment, her relationship with Kevin Federline, and their divorce. I had read the headlines on *TMZ* that said that Federline wouldn't let her in to see her children and her own parents urged her to go to rehab within roughly a week of the day she went into a hair salon and shaved her entire head. *People* told me that she was hospitalized while reportedly "under the influence," and I knew from reporting in the *Mercury News* of San Jose, California, of all places, that she was under a conservatorship. I knew from watching a press event with my own eyes on YouTube that the Vegas residency didn't seem quite as successful as the press made it out to be. And I knew in my heart as a fan that she had struggled. I was worried about her the way I would have been for a friend. I wanted her to be kept safe and loved—and to be left alone.

Today, we know better than to laugh at someone who is clearly in a mental health crisis, or at least we think we do. In 2007, the country was not as generous. Kentwood was swarmed by people. "They didn't want the good stuff. They didn't want [us] being happy about Britney," Fay told me. "They wanted the trash. They felt like any kind of trash was the real stuff. But the real stuff is that we're all real proud of her."

Britney's society, her group, protected her. Folks in Kentwood are still, when you visit, tight-lipped about their relationship with any members of the Spears family. "We've all talked it over and decided we won't say anything," Jansen Fitzgerald, a friend of Britney's, told *People* magazine in 2004. That decision seemed to remain in place when I visited in 2016. When I asked members of Britney Spears's childhood family church about her, they weren't interested in talking to a member of the media. Britney, after all, was a member of their group, and I was not. As more and more people protected her, I began to project feelings onto Britney. It must feel nice, I thought, to have this kind of community. She must feel so supported.

I was using Britney Spears as a mirror. It is hard to remember, as a fan, that you do not know the object of your affection at all, that anything you think that person feels is only your own feeling reflected back at you. All of these wonderings about Britney Spears, about her mental state, what she wanted and how she could have felt, are based on nothing. Sure, I have seen the documentaries, read the articles, and followed her career for a decade, but I know only the version of her curated for public consumption, am only aware of the information that filters out to me through a myriad of sources. I don't know Britney Spears. I have never even met her. Once, during the Femme Fatale Tour, we were in the same room together. But she didn't know I was there. Why would she? In reality, I have no special insight. I do not know her family. I do not know Britney Spears, the person who exists in the world, at all.

But, of course, it feels like I do. The "halo effect," a term coined in the early twentieth century to describe our unconscious tendency to make giant assumptions about people after only one impression, is in play with celebrities. This is the fan's fallacy: to believe that you literally know a famous person just because you consume their art, and follow them on social media, and care about them so much. That's the problem with consuming celebrity gossip as any type of fan: it is far too easy to slip into what I call *entitlement gossip*.

Entitlement gossip is predicated on an assumption that you know more than you do, that the parasocial relationship that exists in your head between you and a celebrity is real. It's projecting the expectations you have for the real friends in your real life onto a public figure. "Why would [insert your favorite celebrity here] not tell me that they had gone through a breakup if it were true?" entitlement gossip asks. "I've bought the albums and the concert tickets, so I should know first," entitlement gossip tells you. "I know better than this reported story, because the celebrity," entitlement gossip lies, "is my friend, and I know she wouldn't do that."

Because gossip is made to bind us to one another, and because gossip historically has been used to communicate about one's own community, allowing one of your precious 150 Dunbar slots to be a celebrity means that you lose sight of them as a person. As an idol, they can be whoever you want them to be, and what most people want is someone to worship, someone perfect, someone whose misdeeds or failures must not be their own fault. And it is easy, when you believe that someone is both your friend and your idol, to expect to be rewarded for your allegiance with intimacy.

I started seriously thinking about entitlement gossip and what it means for the people on the other side of it right around the time my prefrontal cortex finally finished developing (around the age of twenty-five). I went to see Lorde perform at the Barclays Center in Brooklyn, and for the first time in my life I felt old. Everyone with floor seats around me and my friend Aleks was a teenager or the parent of a teenager, and the shriek they expelled from their combined lungs when Lorde appeared on the stage caused us both to cover our ears.

Midway through the show, though, she brought out a surprise guest: producer and collaborator on the album Jack Antonoff, who had just finished playing a set with his band in Manhattan. Aleks and I became the side-eyes emoji. We read the blind items. We heard the rumors. We knew that just months before, Antonoff had broken up with his longtime girlfriend, Lena Dunham. We also knew that the rumors that Lorde and Antonoff were dating were so pungent that both celebrities had been provoked to deny them. So when she brought Antonoff onstage, everyone began whispering, and by whispering, I mean yelling because it was an arena full of people.

They played three songs together, one of which was a cover of St. Vincent's "New York," I swear to God, and she sat—one leg squashed beneath her, one dangling off the stage—staring into his eyes and singing, "You're the only motherfucker in the city who can handle me." Were they flirting? It *seemed* like they were flirting. Were they fucking? It *seemed* like they were fucking.

After the show, that song was all anyone wanted to talk about.

It was all *we* wanted to talk about. We were speculating so fast and so wildly that we were spinning out of control. Was it subtext or *text*-text to sing a song off an album that Antonoff's rumored girl-friend had been a butt model for? Did he look comfortable or embarrassed? "I think Lorde knows that she's a part of this super-gossipy conversation, and that must be exciting. So why not tease the people? Celebrities have that power," Mariah Smith said in a published conversation with Lindsey Weber in *The Cut* the next day.

To speculate on what a very famous pop star does on a public stage with a man she is rumored to be dating is well within the rights of the general public. Gossiping about people with more power and more money than you (even if they are not in your direct social circle) is one of our fundamental freedoms that cannot be stripped away. But there was chatter among the girls around us that stunned me. She couldn't be dating Jack Antonoff, they assured one another, because she had told them specifically that she wasn't. She would not lie to them. She loved them.

Of all the forms of parasocial relationships, this is a mild one: to believe the object of your affection even when all signs point to the contrary is a hallmark of any love affair, even a one-sided one. But what jarred me was how certain the teen girls were that she would communicate directly about what they needed to know about her. Lorde did not know any of them. They were strangers to her.

In her book *My Body*, the model and author Emily Ratajkowski wrote about how a photographer allegedly assaulted her early in her career. The photographer, Jonathan Leder, later showed a collection of nude Polaroid photos of her in a gallery on the Lower East Side in New York City. Ratajkowski's lawyer sent him a cease-and-desist letter, but it didn't matter. "The problem with justice ... is that it costs a lot ... pursuing the lawsuit, costs aside, would be fruitless." Ratajkowski wrote, "By then, the exhibition would have been viewed by tons of people. I tweeted about what a violation this [photo] book was, how he was using and abusing my image for profit without my consent. In bed alone, I used my thumb to scroll through the replies." She wrote, "They were unrelenting. 'Using and abusing? This is only a case of a celebrity looking to get more attention. This is exactly what she wants.'" Ratajkowski compared the displaying of those photos to the invasion of having private nudes stolen and distributed in 2014: an intrusive, personal attack.

Leder claimed that the allegations were "totally false." When asked about the allegations by a fact-checker for *The Cut*, Leder mentioned her nudity in the Robin Thicke music video and added, "You really want someone to believe she was a victim?" In an interview with the *Highsnobiety* website, Leder defended showing these photos by saying, "I think it would have been smarter for her to get behind the photos and embrace them...The people that love these photos are her fans."

That invocation of the fans has since haunted me. This is a man who was profiting off these photos, who Ratajkowski says manually assaulted her without warning while she was upstate for that shoot, for work. It was as if, by invoking the fans, Leder believed that he had played a trump card. What does your own opinion matter, after all, if the people who love you are not upset? It's a kind of twisted, forcible logic that requires that celebrities ignore their own desires, their own interests, their own safety, so long as the people who like them are happy. *Highsnobiety* has since added an editor's note to that interview, stating the site's regret over having published it in the first place.

And while fandoms are not new in any sense of the word, the access that fans have to their beloveds has increased drastically with the rise of social media. Instead of having to wait to see John Lennon or Michael Jackson perform live, hordes of fans have access to celebrities all the time via their Instagrams and their TikToks. It doesn't matter that most of those accounts are managed by professionals, carefully timed to optimize performance, or contain photos from months ago. It *feels* like you, as an individual, have access to this person. You can even DM them if you want.

Researchers are fascinated by this evolution, and in 2002, Lynn E. McCutcheon, Rense Lange, and James Houran created what became the "Celebrity Attitude Scale." Under the model, there are three levels of worship a fan can engage in. At the lowest level is *entertainment-social* celebrity worship. These are people who are fans simply because they like the art created by the celebrity. At the middle level, *intense-personal*, fans engage more with the celebrity but still keep an appropriate distance. Those in the final group—*borderline pathological*—overidentify with the person they follow. Their moods, responses, and interests can be swayed by the celebrity's behavior. Some people have said that they would genuinely commit a crime if asked to by their object of worship. At the height of my fandom, I was probably intense-personal with Britney Spears. Now, I register only at entertainment-social, which is either progress or regression, depending on your perspective.

The scale is based on a quiz given to study participants. It asks fans to describe how much they identify with statements about their favorite celebrity (My Favorite Celebrity, or MFC). The questions range from the mundane—"News about my favorite celebrity is a pleasant break from a harsh world" and "Keeping up with news about my favorite celebrity is an entertaining pastime"—to the extreme—"My favorite celebrity and I have our own code so we can communicate with each other secretly (such as over the TV or special words on the radio)." That last question may sound familiar to anyone who has ever stumbled into the internet rabbit hole of Swifties attempting to red-string deduce their way to the release date of the next album by analyzing Taylor Swift's arm movements during a Grammy speech.

In a study using the Celebrity Attitude Scale, the social scientist John Maltby and his coauthors found that as celebrity worship becomes more intense, individuals begin to (falsely) perceive a mutual relationship with the celebrity, and they become more prone to fantasies and dissociations. One of the quiz questions perfectly encapsulates this (and haunts me): "If I walked through the door of MFC's home without an invitation she or he would be happy to see me."

Celebrities, of course, already know that people believe this. Britney Spears's family no longer lives in their small house with the basketball hoop and a two-car garage; they moved to a new house about five miles outside of Kentwood, a grand mansion set back from the road and surrounded by tall iron fencing. The house is called Serenity, and it was (and may still be) guarded by two large, ferocious German shepherds, because fans would try to climb the fence. At least once, a fan received a court order to stay away from her because he was so hell-bent on getting close to Spears. In an April 2014 research paper, Dr. Kineta H. Hung of Hong Kong Baptist University argued that people who are less invested in celebrities are interested in their behaviors, endorsements, and content because they are entertained by it. But true fans have a different motivation: they're emotionally invested and "attend games, shows, and movies to close the physical, mental, and spatial boundaries between themselves and the celebrity."

In the movie *Ingrid Goes West*, Aubrey Plaza plays a girl so obsessed with stalking people online that she is checked into a psychiatric care facility. However, the moment she is released and reunited with her phone, she moves to Los Angeles to stalk more. She kidnaps someone's dog! She creates whole schemes to inject herself into the lives of her beloveds. It's directed like a horror film, but it's not all that far removed from the reality of fandom. In 2023, Drew Barrymore left a stage when an alleged stalker appeared in front of her during a Q&A. In 2024, a man was arrested outside Taylor Swift's New York apartment on a stalking charge.

The term used for this kind of relationship—believing that you have an actual connection with someone who does not know you exist—is *parasocial*. The term was introduced by the social scientists Donald Horton and R. Richard Wohl in 1956 to describe the way that viewers responded to television personas; they argued that over time people's interest in media characters would increase their importance in a person's life. Social researchers have found that our first encounter with a celebrity (be it on TV or, presumably, social media) is clocked the same way in our brain as meeting a real person. They have also found that fans categorize celebrities in their mind in the same groups as people they actually know. We begin to mistake our consumption of culture for actual interaction. It's just the way our brains work.

Even in my own life, I have seen this happen. When I consume stories or interviews my friends have done, I often forget that they haven't told me those things themselves. And as my podcast becomes more popular, I have begun to experience having fans. I'm not in any way as famous as a pop star, but I can already see how quickly this divide can happen.

Before we even began recording our podcast, my cocreator, Alex Sujong Laughlin, warned me that podcasts in particular are notorious for creating parasocial relationships. Researchers have found that listening with headphones is a superconductor for creating a feeling of emotional connection, because it sounds like the person's voice is inside your head. In my reality, I speak into a microphone alone in my room, facing a computer. But in the consumptive reality, when you listen to *Normal Gossip* (or this book in audiobook format), it sounds like I am with you: on your walk, as you are doing your chores, while you are driving in your car. When I do live events, people often forget to introduce themselves to me. It's strange, to meet someone for the first time and not be told their name. At a Seattle show, when I asked a very lovely attendee why she didn't introduce herself, she told me, "I forgot you don't know me because I feel like I know you." It makes sense: they know my name. They have spent hours with me inside their head.

Perhaps you will finish this book and believe that you know me, that there are pieces of my history so vivid in your mind that it will confuse you if we ever meet in person. But you will be wrong. All of this, the whole book, is edited, carefully scraped of moments that hurt too much or feel too good to give to you. The version of me in this book, even if it were not so carefully constructed, would at its best be outdated. By the time this book comes out, the person who wrote these words will be distant from me. In all likelihood, in a few years I will have no memory of writing most of this. It will fade from me, even as it stays in print.

Depending on where you fall on the Celebrity Attitude Scale, your propensity to consume entitlement gossip increases. Take, for example, the unfounded rumors that Taylor Swift is a lesbian. Gaylors, as these conspiracy theorists call themselves, are convinced that Swift's past friendships were actually romantic entanglements. Friendships, of course, can be emotionally entangled without sexual attraction, but that's not important to the Gaylors. The Gaylors are fans, first and foremost. And they are obsessive ones.

The rumors began on Tumblr more than a decade ago as a kind of private fan experience. I know, because I was there. I loved imagining that Karlie Kloss might be bisexual and going through a friend breakup that meant more than she realized. It was reflective of my own experience, and I wanted us to be the same in this way. "Queer fandoms often foster an especially ardent passion, passed among people who've felt misunderstood and judged for whom they love, finally publicly expressing adoration. The object of their affection isn't real, per se; they're a character, a figment of our shared imagination: a collaged angel, or a shattered mirror showing us shards of one another," the writer Emmeline Clein wrote about the Gaylor and other celesbian theories in the *New York Times Magazine*. Clein argued that this kind of mythmaking and fantasizing about a celebrity's sexuality can be good for young queer people. While reasonable enough, it does not mean that Taylor Swift herself owes us personal details.

The Gaylors broke containment a few years ago and began publishing their theories in the mainstream media (some politely and introspectively, others not) about the sexuality of a woman they don't know. A long, storied, and fucked-up history of outing people who do not wish to be outed was ignored. Because they believe that Taylor Swift is their friend, they are mad that she would withhold this information from them in the same way you might be mad that your roommate was dating someone she didn't tell you about.

The most obvious example of this is a January 2024 *New York Times* op-ed titled "Look What We Made Taylor Swift Do," in which writer Anna Marks laid out all of her "evidence," mostly cobbled-together close readings of Taylor Swift's work product and online behaviors, that Taylor Swift is queer. "There are some queer people who would say that through this sort of signaling, she has *already* come out, at least to us. But what about coming out in a language the rest of the public will understand?" Marks wrote in the paper of record, on a national platform, about a woman she does not know. Her argument, then, is that because Taylor Swift is famous (or perhaps because Marks herself is a fan), we are entitled to this information whether or not she wants to share it with us. I confirmed independently that Marks did not reach out to Swift's camp for comment before the piece ran. And for the record, Taylor Swift is vocally, consistently on record as supporting the gay community but not identifying as part of it.

It's not entirely fair to claim that all entitlement gossip is bad or even desired for the wrong reasons. Most fans want their favorite celebrity to do well and be lauded and happy. The relationship a celebrity has to entitlement gossip can at times be symbiotic. The fans get a feeling of closeness, and the celebrity gets money and attention.

But where to draw the line? When does fan attention creep from adoration through entitlement gossip and into something more sinister?

* * *

This is not to say that I think that the existence of celebrity news is immoral. I don't. I read blind items. I listen to the celebrity podcast *Who? Weekly*. I follow Deuxmoi. Gossip, after all, is democratic in speech, and (in many cases can be) protected by the First Amendment. US government regulation rarely applies to social and private conversation. Even in the case of libel or defamation, it is the duty of the person bringing the charge to prove that not only were the statements published (or said) about them false, but whoever published them *knew* that they had a high likelihood of being false. In the United Kingdom, the burden is reversed: the defendant must prove that what they said was true.

Perhaps the United States' relatively lax libel and defamation laws allowed for the flourishing of the celebrity gossip industry in the early twentieth century. The aforementioned magazine *Town Topics* was meant to be read by members of the community it talked about. The Fitzgeralds read it because the people written about in it were their friends. One of the first gossip magazines marketed to people not in the elite class was *Broadway Brevities & Society Gossip*. The gossip about *Broadway Brevities* itself is immense: that magazine, too, was caught blackmailing, and its founder went to prison for two years. He returned to the public in 1927, and in 1930 the magazine was reformatted to make it appeal more to regular people. Mostly, this was done by filling it with lies, lurid jokes, and suggestive cartoons.

Under the headline "Miners' Hot Holes," for example, was a cartoon of a mine worker bent over in front of a jackhammer. It lasted two years before New York City banned newsstands from selling it, presumably because it was both libelous and scandalous.

As Hollywood boomed and actors like Jean Harlow, Ingrid Bergman, Jimmy Stewart, and Bing Crosby rose in prominence, so did Americans' appetite for information about them. "If the gossip industry had a golden age, it coincided with the 'golden age' of the Hollywood studio system in the 1930s and 1940s," Jeannette Walls wrote in her book *Dish: The Inside Story on the World of Gossip*. "And, like Hollywood during those years, the gossip industry had its constellation of fixed stars." Many credit Walter Winchell, a gossip columnist and radio host, with the creation of the modern-day celebrity concept. Millions of people read Winchell's syndicated gossip column in the newspaper every day. He wrote in slang, without pretension. "Winchell, in such an easy, quick way, could take anybody's career and destroy it," actress Nancy Gray said in the film *Walter Winchell: The Power of Gossip*. He was a master of brief, pungent insults ("Their separation was caused by illness. She got sick of him."; "Anita Colby...will play the role of a high-class bad girl—which is only half correct."). You know he was important to the American public because one of Winchell's most famous sources was J. Edgar Hoover, the director of the FBI.

The heirs to Winchell's throne were two Hollywood women, Hedda Hopper and Louella Parsons. They worked for different syndicates, were open rivals, and were more famous than some of the people they covered. Parsons was called "the Queen of Hollywood," and her reign lasted almost forty years. Studio executives knew that gossip about stars increased public interest in their movies (thus making them money) and so they leaked information to Hopper and Parsons. Both viewed themselves as champions of Hollywood rather than critics of it. Their ire was reserved for each other. If a couple married secretly and told only one of them, the other might ostracize them or ban their names from her column, so that by 1955, when Rock Hudson married Phyllis Gates, one of them called Parsons, while the other called Hopper. When Parsons broke her hip in 1964 at the age of eighty-three, Hopper is said to have stayed up all night dancing in celebration.

After that, though, celebrity journalism became more confined to the lucrative but seedy tabloid industry. In 1953, Walls explains, the *National Enquirer* pivoted to tabloid work and quickly began bribing people for stories. It sent reporters to sort through the garbage cans at important people's houses and publish the contents. By the time *People* magazine was founded and celebrity news returned to a more fond and symbiotic relationship with Hollywood, the *National Enquirer* was so important that they knew that Elvis was dead before his own father did. They were so well sourced within Graceland that the reporter was tipped off and on his way before the ambulance arrived at the house.

The back-and-forth of celebrity coverage, from acting as the mouthpieces of the rich and famous to digging sometimes unethically into the seedy underbelly of their dealings, is the same dynamic we see today. *TMZ* is rumored to have paid off nurses at most Los Angeles hospitals to ensure that they get scoops first, something that is both morally and legally (HIPAA) unethical. And big celebrity magazines like *People* are still running profiles approved by celebrities' camps where the reporters are given a list of topics they aren't allowed to cover. Both have to exist in a celebrity ecosystem: we want to know what celebrities say they are up to and what they think, and we want to know whether or not that is a lie. Our curiosity is at odds with their desire for and perhaps right to privacy.

"We tend to think she lost that All American Girl status when she started losing her mind, but from my seat, after reading *The Woman in Me*, that part of her story makes her more like us than ever. What woman wouldn't go insane, given the circumstances?" Alana Hope Levinson wrote in *GQ* in 2023. Celebrities reach a point in fame where they must either step back from the spotlight (like Beyoncé did) or accept that every second of their lives will be documented and reported on (like Taylor Swift has). There does not seem to be a comfortable middle ground once you reach a certain level of fame.

In every generation, perhaps, a celebrity is driven to the brink by some combination of tabloid coverage and deviation from the norm. The career of the actress Jean Seberg, the star of *Breathless* and an icon of the French New Wave movement, was destroyed by the FBI. Because she had donated to the NAACP and the Black Panther Party, the FBI added her to its slew of COINTELPRO operations to discredit and harass her. Led by J. Edgar Hoover, the FBI leaked a likely false story to Joyce Haber of the *Los Angeles Times* that Seberg was not in fact pregnant with her husband's baby, but with the baby of a Black Panther. Haber ran the story as a thinly anonymized blind item, but *Newsweek* named her directly. All of this was revealed years later after the documents became accessible through the Freedom of Information Act. Seberg went into an early labor following the *Newsweek* article, and her child died. The Federal Bureau of Narcotics under Hoover's leadership also attacked Billie Holiday for her anti-lynching song "Strange Fruit," but its attacks on her were more direct than press articles: they busted her for drugs that many people now believe were supplied by the same agency to have cause to arrest and prosecute her.

In her memoir, Britney Spears wrote about driving in a car and performing a very dangerous maneuver near a cliff's edge to escape the paparazzi trailing her. Reading it, I felt a knot in my stomach. One second later, one wrong turn of the steering wheel, and the story of Princess Diana would have repeated itself in a little more than a decade. Princess Diana married into the royal family and so brilliantly built up press coverage for herself that, following her death, former UK prime minister Tony Blair referred to her as "The People's Princess," and the nickname stuck. "Diana was caught in the trap experienced by every celebrity who invites the media into their lives and then gets angry about the intrusion...she had become a prisoner of the fame she worked so hard to cultivate," Walls wrote in *Dish*.

When she died, people were devastated: sobbing mourners who had never met her described her as a friend. Their connection, built on her strategic and brilliant use of media and PR, felt real. After Diana's death the blame was placed squarely on the paparazzi who had been following her car on the day she died. Later, it was revealed that Princess Diana's driver had more than three times the French legal amount of alcohol in his system when the car crashed. But the narrative still remains focused on the paparazzi, both because of the way that her sons talk about her legacy, and because her death perhaps reflects a larger insecurity within each of us about how much information we believe we are entitled to. "The public, for its part, is indisputably titillated by celebrity gossip but also disapproves of the media for the invasion of privacy required to provide them with the gossip it finds so fascinating," Walls wrote.

It will always be easier to blame *the media* writ large for the treatment of celebrities than ourselves. The paparazzi make money off her, stalk her. We aren't doing that. We are just lapping up the photos they produce like desperate little parched dogs. We, the fans, would never publish the address of a superstar. That could be dangerous for them. But take a drive through Tribeca in New York City and you'll see the line of (mostly) teen girls standing outside the building where Taylor Swift owns an apartment compound.

"It's that her fame was so huge that it made people dehumanize her. They were not able to see Britney Spears as just a person. And I think now that seems like a normal thing to say, but back then, it was radical," Cara Cunningham told NPR in 2021. I watched Cunningham's now-iconic videos defending Britney Spears, the day they came out in September 2007. In the now famous video, Cunningham cries, begging people to "leave Britney alone." I cried alongside her. Cara, I felt, was right. "I didn't want to share anything private with the world. I didn't owe the media details of my breakup. I shouldn't have been forced to speak on national TV, forced to cry in front of this stranger…but I had no choice. It seemed like nobody really cared how I felt," Spears wrote in her memoir.

It was a justified plea. In 2007, photographs of Spears could earn photo agencies millions of dollars because the American public was so greedy for them. As she herself sings on "Piece of Me," "I'm Mrs. 'Extra! Extra! This just in' / (You want a piece of me?)."

In the video, Cunningham begs people to respect Britney's space. She says she is scared that if Britney is not left alone, she might become a danger to herself. "Do we really want to see a twenty-five-year-old woman leave behind two children and die?" Cunningham asked into a camera in a grainy video. "Have we learned nothing from Anna Nicole Smith? I know it's hard to see Britney Spears as a human being but trust me, she is. She's a person."

In light of the *New York Times*' 2021 documentary *Framing Britney Spears*, Cunningham's video seems like a rare beacon of light during a crowded time. Society, the series seems to say, treated Britney Spears poorly. Everyone, it seems to claim, is to blame. But in 2007, plenty of people were on Britney's side, supporting Cunningham, and begging others to pay attention. Mark Stevens wrote in *New York* magazine that with her shaved head, Spears "seemed to be trying, with befuddled brilliance, to tell the truth." Anna Holmes at Jezebel wrote in 2007, "We've been complicit in the frenzy that has enveloped Britney Spears. Day after day, week after week, we taunt her, question her, suggest she could benefit from a lobotomy and gleefully compare paparazzo shots of her to the troubled protagonists of two classic Stanley Kubrick movies. Maybe we do this because we think it is funny, or because it is expected, or because...we have minutes, not hours or days, in which to prepare and present our thoughts about her. Or maybe we are just unoriginal assholes."

Despite the latest revisionism, people were arguing that the incessant media coverage of Britney's breakdown wasn't just inappropriate; it was an invasion of privacy. More recently, we have seen the same kind of argumentation happening in the dissection of Amber Heard's allegations against Johnny Depp. I imagine that in ten years a documentary will be released scrutinizing that trial and the online analysis of it and how cruel, unfair, and rabid the defense of Johnny Depp was. If *Framing Britney Spears* taught me anything, it's that society benefits from claiming that "we" were all wrong about something even when a loud and large group of people said otherwise at the time. It is an abdication of responsibility to extend one's own failure to the entirety of the American population, but it is an effective one. It allows the people who make money off the invasive coverage of celebrities to justify their continued invasion of privacy with the endorsement of the fans.

That's what's so complicated about entitlement gossip for me as both a reporter and a fan. All press is good press, everyone says. That's true if your aim is to be famous and talked about all the time. It's a kind of capitalistic urge to believe that any extra amount of fame and attention is worth it. Assuming that famous people all want to be infinitely more famous forever is part of what enables us to justify our constant invasion of their privacy for our own entertainment.

"I run an Instagram account. It lives in the phone. It's not real life," the woman who runs Deuxmoi told *Vanity Fair*. That's willful ignorance. "I'm also constantly waiting for the inevitable 'you've been served' line," she told Rachel Sylvester in *Cosmopolitan*. You cannot both expect to be served with libel papers at any moment and believe that the gossiping you do causes no harm. But I am not responsible for the behavior of Deuxmoi; I am responsible only for my own behavior and the behavior of my dog, and she cannot read.

It is so easy, through a blinding haze of fandom, to assume we would know what celebrities want and therefore cannot do wrong by them. "The institutionalized gossip of *People* magazine and other such publications is particularly effective...because it allows us to believe that the rich and famous are no better than the rest of us," Ronald de Sousa wrote in *Good Gossip*. On April 1, 2002, *Us Weekly* began running a column called "Stars—They're Just like Us" featuring photographs of celebrities pumping gas and buying groceries and picking their kids up from school. "'Just Like Us' was so successful at turning street photography into a commodity that today, it's obvious many striving celebrities dress up to take out the trash and go to the grocery store," Ruth Graham wrote in Slate. The paparazzi take photos of celebrities doing normal things, so that they never have privacy, so that we (the normal) can feel like they are just like us, so that we can point at their photo and say, "Same," which then allows us to believe that we know exactly how they feel. "[The paparazzi] just kept acting like I owed it to them to let the men who kept trying to catch me looking fat take photos of my infant sons," Spears wrote in her memoir.

Still, I looked at the photos of Britney with her head shaved and thought that I felt her fury and her rebellion and her sadness. But I had no idea how she really felt. I still don't. I thought I did, and at times I felt betrayed by the fact that she was not communicating with me, her fan, about what was going on. I wanted her to tell me that she was okay, and it never crossed my mind that she didn't owe me anything at all.

This, of course, can be used for good or evil. Celebrities can encourage their superfans to donate to causes they believe in or sign petitions, and the fans (because they trust them the way they trust someone they know) will abide. But it also means that when a celebrity is revealed by trusted sources to have misbehaved, fans think they know better. If you believe Johnny Depp is your close personal friend and believe that he would never lie to you, you can ignore any reports or lawsuits or news articles. You know better. Or, at least, you think you do.

* * *

But as uncomfortable and invasive as entitlement gossip can sometimes feel, it's not entirely evil. Fans do often have symbiotic relationships with the objects of their affection. Britney is, in that way, the perfect example of entitlement gossip, because parasociality is also what freed her from an unjust conservatorship.

In 2008, after all the paparazzi attention and the trauma of her divorce, Britney's father, Jamie, got the court system to approve a temporary conservatorship over her estate and her person. She was an adult woman, but legally, she was trapped under her father's thumb. She wrote in her memoir that she could not look at her phone without his permission, much less decide what she wanted her Vegas show to look like. She lived like that for more than a decade: trapped in a prison of the legal system's and her father's making, like a court jester made to perform for her fans without any of her own willpower. In 2019, she paused her latest Las Vegas residency and *TMZ* reported that she had checked into a mental health facility.

In April 2019, the podcast *Britney's Gram* speculated on Britney's curiously quiet Instagram account and released a voicemail from an unnamed paralegal who claimed that they were concerned about Britney's health and well-being. People began to wonder whether the conservatorship that she was under might be oppressive, and they began to fight about it. "I am trying to take a moment for myself, but everything that's happening is just making it harder for me," she wrote on Instagram. "Don't believe everything you read and hear."

There are two ways to interpret that post. One is that Britney genuinely wanted to be left alone and felt that her privacy was being invaded again. The other is that she was so trapped in the conservatorship that this was the closest she could come to pleading for help. It's a leap of faith or (depending on your perspective) a massive delusion to believe the second. With the clarity of hindsight, we know that what happened next was what Britney had intended, but at the time, watching the #FreeBritney protesters outside the West Hollywood City Hall in April 2019, I felt nauseous. By then, I had grown up. Any delusions of intimacy between Britney Spears and me, I had grown out of. But I still worried about her, and my instinct was to take her at her word, not to make it harder for her again.

But I was wrong. "It's no accident that the #FreeBritney movement came during the height of the #MeToo movement—it was a natural outcome for a society grappling with the violence done to women's bodies…And because we still identify with Spears, that cultural movement helped spark the momentum needed for Spears to finally get herself free of the conservatorship," Lyz Lenz wrote in her Substack. Because her fans identified with Britney, felt that she was like them, it was easier for them to fight for her.

In September 2020, Spears's attorney confirmed to the press that the #FreeBritney movement was "far from being a conspiracy theory." The fans had been right. They'd known her, and believed the signs, and fought for her. By the time *Framing Britney Spears* was released in February 2021, the public and the court were ready to fight on her side. By November of that same year, the thirteen-year-long conservatorship was terminated.

"Good God I love my fans so much it's crazy 👀 🖤!!! I think I'm gonna cry the rest of the day !!!! Best day ever … praise the Lord … can I get an Amen 🙏 ☀️ 🙌 ???? #FreedBritney," she tweeted that day, with a video of fans celebrating outside the courthouse. In her memoir, she was even more explicit in crediting her fans with her salvation. "The same way I believe that I can sense how someone's feeling in Nebraska, I think my connection to my fans helped them subconsciously know that I was in danger. We have a connection, no matter where we are in space," she wrote. "Fans of mine—even though I hadn't said anything online or in the press about being confined—they just seemed to *know.*"

The tenor of celebrity world culture in the 2020s seems far more interested in supporting celebrities than tearing them down. But the interest in what celebrities are doing, where, and with what intentions seems only to have intensified. And there are far, far more celebrities than ever. A girl with a viral TikTok becomes a known person to us, we follow her on Instagram, and now her photos are right next to our best friend's memes and our sister's birthday party photos. That intimacy is even more difficult for our brains to comprehend: one person whom we know and love, and one we do not know at all. And to be a fan, to consume, you do not really have to distinguish. "Instagram captions appear like letters from a loved one; direct-to-cam posts seem like FaceTimes from a friend," Amanda Montell wrote in her book *The Age of Magical Overthinking.* "Platforms like Tumblr, TikTok, Instagram, and Patreon offer fans exponentially more access to personal information about their heroes, bridging the parasocial gap to make them feel ever more connected."

The fact that Patreon, where fans pay for extra access to their favorites, exists within the parasocial realm makes this all the more complicated. For many microcelebrities and influencers, their parasociality is how they pay their bills. They need to encourage their fans to believe that they are friends so that they can sell them things. You trust your friends' recommendations, so if your brain thinks an influencer is your friend (or even if you just think she's cool), you'll probably trust her recommendations, too. That kind of power is connected to money, and for many people, paying their rent. Celebrities and non-celebrities are more entangled now than ever before. Everyone is one viral video away from that kind of attention, and most people have at least one person with whom their relationship is more parasocial than social.

Being in a parasocial relationship does not have moral boundaries, but our expectations regarding how and what kind of information we receive from the other party have to be different from those in our real life. It's not so much that we have to leave Britney and everyone else alone, per se, as it is that we have to be willing to listen to them when they speak. The relationship should go both ways, and that means that if I want to stop being a fan of Britney Spears, I can. But if she wants to never make an album again and never perform again, I can be sad, but I have to respect that.

At my high school, whenever a student was brought before the disciplinary committee, a letter including the student's name, the rules they broke, exact details of how they violated those rules and were caught, and their punishment would be posted publicly on a bulletin board outside the dean's office. The justification by the administration was that it was meant to eliminate gossip by making the facts of these cases public. In reality, I remember how we would all run to the board as soon as a new letter was posted, and one of us would read it aloud to the assembled crowd like a town crier.

The Plight of West Elm Caleb

One survival skill that every modern person must acquire is the ability to avoid becoming the Main Character of the internet. Every few weeks, a new Main Character is chosen, their life placed under a microscope, their decisions dissected. The court of public opinion tries them and decides whether they are to be found guilty or (rarely) innocent, and they never get a say in the matter. If the internet says you're a witch, no one cares whether or not you float after they throw you into the river, because you will drown anyway. You don't need to know how to make fire anymore; you need to know how to dodge it when it comes for you. *When*, not if.

In the almost two decades that I have spent with my eyes glued to whichever social media website is hot at the moment, I have seen dozens of Main Characters get run off of platforms and into hiding. I remember when a PR director tweeted something offensive about AIDS, got on a plane, and by the time she landed had become the Main Character. Then there was the young woman whose friend posted a photo to Facebook of her flipping off the camera and pretending to scream at Arlington National Cemetery's Tomb of the Unknowns. There was a young woman who dressed as a Boston Marathon bombing victim for Halloween. There was a media man who tweeted that we should "bring back bullying" and quickly felt that group wrath directed right at him. But there are also the Main Characters that only I remember: a user bullied out of a *Twilight* Tumblr for saying Kristen Stewart couldn't act well enough to seem attracted to a man, a class president being forced to step down from his position because he tweeted about girls wearing leggings as pants. So many Main Characters, and all of them destroyed.

In a world where everything is content ("everything is copy" as Nora Ephron's family once said), everyone is a potential Main Character in someone else's story about the world. My first brush with becoming a Main Character took place on a very short-lived social media platform called LikeALittle that existed, as far as I know, only on college campuses. The premise of LikeALittle was that you could post anonymous messages to people that you might have crushes on. Basically, it was Craigslist's Missed Connections for the Tumblr generation: better designed, more localized, and filled with potential. Quickly, people began posting snippets of conversations they had heard from people they thought were hot.

The only one I ever thought was about me was something to the effect of "girl in the honor's quad ranting about *Middlemarch*... hello." When I read this post, my entire chest flushed red. I was flattered to be the object of someone's attention. But the idea of being the object of so many people's attention (everyone on campus was reading the site, hoping to find a crush), even though I was nameless, filled me with dread. I remember thinking that I would need to be more careful about what I said in public, more aware of my surroundings. Of course, that didn't happen, but the feeling has only gotten stronger as social media has evolved.

All of this is gossip. Discussion of strangers online, even with other strangers online, is gossip. And in some ways the panopticon of internet gossiping at such a scale shows all the goods and evils that gossiping has to offer.

Take, for example, the joy of snooping. There is almost no greater pleasure in my life than being asked to help obtain gossip. Let's say a friend meets a cutie at the bar. They don't know the cutie's last name. All they have is a first name, a physical description, and a crush. I am cracking my knuckles just thinking about this made-up but frequent scenario. I am settling in on the couch with my laptop, and we are going hunting, baby. The internet has made the world so small and our lives so interconnected that with a few tools and the ability to use them, you can find almost anyone. I once found a man seated three rows ahead of someone on an airplane because I found a post from someone in the row behind him where you could see his Instagram handle. It is one of my proudest moments. They did not, unfortunately, get married.

Give me your address, and you can bet all your money that I will be typing that address into Zillow and looking at what your house cost and how many bedrooms it has, and when it last sold. Give me your girlfriend's ex's first name, and I'll find her Instagram page and tell you you're hotter, I promise. Mention in front of me that you haven't been able to find the email address of literally anyone, and I will ruin my own life to find it.

I am professionally nosy, and perhaps more curious than average, but this kind of desire to learn about the world and the people around you is inherent in humans. Compared to primates, humans retain juvenile traits at significant rates. Biologically we are neotenous creatures because of our jaw shape, the fact that our bodies are mostly hairless, our delicate skull bones. And our brains are so big compared to our scrawny bodies. Our neoteny makes us unlikely to beat an ape in a fistfight. They have evolved to be bigger and stronger than we are. But our childlike traits allow us to learn, so maybe we could deceive an ape even if we could not beat her.

We are inherently more curious than, for example, an orangutan. And part of that neoteny is what makes us so fucking nosy. "We are here on Earth to fart around. And don't let anybody ever tell you any different," Kurt Vonnegut said, and he's right. We have evolved to do all sorts of things that (from an evolutionary perspective) are absolutely useless. Reading this book, for example, will not feed your family or protect your body. Maybe there is a way to use it to get laid, but that's not my business. We've evolved to be curious, so you figure it out.

That curiosity, that desire to learn, is also what makes us nosy. Our brains reward us with little hits of dopamine for newness and novelty. Pandora, the first woman in Greek mythology, is a cautionary tale about curiosity. In the story, Pandora is given a jar containing many unspecified evils, and she can't stand not opening it. She opens the jar, and the fiery evils go flying out over the earth. Now we use the idiom "to open Pandora's box" as a warning about the unforeseen problems that might arise from looking where you shouldn't. Curiosity, the stories tell us, is dangerous. It can backfire. But no warning can keep us from our nature.

It is in our biology to snoop, but we evolved to do that within our community. And now our community is…well…everyone in the entire world. And because we leave digital footprints everywhere we navigate to online, it is easier than ever for people to be found.

Kahn, a digital creator on TikTok (@notkahnjunior), engages in what she calls "consensual doxxing." Someone comments on one of Kahn's posts and dares her to try to find out their birthday. In one posted in December 2023, by using tattoos, a combination of people once following the user, and Facebook posts from people who she was friends with, Kahn was able to find the birthday of a woman named Jenny who did not have an Instagram or Facebook account with very little trouble at all.

"I know that my intentions are innocent when I post a video... and I know the person who asked me to find their birthday also has innocent intentions... but the information I find can be used by bad people," Kahn said in a recent post explaining why she does not post as many consensual doxxing videos anymore. She is trying to be choosier about whose information she shares, and now partners with a company that removes your information from the internet and encourages her followers to have their personal data scrubbed.

I also use this service. From experience, I know that other people as nosy as me exist in the world. The longer you spend being a snoop online, the more you realize that there is so much information to be had about a person if you really want it. It's fairly easy to find someone's email address, where they live, and their birthday. If you had malintent, it would be only a few more steps to find something like a maiden name, and suddenly you don't need anything except a big password breach to steal someone's identity.

The internet is what you (and others) make of it. The fear that what is fun and silly online can radiate into violence or misery offline is based on history, not nightmare. We have seen over and over again the power that the internet has to identify, locate, and judge a person we've never met. Perhaps earlier in the rise of social media, that ability felt like justice. "In those early days [of social media], the collective fury felt righteous, powerful and effective. It felt as if hierarchies were being dismantled, as if justice were being democratized," Jon Ronson wrote in the *New York Times Magazine* in 2015. "I also began to marvel at the disconnect between the severity of the crime and the gleeful savagery of the punishment. It almost felt as if shamings were now happening for their own sake, as if they were following a script."

These shamings are gossip: we are talking to one another about someone who we do not know at all. But they're also gossip in outcome. Gossip reinforces social norms within tight-knit communities—it is an extralegal solution to enforce the community's ideals and powers.

In the eighteenth century, the philosopher and social theorist Jeremy Bentham designed a prison that he called the panopticon. The building would be round, and all of the inmates' cells would face a central rotunda, where the guards would be stationed. The guards, then, could watch the inmates without the inmates knowing for certain that they were being watched. The central tower would be subject to periodic observation by the public. He envisioned everyone watching one another as a kind of police state to create good behavior. The Austrian sociologist Christian Fuchs argues that social media exists within a panopticon in which Meta, TikTok, or Snapchat sits in the center, and we—with all our data and messages and cookies—are the ones being watched. We, the users of social media, are inside our little jail cells, while the big corporations sit in the tower watching us.

As the narrator of Jane Austen's *Emma* says, "Human nature is so well disposed towards those who are in interesting situations, that a young person, who either marries or dies, is sure of being kindly spoken of." The communal aspect of gossip is how we create and perpetuate norms within our groups. Say our society has decided that wearing blue is immoral and bad. If we saw someone from our community wearing an all-blue outfit, we would tell our friends: here is a member of our community actively doing something we all agree is wrong. No blue is allowed here! Even if none of us were to directly confront the blue wearer about the behavior, it is uncomfortable to be gossiped about, and probably eventually the blue wearer would either stop wearing blue in order to maintain peace within the community or leave and find a space in which wearing blue was not villainized.

In modern-day American society, wearing blue is fine, but something almost universally disliked is being a fuckboy. Let's take the contemporary cautionary tale of West Elm Caleb as an example.

In January 2022, Mimi Shou posted a funny video to TikTok about being ghosted by a guy she had a great first date with in New York City: a classic tale of heartbreak and annoyance. Mimi Shou posted four videos that week about her dating mishaps in NYC, but only that one created a sensation. The video itself is vague, but she captioned it "This one's dedicated to Caleb." The video had a subject, the ambiguous Caleb. And because the internet is both infinite and hyperlocal, other women in NYC saw the video and began commenting about a man named Caleb who worked at West Elm. Ironically, this was not the Caleb that Shou had gone on a date with. She had been ghosted by another tall NYC Caleb.

A few days later, Shou posted an update video explaining that someone had slid into her DMs and told her all about how a man named Caleb who worked at West Elm (whom she had not met up with) was love-bombing her on Hinge and then ghosted her. Information is coming from an unidentified source talking to Shou, whom we do not know, and the information that source is presenting is that a man she has not met was overly affectionate with her over text and then stopped talking to her. This is not a crime. This is barely even a faux pas in the realm of dating. Hitting it off with someone, not meeting up, and then falling out of contact is pretty much par for any dating interaction in any major city. One real criticism that emerged from the women telling stories about this man was that he sent an unsolicited dick pic.

Women advising other women about men in their communities who seem dangerous happens online in less unchecked ways. Many cities have Facebook groups called "Are We Dating the Same Guy?" or "Vouched Dating," where members gut-check men they have questions about to see if they are duplicitous. These groups have millions of members, and are not fact-checked, and scattered lawsuits have been filed against them for defamation. But they are theoretically contained within a single community (a city). The rules of "Are We Dating the Same Guy?" groups also warn users to "Please be mentally prepared for the possibility that things you say here may get back to who you wrote about."

There is another version of collaboration against a shared enemy that is intimate. In the movie *John Tucker Must Die*, the three concurrent girlfriends of John Tucker team up to ruin his life. But they do so on their terms, within their community, and for the very real reason that he was dating them all at the same time.

Because the allegations against West Elm Caleb were happening outside of any protective privacy barriers, the panopticon of social media could do something very strange and very surreal. "Tiktok has made every city TINY," a user commented on Shou's explanation video. But what TikTok actually does is make tiny things seem infinite. Many have speculated that the TikTok algorithm can connect you to people who have your phone number. That means anyone whose number was in Caleb's phone would be connected to all of the other people in his phone. The TikTok algorithm, *Wired* reported, connects people who have one another's cell phone numbers. Every single person with a stake in this drama was apparently linked to the video, making it seem more relevant and more universal than it actually was.

As of this writing, the original video had just over seven hundred thousand views, so it was by no means the most popular video on TikTok, but when it was first posted the spread was immediate. Several women posted videos explaining their experiences with him, and the playlists he'd given them, and the similar lies he'd told them. Buoyed by their camaraderie, women revealed his last name and posted his dating profile on TikTok. Strangers began commenting on the official West Elm Instagram page. Shou (who, remember, had not dated him at all) posted another video with text overlaid that read, "When you're the girl that single handedly exposed a Hinge villain and united half the girls in NYC." This video got more than 2.5 million views.

In *Gossip*, Patricia Meyer Spacks wrote, "Gossip may damage others, both by threatening their reputations and by converting people into fictions." West Elm Caleb became not just *a* fuckboy; he was *every* fuckboy who had ever ghosted any woman on any date. As a fictional character (which to most people he was), he could be purely evil. The witch hunt against him could continue unabated until the internet found a new target. "In less than a week, a person who seems to be a pretty normal twentysomething single has become a symbol of something larger, a punching bag meant to represent the millions of brief but bad exes those perpetuating an online harassment campaign against him have likely experienced themselves," Brittany Spanos wrote in *Rolling Stone*.

It is as if the screen between the viewer and the person being indicted on the front page of the internet allows us to develop a kind of brain worm, let's call it West Elm Caleb–itis. It convinces us that not only is it our right to know what is happening among everyone in the whole world, but it is also our job to legislate it.

The West Elm Caleb saga began almost immediately after "Couch Guy," another exercise in projection where strangers on Tik-Tok judged a man's response to his girlfriend showing up to surprise him and (with absolutely zero evidence except vibes) accused him of cheating. His girlfriend's cute nineteen-second video received more than 64 million views and was covered by a whole host of major media outlets, including *The View*. The hashtag (which included videos dissecting the original video) had more than a billion views. The "Couch Guy," whose real name is Robert McCoy, later wrote in an article for *Slate* that people in his building posted on TikTok promising to surveil the people coming in and out of his apartment and report back. "This tabloid body language analysis—something typically reserved for Kardashians, the British royal family, and other A-listers—made me, a private citizen who had previously enjoyed his minimal internet presence, an unwilling recipient of the celebrity treatment," McCoy wrote.

"A life had been ruined. What was it for: just some social media drama? I think our natural disposition as humans is to plod along until we get old and stop. But with social media we've created a stage for constant artificial high dramas. Every day a new person emerges as a magnificent hero or a sickening villain. It's all very sweeping, and not the way we actually are as people," Jon Ronson wrote in his 2015 book *So You've Been Publicly Shamed.* To exist in the world now, be it in public or private, is to risk becoming the Main Character of the internet just for living your life. It isn't just the media companies in the center of the panopticon anymore; we are all inside the panopticon, our cameras pointed at one another, with little regard for the ramifications of that surveillance.

* * *

The feeling I got sitting in the quad, reading a little anonymous post about me, is ever prevailing now. Strangers all around us are recording video in public all the time. They are posting those videos to social media or recapping them into a front-facing camera, knowing that their audiences will eat up other people's drama that they have scavenged in the wild, and that they will be paid for that content.

In September 2023, TikTok influencer Kellie Yancy overheard some women gossiping about a friend while out at brunch. In the front-facing video she posted to TikTok afterward, she seemed to believe that she was doing a moral good when she said, "Whoever Sarah is, your friends is over there talking about you." She went on, "They said that your coochie was out on the video…she said you dress sleazy everywhere the fuck you go." And then she flipped the camera and pointed it at a table of women. In less than a week, the video was viewed 1.2 million times.

This kind of video has become more and more common. A creator in public overhears something (out of context) and, without addressing the situation with anyone in the direct environment, they post a video to TikTok to put them on blast. With the reach and breadth of the internet and the encouragement of "stalking" culture online, videos like Yancy's aren't just recounting a problematic thing overheard; they are a call to action—in this case, to find the women in the video, to find the "Sarah" they were talking about.

Yancy ended up deleting both the original video and the TikTok Live she posted to announce that Sarah had messaged her and asked her to take the video down because she had been receiving threatening messages and because of the impact of the video's virality influencing her business.

"Content has grown to encompass practically anything you can point your camera at," CT Jones wrote in *Rolling Stone*. "But with that growth, building out a self-imposed surveillance state doesn't just become a danger, it starts to feel like an inevitability."

To make all of this a little more ethically dubious, add in the fact that in the creator economy, attention equals money. Telling stories about other private citizens online without regard for discretion or their best interest can be profitable. Utilitarianism has died a rough death in the content mines, because views equal money, and if the pursuit of views is unchecked by ethics, then other people's privacy becomes irrelevant. Everything and everyone is content, baby. The public is now a stage on which I can perform. Everyone else is a minor character in the play of my life, and their harm does not exist to me, for I must post. And if a life or two are destroyed for a few weeks, but I gain followers, isn't it worth it?

In 1975, the panopticon was repopularized by the French intellectual and critic Michel Foucault. In *Discipline and Punish: The Birth of the Prison*, he discussed how we obtain both power and knowledge, with the panopticon as a perfect metaphor. The person in the center (the guard), who sees everything and knows everything, derives power not only from their station but from that information. "By being combined and generalized, [the people involved in the panopticon] attained a level at which the formation of knowledge and the increase in power regularly reinforce one another in a circular process," he wrote.

This is most dangerous at the state level. One of the most notorious and widespread surveillance programs ever invented was the East German state security agency called the Stasi. The Stasi, like the KGB, was meant to enforce state authority in Communist East Germany. It did so by creating a massive network of civilian informants and widespread surveillance. When you visit the Stasi Museum in its old office in Berlin, you walk into a horrifying amount of information. It is, in some ways, the dream of a gossip. Because the files were largely declassified after Germany's reunification, German citizens can inspect their own files: all the transcripts of recorded phone calls, all of their letters. The museum shows how the agents tapped phone calls, the notes they took, and where they stored tips sent in by informants. It is a massive trove of stolen information. A few Stasi agents were later prosecuted, and Germany now has some of the strongest personal privacy laws in the world.

Recording people in public as individuals does not create the exact same panopticon that the state generates by wiretapping or privacy invasion, but it does make the state's ability to monitor us even easier. We have created our own surveillance state willingly, and we applaud ourselves for doing so.

West Elm Caleb–itis convinces us that one person's life or day can be played with in exchange for our own increase in power. It's a severely capitalistic and consumeristic mindset to use the joy of snooping as a form of punishment. Gossip can be used as an extra-legal form of justice, but as the internet shrinks the world around us and the people in charge of tech platforms realize that we love drama and gossip enough to keep scrolling, we are at risk of throwing our own into the gallows and corrupting the joy we are able to find in satisfying our curiosity. The problem is that it is fun to be neotenous, to learn about the world around us, to dig where we aren't supposed to, to gather information we aren't supposed to have.

Applying gossip as a regulatory force to strangers has the potential to create harm. The mob that trails West Elm Caleb knows neither morality nor mercy. There is no end to the aim of the group. What exactly did society want from this man? Or from Couch Guy? Or from any other Main Character? An apology? A disappearance? A mutual shared enemy on which to project all its fears of and frustrations with the modern dating scene? Do we want the internet's equivalent of Cersei paraded naked through the streets while everyone yells "Shame!"?

As clear as all of this feels, though, I forgot my own stance. Caleb has disappeared from the internet almost entirely since his brief brush with fame and shame. He apparently does not post anymore. But to write all of this about him, to bring him back into the public eye to prove my point without warning him that I was going to do so felt unfair. The journalist in me believes in asking for comment, but to do so, you need someone's contact info. He has no Instagram or X account. He definitely doesn't have a public TikTok. Only his LinkedIn listing still remains. But as I've admitted, I am more powerful than a Google search engine. I used every tool at my disposal, and I found him: his email address, his phone number, where he lives. It didn't feel good to write him an email. Invading someone's privacy never does. But I did send it.

My curiosity about who he is now, and what he thinks of all of this, and how he's survived all of this attention outweighed my belief that he would not want to hear from me. He did not respond to my email, and I cannot say that I blame him. I wouldn't respond to me, either.

The experience of watching reality TV at the same pace as other people is so much more satisfying than bingeing. Gossiping as the show unfolds heightens my experience, intensifying my emotions and righteous opinions regarding a group of complete strangers in a ridiculously stupid experiment. After picking apart every contestant and interaction with a fellow fan, I enjoy the second wave of gossip flowing from social media even more. As the nation picks sides, choosing the favorite couple, naming the villain, and roasting the cringiest moments, I have my own fully hashed-out opinions, carefully curated by gossip, to compare.

Knowledge Is Power

Before the fight breaks out, the women of *The Real Housewives of Salt Lake City* are seated outside. Their hair blows in the wind. They are seated at tables that have been pushed together into a triangle. They are in Bermuda. The dinner, which is a birthday dinner for Monica Garcia, is Bermuda Triangle themed. "I know who you really are," Heather Gay says. She pauses for effect. "Who you really are is the cyberbully internet troll Reality Von Tease."

To understand why all hell breaks loose after this, you have to understand that this was the finale, the culmination of all the plotlines that were born over the course of the season. Monica Garcia is the new girl. She was brought onto the show after a former housewife, Jen Shah, was caught running a telemarketing scheme targeting elderly people and went to prison for conspiracy to commit wire fraud. Jen is the enemy of the housewives, their former friend who was revealed to be a scammer and scammed many of them. An Instagram account had spread gossip about Jen and occasionally also made fun of the other housewives.

What Heather is accusing Monica of is not only running that Instagram account (Monica admits that she helped with the account) but intentionally hurting the other housewives by posting negative things about them. The betrayal is an intimate one: you, our contractual friend on this TV show, have betrayed our confidence. Heather also goes on to accuse Monica of a conspiracy; she chose to work for Jen (she did) in order to create a scenario where she could worm her way onto the show (not true that we know of).

As the fight progresses, the tightly built reality TV facade begins to bleed around the edges. In the background, the viewer can see a member of the crew scurrying quickly around the deck looking for something. One of the cameras is jostled a little as the operator moves it to a more advantageous position. Producers have edited in screenshots of a housewife's DMs to the accused account and clips from the past, while in the present, at the triangle table, women point at and scream over one another. Near the end of the scene, Heather stands to make the argument that the reason they are all reacting so strongly to an Instagram page that helped reveal that their former friend Jen was a fraud and an abusive employer is that they were gaslit and hurt by Monica.

On no level is Monica's posting about Jen's abusive behavior the same as Jen's actively lying to them for years and, according to Heather, giving her a black eye (?!). But it is absolutely excellent television. The wind is whipping around like it was paid for by the production team. The housewives who are not yelling are wrapped up in little blankets, cowering, on the verge of tears.

Two million people watched that finale. Jennifer Lawrence called it "the best reality TV finale, I think, ever" and said she would give the women on the show her Oscar because they deserved it. It is juicy and messy—and perfect.

But there is one line in the scene that has buried itself in my subconscious, so that it rings out in Heather's cadence, her hand hitting her other hand, anytime I hear one of these words. "Guess how you know I'm telling the truth!" Heather yells. "I have your perfect formula: Receipts. Proof. Timeline. Screenshots. Fucking everything!" The line was so instantly iconic that it became a meme: people on TikTok remixed it as house music or to the tune of Chicago's "Cell Block Tango." Receipts. Proof. Timeline. Screenshots. Fucking everything!

Like a prosecutor, Heather built her case on evidence; she laid it out on television, and she felt vindicated. In a way, she was. Monica was not asked to return to the next season of *RHOSLC*.

What is so riveting about this scenario is that gossip plays a huge role in all reality television. Gossip is one of the genre's greatest plotlines. Who knew what and when, and who did they tell? In the same way a murder mystery pivots on learned information, so do the minor dramas of reality TV. And like real life, the people on reality television believe that gossip can save them.

When Heather presented her theory and built it up with concrete documentation, what she was trying to do was control the situation around her. We gossip because we want to believe that if we just know enough, we can keep ourselves safe and control our future.

* * *

Knowledge is power, and reality television is a kind of warped mirror. It shows us who we are, what we want, and how we relate to others. One of the many things it reflects is that gossip is how we decide whom to trust and whom not to trust. It helps us decide who is safe and who is not, who will protect us and who won't. Gossip is how we build our communities, and watching people build (and destroy) communities on television is still social learning.

"One unique appeal of this genre is that it involves real people ostensibly reacting to real-world stimuli, which facilitates our

149

putting ourselves in the participants' shoes. (Would *I* have told Shannon that Vicki was talking behind her back? What protein would *I* have selected for the barbecue challenge?) Reality television places its viewers in the driver's seat in ways that scripted TV does not," Dr. Danielle J. Lindemann wrote in her book *True Story: What Reality TV Says About Us*.

The current form of reality TV is most often said to have begun when *The Real World* premiered in 1992. Over a single decade, *The Real World* took over television. By 2003, more people were applying to be on the show than were applying to Harvard. Since then, reality television has rocketed in importance, and social scientists have been trying to nail down exactly why we like it so much. In their seminal study "Why People Watch Reality TV," published in 2004, Steven Reiss and James Wiltz at the Ohio State University asked 239 adults to rate the importance of sixteen different motives as well as how much they watched and enjoyed different reality television shows. Some of the sixteen motivations were power, curiosity, independence, vengeance, honor, and romance. For each motive, an animal behavior and a joy are also applied. Independence, for example, is a desire for autonomy; the animal behavior is "Motivates animal to leave the nest, searching for food over larger area," and the joy found is "Freedom."

Reiss and Wiltz found that viewers of reality TV are motivated mainly by "status," defined as a "desire for prestige (including desire for attention)," and that prestige can grant "self-importance" or attention. They hypothesized that status-motivated people might consume more reality television because they want to feel more important than people on reality television (another study has found that reality TV viewers do not derive pleasure from the humiliation of participants and instead are willing to participate in the shows themselves) or because reality television implies that ordinary people (i.e., them, the viewers) are important. As a longtime reality television watcher, though, that feels a little weak to me. It seems more likely that people motivated by status would be drawn to reality television because they are looking for a playbook.

This is more obvious if you think about competition-based reality TV: shows in which normal people are gathered from the real world and set against one another to win a (usually but not always) monetary prize. This includes shows like *The Bachelor*, *Survivor*, *The Apprentice*, *Big Brother*, and *Farmer Wants a Wife*. To differing degrees, all of these competitions require strategy, and gossip can be used as a tool in each of them. On reality TV, gossip can be a lifeline or a death sentence; it can sway a suitor to send you home or convince one that you're the real deal.

Mark Burnett, the executive producer of *Survivor*, told Mediaweek in 2000, "Viewer interest in [*Survivor*] will lie less with watching who takes home the cash than it will with observing how the game is played." The bet he made paid off. Every week, some friends and I watch new episodes of *Survivor* together. Of course, we have favorites that we would like to win, but that's not really the point. The point is to dissect the moves: Who is playing a bad game? Who is sneaky? Who would we be?

But why? Why do we care so much about how these games are played and what strategic choices people make? Maybe we watch reality TV because we are trying to learn how to exist in the world. "Greater intelligence in primates likely evolved because being able to keep track of complex social relationships in groups gave individuals an advantage," Dr. Joe Stubbersfield, a senior lecturer in the propagation of narratives and cognitive bias at the University of Winchester in the United Kingdom, told me. We are inherently, evolutionarily built to do this kind of evaluation of others and try to learn from it. It's possible that watching reality television gives us a way to observe social interactions from every possible angle, thus understanding the way we interact in the real world.

I certainly feel myself identifying with contestants on reality competition shows, and the shame I feel when they make a bad choice is almost personal. I feel like they are embarrassing *us*, the stereotype we both belong to. This is, of course, partly a parasocial projection, but it is also the way that reality competition shows encourage you to relate to them. The entire confessional booth concept makes you, the viewer, feel like you know more than everyone on the show does, even if you know in your heart that the whole thing is tightly edited. In 1959, the sociologist Erving Goffman argued in *The Presentation of Self in Everyday Life* that people exist in the world based on how they think they will be perceived. He called this "presentation of self." He believed that while we can relax in private (even when we are doing things like watching reality TV), we are performing how we think we are supposed to behave in public. There's some tangible evidence for this in relationship to reality TV. For example, watching the show *16 and Pregnant* reduced births by teens, according to a study published by the National Bureau of Economic Research.

"While the average viewer may not be able to relate to eating grubs on an island or sliding into a sparkling sheath dress for an elaborate rose ceremony, these shows lay bare the forms of interaction that dominate all of our lives. They're mirrors of our most basic and immediate social groupings," Lindemann wrote in *True Story*. And with millions of people watching these competition shows, that means that we as a society are collectively learning from the actions presented to us. We are building road maps for how to create status for ourselves within social groups from the way people on our screens behave.

A common practice on reality competition shows is "the Tattle." A term coined by Joyce Chen on Refinery29 in 2019 when speaking of the *Bachelor* franchise, the Tattle is "what happens when some drama goes down in the mansion, and one or multiple men feel the need to go running to the Bachelorette to let her know that so-and-so is not here for the right reasons, or that what's-his-name has been acting super sketchy when she's not around." In season eight of *The Bachelorette*, one of the terrible contestants said a slew of ugly things about the lead, Emily Maynard, including that she was an "exhausted sick mother" and that her daughter was "baggage." In the episode, you see the men sitting around gossiping about this, talking about how mad they are that he would say that. Only one of them, Doug, who is a dad himself, decides that it is serious enough that she needs to know about it. He goes and tells Emily, who in one of the most iconic lines in *Bachelor* franchise history declares that she wants to "go West Virginia hood rat backwoods on his ass." She sends the annoying man home. Doug, who did the Tattle, lasts a couple more weeks before exiting the show.

The Tattle is theoretically a strategy play on dating shows. But if you watch enough of them, you learn that it rarely works. The messenger usually gets shot. The lead can't shake the association of the bad feeling from the information with the person who brought it to them. One of the most recent *Bachelorette* tattletales was Adrian Hassan on Charity Lawson's season. Annoyed with how immaturely some of the other men were behaving, Adrian told Charity that he thought some of the men were acting as though they were on spring break. Then he snitched that one of Charity's favorite men had called her "classless." In that moment, Charity told him that she appreciated his honesty. However, the accused happened to be at the top of the pack, and so Adrian was sent home in the next week's episode.

The Tattle is a game mechanic that exists in every reality show in different ways. Knowledge about other contestants can always be played to your advantage if you do it correctly. And the way to get that knowledge is to gossip.

Everyone on a competition reality show has secrets. Contestants are dropped onto an island or into a mansion with no knowledge of one another and no assumptions. You get to start over. What you reveal about your past to the people on the show is entirely up to you. Contestants on *The Bachelorette*, for example, frequently hide the fact that they are divorced until they receive a one-on-one date with the lead, the assumption being that the bias against divorcés will outweigh any chance they might have to make a good first impression. Contestants on *The Mole* may hide that they are trained in forensics. Contestants on *Survivor* hide that they are lawyers. On almost every reality show, cops hide their profession, though that may be because of the possibility of well-earned disdain. Gossip and the revelation of motives, secrets, and moves is one of the only social currencies these shows have, so if you keep your own secrets, no one has anything to use against you, and if you have secrets to trade, you can gain allies.

Almost immediately in the game of *Survivor*, secrets and collusion became the major currency. In episode five of the first season, "Pulling Your Own Weight," the eventual winner, Richard Hatch, set the standard for how the game would be played. Hatch's four-person alliance colluded in secret, walked purposefully into tribal council, and coolly voted Dirk off to maintain the strength of their group. It took the other members of the tribe weeks to catch on to the alliance. Now, within the *Survivor* community this kind of voting is known as "blindsiding," and it is the way that most players are voted off the island. The only way to keep from being blindsided is to have good sources. One of the biggest brags a contestant on *Survivor* can have is that they were always on the right side of the vote. Their alliances were strong enough and their knowledge correct, so they were never surprised by who was sent home. But in a show that is all about who knows what, where (as they always say) knowledge is power, feeling confident that you actually know what is going on is almost impossible.

The creators of *Survivor* know this and have frequently made changes to the game to encourage the players to gossip. In season eleven, the show introduced the concept of "hidden immunity idols." A hidden immunity idol is a one-and-done object that players can find to save themselves from being voted off the island. Sometimes players find or earn clues to help them find the idols, and sometimes they just dig inside the roots of a tree, get lucky, and find one. So if you are going to be voted out and you play your immunity idol correctly, you will be safe and the person with the next most votes will be sent home. Since season fourteen, idols can be played only before the votes are read, so to use one effectively, you have to know that you are in danger. This means that survivors need to determine whether they might be on the wrong side of a blindside and then play the idol before the votes are revealed. If they are too cocky (as almost everyone in season forty-six was), they will be sent home with the idol in their pocket. Or if the gossip they have gathered is incorrect, they will waste the idol.

A perfect play of this kind of gossiping occurred in *Survivor: David vs. Goliath* in season thirty-seven. The premise of that season was that some people in life are Davids (scrappy, uphill fighters, underdogs) and some are Goliaths (titans of industry; Mike White, the creator of *White Lotus*, was on that team). At one point in the season, everyone was merged into one tribe, but the players still felt an intense allegiance to their original David and Goliath tribes and were voting accordingly. There were twelve contestants left: seven Goliaths and five Davids. The Davids were in trouble. As the minority alliance, they were in danger of being picked off one by one until only Goliaths remained. The Davids planned to vote for Angelina Keeley, and the Goliaths planned to vote for Christian Hubicki.

But one of the Davids, Nick Wilson, had a hidden immunity idol. He created a smaller alliance of only three Davids, and they concocted a plan. They had an idol. But they believed a rumor that a member of the Goliaths had an idol, too. So the three of them didn't vote for Angelina as planned; they voted for John Henningen, whom no one was targeting at the time. Then they continued to talk about voting for Angelina to throw the Goliaths off the scent. It worked. At the tribal council, the new small alliance of Davids played their hidden immunity idol for Christian, and the Goliaths played an immunity idol for Angelina. When the votes were read, seven votes for Christian and two votes for Angelina were nullified by idols. That left only the three votes from the small alliance, so John was sent home.

This is the kind of four-dimensional he-said-she-said chess that most of us can only dream of. It's such a strong social game that one member of the alliance, Nick, used this event as the argument to win the whole season. The fallout from that action, though, was hurt feelings. The two other Davids who hadn't been included in the plan felt slighted. By gossiping without them, the smaller alliance proved (according to those players) that its members did not trust them. They voted together for a few more episodes, but the trust was gone. Gossip can bind you to others, and it can also exclude others from your group.

Experiments by researchers Matthew Feinberg, Robb Willer, Jennifer Steller, and Dacher Keltner have shown that not only does the threat of being gossiped about deter untrustworthiness, but spreading rumors about people who have behaved badly can indicate to our friends and acquaintances that we are trustworthy. Their experiments indicate what we think to be true through the Tattle: if it is perceived that you are sharing gossip only so that people will trust you (i.e., for personal gain or being there for the wrong reasons), it will backfire onto you and you will be perceived as less trustworthy. But if you give someone information that they can use for their own schemes and perceptions, they will trust you more.

As the game of *Survivor* has evolved, the advantages have become more and more specific. One of the best is called the

"Knowledge Is Power" advantage, which allows a player to steal an idol or other advantage if they know who has it on their person. It's a perfect symbol of the game as a whole; it is just as much of a benefit to know who has an advantage as it is to have one. Your intel can keep you safe. As long as it's right.

* * *

But that's not entirely true, is it? I want to believe that understanding how the world works can keep us safe, but this is the false security of gossip. Knowing crime rates does not prevent crimes from happening. Knowing that someone was scammed out of $50,000 does not prevent you from being scammed in the future. Knowing that someone else's girlfriend cheated on her after they stopped sharing locations does not mean that if you force your girlfriend to share her location, she won't cheat on you. Knowing that you might be voted off a show certainly gives you a chance to fight against it, but that alone isn't enough to prevent it.

For Heather Gay, having the receipts, proof, timeline, screenshots, fucking everything might have been enough to get Monica removed from the show, but it wasn't enough to stop the whole thing from happening. Knowledge may be power, but it is not omnipotent. And it's worth noting that gossip is not the same as knowledge. Gossip includes a hefty spirit of doubt.

My favorite reality game show, *The Traitors*, puts strangers together in a mansion and pits them against one another, forcing them to gossip to survive. It is based on a Dutch television show that premiered in 2021 called *De Verraders*, and it is very similar to the party game Mafia or Secret Hitler. The premise of the show is this: twenty or so contestants arrive in a house. Somewhere between two and four of them are then chosen secretly by the show to be "Traitors." At night the Traitors murder one of the "Faithful," removing them from the game. The next day, everyone sits around a big table and fights about who they think the Traitors are. The goal of the game for the Faithful is to vote out every Traitor, because at the end of the game, if even one Traitor remains, they take the entire prize pot of money. In the American version, the pot is worth about $250,000. However, if everyone remaining is a Faithful, they split the money evenly. Practically, this means that the entire gameplay of the show is gossip.

Because of the way the game is constructed, the Traitors know everything. Each knows who the other Traitors are, and they know who they want to murder. They also sit in on the conversations with the Faithful, who are blind to their existence. For the Faithful, the game relies on instinct. There is no knowledge. A Faithful's win, in the current iteration of the game, almost requires a Traitor's mistake or a huge amount of luck. The first season I watched was the UK version when on vacation with a group of my friends in London. I knew from the first episode that the show would rule because viewers are told who the Traitors are the moment they are chosen. You can watch them play, watch them manipulate, cast suspicion, and create chaos.

In the first episode, the host walks around the table while everyone else is blindfolded and places a hand on each Traitor's shoulder. Among others, she chooses Alyssa Chan, a business management student from Ireland, who smiles under her blindfold. The moment the participants remove their blindfolds, the game begins. Chan leans over to the person next to her and points out something subtle: the woman across from them did not raise her glass to cheers. Isn't that a bit suspicious? The woman, Nicky, who didn't toast is voted out at the next elimination ceremony. Alyssa had her removed from the game with one phrase. It's a masterful use of gossip. But it's also gossip that she's able to deploy effectively because she's a Traitor.

Because the contestants are never given clues to the identities of the Traitors and because they have no phones and no contact with the outside world, the gameplay of the show is social observation. If someone doesn't clap hard enough when the Faithful are mentioned, jokes lightly about being murdered (a fatal flaw), or is too good at positing how the Traitors might think, they will be voted out. Early in the game, there is so little evidence to go on (you do not know these people, and there are so many to choose from) that the odds of picking a Traitor based on observation are the same as if you were to draw a name from a hat. But everyone is convinced that they have seen something or heard something and that their career (be it as a detective, a schoolteacher, or a surfing instructor) has uniquely prepared them to read other people.

"Once the assembly has broken up and these social influences have ceased to act upon us, and we are once more on our own, the emotions we have felt seem an alien phenomenon, one in which we no longer recognise ourselves," the French sociologist Émile Durkheim wrote in *The Rules of Sociological Method* in 1895. Daily, this happens to the players on *The Traitors*. The participants walk into the room and confidently vote out a Faithful, and then they all sit in a daze, unable to understand how just a minute before they had been so confident that the person in front of them was a Traitor. As a viewer, you can see how the actual Traitors manipulate situations by the way they gossip strategically about other players, the way they share information with a close few allies who will vouch for them even though they should not do so. The Traitors' greatest enemy is their own feeling of guilt, their ability to lie to people they are learning to like. The Faithfuls' greatest enemy is the all-knowing Traitors.

Because reality television is meant to be "real," the reflection it shows us of our own existence isn't always the one we want to see. On reality television, gossip can be your lifeline, but it can also be your downfall. In *The Traitors Australia*, season one, for example, one of the Traitors, Marielle Intveld, who played an excellent game and made it to the top eight before being discovered, undid all her weeks of work with one little mistake: the gossip she shared was a lie. After the Traitors had murdered someone the night before, she told a remaining player that the murdered player had pointed the finger at someone else. But that was a fatal flaw. The person she attempted to gossip with had been allied with the murdered girl and therefore knew that Marielle was not telling the truth. And why would someone lie about what a now-dead player had said if not to shift the attention away from herself, a Traitor? She knew who the Traitors were, and she misplayed her hand. The woman who questioned her was able to rally everyone else, and at the next vote, Marielle was sent home.

Especially early in *The Traitors*, the players are easily swayed by one another. In 1972, the social psychologist Irving Janis coined the term *groupthink* to explain poor foreign policy decisions that led to the Pearl Harbor bombing and the Bay of Pigs invasion. Groupthink is when members of a small group accept a *perceived* consensus. So even if many members do not think that Nicky is a Traitor simply because she didn't raise her glass to toast, if they notice that the majority of others seem to be leaning that way, they will follow the herd in order to reach a consensus. On *The Traitors*, if you vote against the majority group, you are often questioned, which can very rapidly raise the risk of the conviction of being a Traitor. Groupthink is gameplay.

This is one of the less positive reflections that gossip on reality television can show us: that we are prone to using gossip to reinforce the perspectives of the majority. If one person decides that another is untrustworthy, their entire gameplay can fall apart. "The genre is a fun-house mirror, to be sure, but one that powerfully reflects the contours of our social world. It takes the elements that are central to our culture—our collective preferences, our norms and taboos, and the jagged edges of our social inequalities—and beams them out to us in frenetic detail," Dr. Lindemann wrote. That means that the way in which contestants gossip about their peers on reality TV reflects the same racism, classism, and sexism that exists within our societies. The psychologist Erin O'Mara Kunz at the University of Dayton and two coauthors examined 731 contestants across forty seasons of *Survivor* and found that both women and people of color are less likely than white men to make it to the individual competition stage of the game (the merge).

What I love the most about *The Traitors* is how we the viewers are omniscient. We can watch a nice guy (like Harry Clark, the winner of UK season two) look into his friend's eyes and lie. As a Faithful, we might have had suspicions about Harry, but as a viewer, we can see exactly what he's doing. In confessionals, he explains himself straight to the camera, and to us the viewers. If part of why we watch reality television is to learn how people behave, there is no greater vantage point to observe from than in front of the television while *The Traitors* is on. The players function on hearsay, on guesswork, on hope, but we the watchers have power. We know it all—or at least it seems like we do.

That's one of the interesting things about reality TV: it's real and it isn't. It is tightly produced and tightly controlled. In the second season of the American *The Traitors*, instead of sending players to the round table to banish a player, producers sent them to the woods to play a game. The game they played frayed the alliances the players had built by asking each person to choose one person to save from that night's murder. Players often complain on the show that they did not sleep well because they are worried that they may be murdered, so a night without worry is a night of blissful rest. On the Reddit afterward and in my own group chats, people gossiped about why the producers would choose to change the game at the last second. Maybe, we guessed, someone they wanted to keep on the show for dramatic reasons looked like they were going to be voted out.

Two players in this game concocted by production were playing their own emotional game as well. Chris "C.T." Tamburello and Trishelle Cannatella have been linked since their appearances on different seasons of *The Real World* in the early 2000s. They competed together on *The Challenge: Rivals II* in 2013, and their relationship was so tumultuous that Trishelle ended up dropping out. She emphasized in interviews that she thought he was "horrific." Clearly, they were cast together on *The Traitors* as rivals. Anyone who had watched them on other shows, including other players inside the castle, would have known that instinctively. When *The Traitors* began, however, Trishelle told *People* that she thought C.T. had changed. They seemed to be making an early alliance.

But in the nighttime game of survival, C.T. saved someone else instead. They'd known each other for years, and Trishelle expected their alliance to keep her safe. Trishelle's feelings were hurt. But at least from the way the episode was produced, Trishelle did not seem to be in real danger of being murdered. So it was easy to side with C.T. in their fight. I, the viewer, had knowledge of the greater social dynamic at play. Watching a scene like that is great for social learning. You know that Trishelle is being a little dramatic, but the stakes for her are clear: she feels certain that she is in danger, and C.T. does not.

After the game, Trishelle cried in the castle, telling C.T. that she felt like he didn't care about her. "If we're playing the game, it's not about friends," he said, a common refrain on all of these shows. But as much as reality television is constructed and manipulated, the people on it are real. Of course, Trishelle was upset about not getting a good night's sleep, but she was more upset because of their shared history, because being on the game is still part of your life. She and C.T. will continue to see each other outside the game. Not only did she feel like she was being sentenced to death; she felt like her friend had done it.

Reality TV is so delicious because of how blurry the line between people's real lives and the story we are being shown on-screen is. Lindemann told me in an interview that her students are "pretty savvy about reality TV not being real." They know that producers exist. They aren't naive enough to buy everything they're sold wholesale. And because of that they bring other bits of information to their discussions of reality shows. Instagram posts, rumors, blind items, and Reddit threads. The show is someone's life, and if you can decipher the cracks between reality and reality television, you can feel like maybe you've found truth.

One of my favorite small production tricks is commonly featured in *The Bachelor* franchise. The lead will be talking to someone in a room with the door slightly closed, and the camera will show us a woman in a beautiful dress, a little tipsy, with her ear pressed up against the door. She is talking. Usually she's talking about how she's jealous or how the woman he's talking to is wrong for him, and from the angle of the camera shot down a hallway, it looks like she's talking to herself. In the world of reality TV, a producer is usually standing just around the corner. The woman talking is made to look mildly unhinged while being prompted by someone wearing a headset who we cannot see.

The same happens with the editing of reality TV. For years, Mariah Smith ran a column called "Keeping Up with the Kontinuity Errors" for *The Cut* in which she compared the plotlines appearing on *Keeping Up with the Kardashians* to the posts the Kardashians made on social media. Using their outfits, locations, and press appearances, Smith determined the real dates of each scene's filming, pointing out when they had been filmed at a totally different time from the event they were referencing. In 2017, for example, Kim Kardashian's photos for her new KKW Beauty line were so heavily fake tanned and contoured that people accused her of being in blackface. The photos were released on June 14, 2017, but the scene that eventually played on *Keeping Up with the Kardashians* in which Kim reads the comments online and nibbles her finger in anxiety wasn't filmed until August 4, allowing Kim to craft a public show of remorse. We have no idea whether she actually felt it.

The Kardashians are also savvy enough to use the real world to promote their stylized produced reality. As Morgan Baila laid out in Refinery29 in 2019, the biggest headlines in the Kardashian family history (pregnancy announcements and a cheating scandal, for example) were all apparently leaked to news sources in the lead-up to a new season of the show. It's a brilliant PR use of the celebrity gossip machine, but these are also their real lives. Kylie really was pregnant when her pregnancy was announced. Tristan Thompson really did cheat on Khloé with Kylie's ex–best friend, Jordyn Woods. But all of the reporting about reality television, gossip about who did what when, helps us construct a version of the reality we ourselves live in that feels even more real.

The knowledge that we gather outside the game gives us power to help us decide what exactly to believe about what we see on TV. Part of the joy of watching reality TV is the gossip that exists outside it. Think about the *Vanderpump Rules* saga "Scandoval," when Tom Sandoval was revealed to be cheating on his girlfriend of nine years, Ariana Madix, with another cast member and her close friend Rachel "Raquel" Leviss. Madix and Sandoval were many people's favorite reality television couple, including mine. They had been together in the public eye for a decade, and then suddenly reports were all over TikTok that they were splitting up. It was confirmed by *TMZ*. Immediately, fans began doing private detective work. I remember reading a Reddit thread (since deleted) late at night on my phone about how the Scandoval affair had begun months before in the summer, clicking on Instagram links to see who was in the background of photos, zooming in like I was on an episode of *Law & Order: Special Victims Unit*. What followed next was weeks of lawyers' statements, Instagram apologies, and leaked stories about fights on set.

The voyeurism of reality television is never more satisfying than when the drama is ongoing. An entire infrastructure of reporting and rumor and drama exists outside the actual aired episodes. Reality television is never more successful at giving people something to talk about than when what is airing on television is playing out at the same time as the actual drama happening in the real world. That was why *Vanderpump Rules* producers aired three reunion segments in a row to sum up the drama over the course of the summer. When production and editing are added to the stories of real life, we can see it all in one beautiful swoop. After months of eating crumbs, it felt like being fed a full dinner.

Still, when I discuss reality television with friends, the problems of the people on television feel so separate from ours. We would never be blindsided. We would know who the Traitors are. We wouldn't be cheated on. The joy of watching a live reality television show, perhaps subconsciously, is that the separation is never truer. Something bad or difficult is happening to someone else, not to us. It is easy to believe that we will learn from their mistakes. We feel that the knowledge we gain from watching them will buoy us against harm.

"We perform verbal acts as well as other acts…in order to extend our control over a world that is not naturally disposed to serve our interests," Barbara Herrnstein Smith wrote in *On the Margins of Discourse: The Relation of Literature to Language*. Reality television's most important reminder is that no matter how much gossip you obtain and how well you deploy it, you are still just human. All it takes is one person to lie effectively to you for all of your social gathering to come to naught, your torch to get snuffed, your name to be written down, or your contract to fail to be renewed for the next season. All the receipts, proof, screenshots, timeline, fucking everything that you gather and present cannot give you complete control, because each of us is not the center of reality. Reality exists without us, which is a comforting reminder.

Maybe the reason we love reality television gossip so much is that it is more concise than the narrative arcs in our lives. We can see what matters to us as a society in a neat little diorama. In a couple of hours of bingeing, we can see the decision-making process, the action, the ramifications of that action, and the fallout. The storylines complete themselves in front of us. And with that knowledge we return to the actual real world to try to build alliances and trust for ourselves.

When I was a freshman in high school, I believed that the seniors' prank was letting three pigs loose in the school labeled 1, 2, and 4, the story being that school officials would be looking forever for a pig number 3 that didn't exist. I have repeated this story to everyone until just recently, a friend told me that this is an urban legend that many preteens are led to believe happened in their hometowns. Now I'm wondering how many people over the years heard me tell the story and just nodded along, knowing it wasn't true. Also, I'm thirty now, so I believed and retold this untrue gossip for like sixteen years.

The Truth About Urban Legends

Sometimes a piece of gossip comes in hot and exciting but not quite right. The pacing is off, maybe, or the ending. There is nothing I love more than taking a morsel of gossip and sprucing it up, placing in extra relevant anecdotes, building four walls around the story, and then releasing it into the wild by telling it to as many people as possible. When I tell a story well enough, it cannot help but spark in the tall dry grass and catch. And for a prolific gossip, the true sign that you've constructed a banger is when someone you don't know very well tells that same story back to you later with all the same beats and inclusions you added, without knowing that you were the one who set it off in the first place. I always feel sentimental when this happens, as if my prodigal story has returned home at last.

Some gossip I know, from the moment I hear it, is that kind of gossip that will swirl around and around, growing from the ground up like a dust devil until it demands everyone's attention. One of those stories is what I affectionately call "the Poop Ziploc Story."

The first time I heard it was when a listener called it in to *Normal Gossip*. I remember it like this.

A friend of a friend, let's call her Clara, had tough luck dating. She was living in a big city, going on all of these awful dates, when finally, one night she goes out with a great guy. They hit it off immediately, and she really likes him. It's the first promising date she's been on in ages. They go out to a multicourse meal, and she has a great time. He's so courteous and caring. He tells her that he has an early flight out but that he would love for her to come over to his place anyway. The doors autolock, so she can stay, sleep in, and leave whenever she feels ready the next day. So Clara goes home with him! The sex is great!

In the morning, sure enough, he kisses her goodbye and leaves early. Clara dawdles around the apartment a bit. She drinks coffee, and suddenly her body remembers the multicourse meal. She has to poop! She has to poop now!

Clara goes to the bathroom, shits, and, in the worst nightmare possible, the toilet will not flush. She tries again; nothing. She's desperate and panicking. She likes this guy so much! She cannot leave a giant shit in his apartment! So she grabs a Ziploc bag, fishes out the poop, and decides to carry it out with her.

She stops on her way out to write him a little note that says something like "I had a great time, hope to see you soon!" and scurries out of the apartment. It is only when she hears the sound of the door automatically locking behind her that she realizes she left the Ziploc bag of her poop on the counter next to the note.

This is a horrifying piece of gossip. All of the decisions made in the story are so clearly rooted in fear that you cringe the whole way through it. Even though I have heard it a hundred times, it still fills my body with dread. It's also hilarious, so we added it to an episode of listener-submitted gossip. Immediately, our inboxes were filled with people *certain* that we had fallen for a trap. It was an urban legend, they claimed; it wasn't real. Already, this is a reach. Just because something is an urban legend doesn't mean it isn't real. But was it an urban legend at all?

Jae Towle Vieira and Alex Sujong Laughlin produced a follow-up episode in which they tracked down the person who had submitted the story. She was certain it had come from a real friend of a friend of a friend. It wasn't an urban legend to her; it was thirdhand gossip. When they poked a little further, they found that the story had been told in various versions with subtle differences as far back as the early 2000s and in more than three countries. They spoke with a man who had directed a short film about the story, which he also thought had happened to a mutual friend of a friend, and heard from a woman who was certain she had heard the story at an event for World Toilet Day. We released the follow-up episode, presenting all the research and the muddiness of the story, questioning the hard line that people had been so fast to draw between urban legend and truth, only to receive even more baffling responses.

For days after the follow-up episode, my DMs were full of first-person stories that were shockingly similar to the urban legend. Someone swore that she had once scooped her poop out of a toilet and thrown it out a window into a public park so that she could retrieve it later and throw it away. Someone else told us a story about how they had let a girl sleep in their apartment in college and she had peed in a cup and left it on the desk. Another woman wrote in to tell a story of scooping her poop up and hurrying it to an outside trash can before her complicated situationship could emerge from his room. Another swore that the same thing had happened at their workplace. On and on it went. The majority of the stories had poop in a bag. Some of them had automatic doors. A few people pointed us to a BBC story from 2017 where a woman became stuck in a window after trying to remove her poop from the bathroom and had needed to be rescued by the local fire department, which is somehow worse than the original.

There were so many variations on the tale, all of them slightly different, from different places and different years, but none of them was quite right. Women all over the world, it seems, are scooping their shit out of broken toilets and trying to hide it through various means. Maybe Ecclesiastes was right and there really is nothing new under the sun. Was the original story just another woman digging her poop out of her date's toilet? Or was the story we'd heard first some kind of Frankenstein's poop story, an amalgamation of hundreds of worst-case scenarios wrapped into one neat urban legend?

The Poop Ziploc Story carries the moral that you should not poop at your hookup's apartment, but it also displays the value of our culture: that pooping is embarrassing and funny. But even that distinction feels difficult to me. There are plenty of stories that occur in a particular time and place, and thus would be categorized as gossip, that carry important mores and values regardless of their veracity. Once gossip reaches a certain critical threshold of attention, it morphs. The names of the people involved are no longer as important as the themes of the story, what it tries to teach us, what truths it seeks to reveal. What the people barking that the Poop Ziploc Story was an urban legend were really saying was that it was too widespread to be called gossip anymore. If they had already heard it, it couldn't possibly be gossip. But gossip can only really grow up to be one of two things: an urban legend or a conspiracy theory, or sometimes both.

* * *

Every year, my middle school held a career week. Adults used one of their few PTO days to appear in our Axe deodorant–laden halls and tell us stories about wearing suits, having a boss, and whatever else it was that they did. As part of the curriculum, we were given personality quizzes meant to point us toward potential careers and off periods to consider what we could make of our lives, how we would create meaning and money for ourselves. We were also, of course, twelve and thirteen years old, so all of this caused almost as much commotion as the quizzes we took before Valentine's Day (we had to pay money to find out who we were most compatible with). Those were acceptable forms of horoscope for an early-aughts Republican district. The compatible crushes were all of the opposite sex, and my career test said that I would do well in the military.

As a small, wily preteen who knew every word of "American Idiot," I hid my results. I could not imagine anything lamer or more upsetting than being told I had the personality for the military. They might as well have told me that I was a piece of raw dough, useless if not for the molding of some greater industrial complex. I was still reeling from this result when we were led to the library for the afternoon's seminar. My closest friend was a girl named Alexis who wore chokers and black T-shirts and had introduced me to My Chemical Romance, so I had anointed her the coolest girl I'd ever met. Alexis told me in the hallway on our way to the library that her career quiz had granted her a sparkly, beautiful future as a musician. So of course I lied and told her that the personality test had prescribed me a beautiful future as an artist. Alexis nodded. Of course our futures were bright. Of course we would be best friends forever. We were still whispering, now seated crisscross applesauce on the scratchy library carpet, when the career adult arrived.

Alexis elbowed me. This adult was not in a suit. This adult was not a man. And, unlike every other woman who was allowed to speak at career week, she was not a teacher or a flight attendant. She was very short, shorter than we were, and we were still children, and she was wearing many gauzy, loose layers despite the Texas heat. Her hair was long and curly. Her glasses were thick and round. She looked like a witch from a Disney Channel original movie, and she did not stand behind the pulpit they had set up for her. No teacher needed to step in and hold a hand in the air, crying "Quiet coyote!" to get everyone in the room to stop talking, because the woman's entrance carried with it a wake of silence.

The woman sat on the ground. She told us that she worked as a storyteller. It was, she told the room of preteens, the world's second oldest profession (she did not tell us the first). I do not remember if she introduced herself. The few remaining contacts I have left from middle school do not remember her name, either. But they all remember her presence, and—most importantly—the story that she told.

The story, as far as we can collectively remember it, went something like this:

> In this very town, a long, long time ago, a terrible tragedy occurred. A group of children, just like you were a few years ago, piled into a long yellow school bus and left for the day on a field trip. They spent the day outside, under the sun, and on the drive home curled up on the plasticky seats of the bus, warm and drowsy, and fell asleep. It was night and dark and muggy by the time they got close to home. The teacher was driving the bus over a set of railroad tracks when the bus died. She cranked the key. Nothing. She cranked it again! Nothing. And when she looked up, she saw it: a train barreling toward them, its headlight extinguished. She barely saw the

train before it was upon them, and though she raced to save the children, the train was too close and moving too fast. The train barreled into the bus, cutting it in half and throwing the teacher through the windshield. She lived, but the children were not so lucky. They were all killed instantly.

The teacher mourned. She berated herself. She wished for death, and she tried to find it one night, a few weeks later, when she drove her car back onto the same train tracks and turned off the ignition and the headlights to wait for her own collision. She heard the train and saw its bright light, heard its honking, and then the whispers began, and their small voices were so familiar. Right as the train approached, her car began to roll forward. It was safely on the other side of the tracks when the train barreled by. The teacher rushed from her car, terrified that the good Samaritans who had saved her had been smushed by the train: her life again saved in exchange for someone else's. But after the caboose rolled through, there was nothing on the tracks, and she turned back toward her car, and there on the back of the trunk, stamped into the dust, were ten pairs of tiny handprints.

We were transfixed. For years, I retold versions of that story around campfires, always being sure to note that it had happened right there, in the town where we lived, where nothing ever happened. Much later, haunted by the indelible memory of those handprints, I researched the story only to learn that it had not in fact happened down the road from where I grew up, unless you consider the entire United States highway system to be a single road. The story seemed to derive from a true story, at least. In 1938, a group of schoolchildren had been killed on the train tracks. The teacher had been a nun. The bus had stalled and wouldn't run. The nun had lived, but many of the children had not.

The storyteller's version wasn't true, but it wasn't quite fiction, either. No one spun these ideas out of the air and built them into a narrative. They came from a real event. But the tone of the story wasn't built of tragedy or warning or fear (though it contained all of those emotions); it was told by the transfixing woman as entertainment: the words dripping with scandal, the pacing built to make the hair rise on our arms and a chill run down our spines. Like many stories I loved during my childhood, this one was an urban legend.

Years later, when I reported a story about urban legends for *Thrillist*, I spoke for hours with Andrea Kitta, a professor and folklorist at East Carolina University. "We want to know where something comes from, and we do look for print versions," Kitta told me. I also noted at the time that Kitta had told me that "these stories have the advantage of never being so complicated that they couldn't have actually happened or that multiple people couldn't have invented them separately." The story about a blind girl who thinks her dog is licking peanut butter off her foot all night long and later finds out a man sneaked into her house, killed the dog, and licked her foot did not actually happen to my friend's older sister's friend. The party tale about a girl who babysits a dog (apparently dogs frequent the types of tales I'm familiar with), watches it die, and tries to transport the dog in a suitcase via the subway, only for it to be stolen by a man who thinks it's heavy and expensive electronics, did not actually happen to someone's ex-roommate's ex-boyfriend's sister. Maybe they did. But it's unlikely. What's most likely is that they are legends we've crafted for ourselves to hand out like candies at Halloween.

An urban legend is a product of an eerie experience plus time. One of the urban legends near where I grew up concerned an old rusty bridge called Old Alton Bridge. Or, as we called it, Goatman's

Bridge. Legend had it that if you drove over the bridge at night without your headlights on, the Goatman (half goat and half man) would come out. You can no longer drive over the bridge, so we never got to test it out firsthand, but I spent a handful of Saturday nights turning off a flashlight and walking across the bridge with my hair on end. I never questioned why you had to have your headlights off to see the Goatman. I assumed it was just because everything is scarier in the dark.

But last year I learned another version of the story. In the 1930s, a Black man named Oscar Washburn had lived on the north side of the bridge. He made his money raising and selling goats and became known as the Goatman. He put a sign on the bridge to direct people to his house, and perhaps because of the sign and his success, the local Klansmen tried to kill him by hanging him from the bridge. When they threw him over the side of the bridge, with the noose around his neck, though, Washburn disappeared. The Klansmen then killed all of Washburn's family. It was said that they had driven to get him over the bridge with their headlights off, which was where the legend came from.

"The lack of verification in no way diminishes the appeal urban legends have for us," the folklore scholar Jan Harold Brunvand wrote in his 1981 book *The Vanishing Hitchhiker: American Urban Legends and Their Meanings*. "We enjoy them merely as stories, and we tend at least to half-believe them as possibly accurate reports."

If a story like the one about the ghost children on the bus was at one point printed in a newspaper, that meant that a reporter had to have found out about it somehow, which means that it might very well have begun as gossip. So the gossip about a bus being hit by a train becomes a newspaper article about a tragedy, which becomes hushed whispers in the community. Then when another story (about the ghosts of the children pushing the car off the track) appears in the community, the two stories become intertwined. The new story is picked up by the storyteller and brought all the way to my home-town, where it is told to me. I then tell the story for years before transcribing it here in this book, spreading it even further.

Unlike regular gossip, an urban legend is first and foremost a story. It contains the traditional elements of storytelling: a setting, a plot, a climax, and usually a denouement. "Urban legends are nota-ble for their variation," the psychologists Nicholas DiFonzo and Prashant Bordia wrote in a paper dissecting the differences among rumor, gossip, and urban legends. "The same urban legend—with details adapted to the current place and time—shows up in different locales and at different times." An urban legend is always happening where you are because its story has been moved to meet your loca-tion. The goal of the urban legend is not to source information that can help you in the immediate moment, to protect you, or to give you intel on others. The goal of the urban legend is to convey some kind of moral truth, some value that we as a society hold.

Many urban legends carry an element of horror. It can be the embarrassment of your poop not flushing, the fear of the Goatman's ghost, or the disgust of imagining Walt Disney's body in a cryo chamber deep beneath Epcot. You won't catch me saying "Bloody Mary" three times while looking in a mirror, and if I hear my name in the Appalachian woods, no, I did not. It doesn't matter to me if they're true. I won't be testing them.

* * *

In a classic American legend, George Washington confessed to having chopped down a cherry tree because he could not lie. That story exists because a popular history writer, Mason Locke Weems, included it in the fifth edition of his very popular biography of George Washington after the latter's death. The anecdote was not included in the first four editions and has never been independently verified. Yet it has remained a popular legend in American culture because of the value it espouses: that honesty is more valuable than trees.

Gossip about presidents and other powerful leaders almost always carries with it a hearty helping of moral determination, but only sometimes does it remain an urban legend. Throughout the history of politics (American and not), gossip has swirled around people in power. They are celebrities, after all, so we talk about them. There was gossip about Pericles and how he might be keeping his helmet on to hide his pear-shaped head. It's said that Mark Antony spread a rumor that Augustus had slept with Julius Caesar. There was also talk that Mark Antony had married Cleopatra even though he already had a wife. As Oscar Wilde wrote in *Lady Windermere's Fan*, "Gossip is charming! History is merely gossip. But scandal is gossip made tedious by morality."

You can tell a lot about a society at a particular time by which pieces of gossip are elevated into scandal and which are allowed to slip meekly away with the wind. "The gossip that reverberates and endures isn't necessarily true, but it usually reflects something real about the target, or the national anxieties at a given point in time," Gail Collins wrote in *Scorpion Tongues: The Irresistible History of Gossip in American Politics*. This, of course, is true for more than just presidents. We gossip about traits and behaviors we think are inappropriate and uncouth. We gossip about teen pregnancy and sexual promiscuity because the United States is at its core a Puritan nation with prudish beliefs. We gossip about women neglecting their children because we are afraid of women's liberation.

On the political front, there was gossip that Martin Van Buren, who had been Andrew Jackson's secretary of state, and was president during the financial panic of 1837, was living lavishly. There was gossip that Abraham Lincoln was part Black, an expression of Americans' anxiety over slavery in the lead-up to the Civil War.

Gossip swirled that John Adams *loved* British things, just as the new nation was struggling to find its footing. William Henry Harrison is best known for serving only thirty-two days as president because, the story goes, he gave such a long inauguration speech in such cold weather that he caught a cold that developed into pneumonia and died. He was the first president to die in office, and that was fairly fitting since rumors had swirled around him during the campaign that he was already dead and performing an early staging of *Weekend at Bernie's*. Scholars think that those rumors might have been why he gave such a long speech. Rumors are always based in something, and if they aren't based in actual reality, they're often based in anxiety. We are afraid of something, so we worry that people with power are exacerbating the situation.

John F. Kennedy was maybe one of the best gossipers and gossip subjects the United States has ever seen. It is noted in many biographies that he was constantly asking members of his staff for gossip, maybe because he had so much of his own. He was rumored to be sleeping with Marilyn Monroe even before she sang that sexy rendition of "Happy Birthday." Whether he was or wasn't, the stickiness of that rumor in particular, when certainly other presidents had cheated in the past, could have reflected the country's insecurity about inaugurating the first Catholic president. It could also just be that he was young, hot, and an undeniable flirt.

My favorite piece of presidential gossip comes from the first Clinton administration. Anyone who has toured the West Wing of the White House can tell you that it is a shithole. The ceilings are low. Every renovation seems to have been done as cheaply as possible. The hallways are sporadic and narrow. It's optimistic, really, to think that most presidents are far more worried about doing good for the country than they are about the state of their living and working quarters. When you are inside the West Wing, especially if you are there while people are working, the noise is overwhelming. There is very little privacy in a space overrun by people and even less in a place where everyone is nosy.

Knowing that, it is easy to believe, as Kate Andersen Brower wrote in *The Residence: Inside the Private World of the White House*, that florists, butlers, chefs, and all sorts of other workers would hear conversations they weren't supposed to be privy to. Brower spent hundreds of hours interviewing these employees. She wrote about how the White House staff viewed the Clintons as being paranoid, which is easy to believe since the first giant rumor of the Clinton administration (the ones after would be much, much bigger) came just weeks after the family moved in.

In late February 1993, the *Chicago Sun-Times* reported that the Clintons had fought in the White House and Hillary had broken a lamp. This story was credited to "wicked Washington whispers." In my experience of living in DC, whispers circulate for weeks, sometimes months, before a reporter gathers enough on-the-record sourcing to be able to print something definitively. *Newsweek* wrote shortly after that "dinner parties were buzzing with stories of Hillary throwing—take your pick—a lamp, a briefing book or a Bible at Bill."

When Katie Couric asked Hillary Clinton during a televised 1993 White House tour to point out where she had tossed a lamp at her husband, Hillary joked, "I'm looking for that spot, too." When *The Residence* was published in 2015, it contained not one, not two, but three salacious stories about Hillary throwing something at her husband. The *Washington Post* article questioned whether Brower's sources had actually witnessed some of the events they had described, but veracity is never the point of rumors of this sort.

Is it possible that Hillary Clinton threw a lamp at Bill Clinton at some point during his presidency? Sure, I guess so. He had an affair with Monica Lewinsky, who at the time was an intern. She had plenty of reason to be mad about that. But a good piece of gossip does not require veracity to tell us something about ourselves as a nation.

"The lamp story grew and grew because Hillary Clinton stirred up anxiety in many Americans, and the story about her smashed lighting fixture helped them express it without directly confronting the things that were bothering them...by passing along the rumor that Mrs. Clinton had physically attacked the president, people were expressing their secret fears that she (and maybe by implication all women) would try to push her husband aside and run things herself," Collins wrote in *Scorpion Tongues*.

What is certainly true is that Americans were concerned about having a professional and capable first lady. They made jokes about who the president *really* was. They worried that instead of electing Bill Clinton, they had elected his wife. A national insecurity existed about the role of women and the kind of power they might have going into the new millennium.

"Rumours are essentially unofficial things. No public statement by a government or a government agency, for example, no matter how far removed it was from an original eyewitness account, could be a rumour (though, of course, it could confirm a pre-existing rumour or be responsible for starting another rumour)," researcher David Coady wrote in his 2006 article "Rumour Has It." For the president or first lady, once a rumor has begun to swirl, no number of White House press briefings is going to make it disappear.

As far as presidential rumors go, perhaps all of them can be classified as both gossip and urban legends. But there is always a risk of their evolving into something more sinister. When people in power are involved in stories about morality, they can easily slip into conspiracy theory. A conspiracy theory arises when an urban legend is given a powerful villain. For the story about the lamp being thrown to become a conspiracy theory, all it needed was a cover-up campaign. Does the White House not want us to know something? Is a (real or imagined) cabal making decisions about what we the people get to know? A conspiracy theory is a kind of dark lord rumor. It is more sinister, even when it is playful. It has intent.

During Barack Obama's presidential campaign, the most potent rumor about him was that he was not a US citizen and therefore could not be president. Obama's father was from Kenya, but he himself was born in Hawaii, making him a natural-born citizen. The campaign provided a digital photocopy of Obama's birth certificate and allowed people to view the hard copy. But still the rumors persisted. The Obama campaign wrote that the rumors "aren't actually about that piece of paper—they're about manipulating people into thinking Barack is not an American citizen," a clear response to national anxiety about the nation's first Black president. Researchers have found that people who believe the noncitizen rumor are politically knowledgeable and have very high racial resentment. The "birther movement," as it would come to be called, evolved into a conspiracy theory.

In *The Conspiracy Theory Handbook*, the psychologists Stephan Lewandowsky and John Cook argued that there are seven traits of conspiratorial thinking. They even created an easy-to-remember acronym: CONSPIR. A conspiracy theory is contradictory (C) because conspiracy theorists can simultaneously believe two things in direct opposition to each other. To a conspiracy theorist, Princess Diana could have either faked her death or been murdered. The belief system must also contain overriding (O) suspicion: the official account must always be wrong, and anything that does not fit into the predetermined belief must be ignored. Importantly, the disregarding of those accounts is because of their nefarious (N) intent. The people behind the conspiracy are never acting with goodwill. And even if part of the theory is proven incorrect, theorists persist in the deep feeling that something (S) must be wrong. They themselves are the brave individual willing to fight on behalf of whatever persecuted (P) victim exists, and this aim is completely immune (I) to evidence. Conspiracy theorists believe that very little happens by accident; all random events can be reinterpreted (R) as part of a greater whole.

The birther movement is most clearly a conspiracy theory through overriding suspicion and immunity to evidence (because no number of scans or photographs of Obama's Hawaiian birth certificate can sway the belief), as well as in nefarious intent (because it is presumed that the lie was put forward to steal the presidency).

Conspiracy theories posit that something (though it is not always clear what) is being hidden from us, the people, and that knowledge should be ours. Does the Pentagon have knowledge of aliens? Was Princess Diana murdered? Is Taylor Swift being paid by the NFL to date one of its best players? Is Avril Lavigne actually dead? Is the earth a flat disc infinitely propelling upward? Even in their tone, conspiracy theories do not sound the same as rumors. Even when the undertone is not as bleak as government cover-ups and secret sex rings, conspiracy theories are presented with the underlying assumption that the teller knows the truth and is trying to evangelize it to you, so that you will be converted to their belief that jet fuel can't melt steel beams or whatever, whereas gossip is told from a position of questioning.

"Truth and fact-checking travel along the same paths that conspiracies do. But the truth is often complicated, shaded, and demanding, and there's no denying that it often lacks the powerful, emotional, gut-level appeal of a conspiracy," Anna Merlan wrote in *Republic of Lies: American Conspiracy Theorists and Their Surprising Rise to Power*. And it is so much *fun* to believe a conspiracy theory.

There is no high quite like hearing a good conspiracy theory for the first time. Because a good conspiracy theory is built of gossip that has flown too close to the sun and been burnt to a crisp, there's always a hint of truth there. I remember the first time I heard that

Melania Trump had been replaced by a body double. It was 2017, and I was living in Washington, DC, and out on a walk with my friend Olivia. The conspiracy theory hadn't quite caught steam yet, but she showed me the photo on her phone.

In the photo, Melania was on the tarmac at Palm Beach International Airport on her way to Mar-a-Lago with President Trump and a Secret Service agent. The agent was wearing a black suit with a white undershirt and (as is the Secret Service's MO) pants that didn't fit quite right. In the harsh sunlight, the agent's facial structure looked vaguely similar to the first lady's. Their hair was the same color. "People think this is a body double," my friend said, sliding her phone across the table. Ignoring the fact that it would be very sloppy of a presidential administration to choose a body double for the first lady and then allow the two of them to be photographed together on a tarmac, they also looked physically different. The agent was a good six inches shorter than the first lady and had a much more athletic frame. Still, it was funny to imagine the first lady having a body double like she was Angelina Jolie in an action movie, so I laughed and did not think much of it.

In October 2017, the theory went mainstream when Joe Vargas, the founder and CEO of a CBD retailer, tweeted a screenshot of Melania on cable news next to a (probably photoshopped) photo of her that he had found on the internet. The White House denied that the first lady had a body double. A former Secret Service agent denied that the Service used body doubles at all. The Trump administration, however, lied almost constantly about almost everything; the *Washington Post* counted more than 30,500 false or misleading claims that the president managed to tell in his four years in office. So why should a statement from his White House mean anything?

Every six months or so during the first Trump administration, the rumor would pop back up. Melania would be photographed in an unflattering light or not wearing heels or with stronger contour makeup than usual, almost always wearing oversized sunglasses, and the conspiracy theory would scurry back into the limelight. That was particularly funny because Melania so rarely spoke to the press.

Personally, I do not think the first lady of the United States had a shoddy body double who was trotted out to hold hands with the president whenever she didn't want to. Melania missed enough important events to make it clear that the administration was perfectly happy with Trump's appearing alone. But I am interested in why this piece of gossip was particularly sticky.

"The idea of someone impersonating the first lady to fool the American people relies on the idea that the *real* first lady is off doing something else and abdicating her duties," Alex Abad-Santos wrote in *Vox* in October 2017. "This aligns with the narrative that is often applied to Melania Trump, especially by observers on the left." The insistence that the body double existed, even when facial recognition software was used, spurred that belief into the realm of conspiracy. It was a little taste of gossip, then, that people felt might be true even if they could not prove it.

If the last twenty years of American politics have taught us anything, it's that it is more important to many people that something *feel* true to their personal experience than it is that it *be* factual. Conspiracy theories function on the same saturation premise that fake news does. The more you hear a story, the more likely you are to believe it. A 2015 psychological study found that knowledge does not hold enough weight to fully counter incorrect claims that are repeated. If we hear a story that seems true, we might believe it whether or not it is false. The numbers say that Joe Biden won the election in 2020, but plenty of people acted against those results by storming the Capitol because the facts might be lying. It felt like they were lying. And even though it has been proven over and over again that the 2020 election was not stolen, elections (like Lyndon Baines Johnson's Senate Democratic primary runoff in 1948) have been stolen in the past. But skepticism is not the goal of conspiracy theories. The goal of a conspiracy theory is to other someone or something.

A conspiracy theory, unlike an urban legend, does not just reiterate a moral of society but indicates that someone is behaving badly. There is always a villain in a conspiracy theory, and the villain is almost always a bastion of power. The White House is lying about the first lady's body double. The British royal family is lying about why we haven't seen Kate Middleton. The Illuminati are controlling the media and were responsible for the French Revolution. At their most sinister, conspiracy theories can be a way to justify hatred against a specific group of people. They can show us at our ugliest, becoming vehicles for racism, antisemitism, homophobia, transphobia, and sexism.

What kept the Hillary Clinton lamp rumors in the realm of rumor rather than conspiracy theory is how mundane the story was to begin with. The original 1993 *Chicago Sun-Times* article quoted an unnamed White House source who said that the lamp in the family quarters, which belonged to the Clintons, "wasn't a priceless antique, or anything like that." It was so specific, so mundane. In that rendition of the gossip, she hadn't even thrown the lamp, she'd only broken it.

But at its heart, it is gossip about marital troubles. Throughout Clinton's first term, gossip swirled about his ogling women and having affairs. But the Hillary rumor was the one that dominated that first term. Frank Rich in the *New York Times Magazine* described the view of Hillary at the time as that of "a lamp-throwing Delilah, emasculating her weak husband." There's no conspiracy theory there, only the mundane drama of a marriage elevated into the spotlight. In a 1996 interview with Barbara Walters, Hillary brought up the lamp. There's a kind of winking note in her voice when she says, "I mean, you know, I have a pretty good arm. If I'd thrown a lamp at somebody, I think you would have known about it." Or maybe there's no winking in her voice and I am hearing only what I want to hear: a tone of vengeance, a twinkle of chaos. That's how a legend is born, after all: imbue a little gossip with magnitude and enough time, give it a moral that rings true to people, and watch it grow.

Once gossip becomes so big that it has a purpose, be it in the haunting of an urban legend or the ugliness of a conspiracy theory, it becomes a mirror. The truths inside a gossip that big aren't in the details. Urban legends and conspiracy theories tell us who we are, the good and the bad. They show us our values, whether honesty and helping others or hate. It is easy to dismiss a story that has spread so far, a gossip that has grown so large, by saying that it must be untrue and made up. But if we can see beyond the haze of our skepticism, inside such stories, whatever you want to call them, are the truths that make us who we are, just waiting to be found.

The Poop Ziploc Story isn't just an urban legend to me anymore. When I tell it now, it is firsthand gossip. I've confirmed it. I've spoken to someone it happened to. The details I now have are verifiable. I know where the story took place and with whom and how it ended. The incident really did happen to a friend of a friend, in this town. But then again, that's how all urban legends begin, isn't it?

I'm a huge fan [of a podcaster who] basically interviews other experts in a variety of fields. A few months ago, a journalist wrote a piece about how he was cheating on a gf he had and how he treated her pretty bad. I think he had something like five girlfriends at one time... it definitely wasn't a good look, but it also has little to do with his professional work. I still listen to his podcast, but now I have an ick feeling about him I can't shake! I feel like his work brought a lot of good into my life and it's been now tampered by this knowledge I have of him as a person. It's a piece of gossip I wish I'd never heard!

My Life with Picasso

Pablo Picasso was everywhere in 2023. It was the fiftieth anniversary of his death, and it seemed like every museum had one of his paintings on display, if not a whole exhibition devoted to his work. I looked at his work in museums in Los Angeles, Seattle, New York City, London, Philadelphia, and Austin that year, which is to say nothing of the hundreds of his pieces I've seen over the course of my life. Picasso was an incredibly prolific artist, and he lived a very long time, so there were plenty of canvases, drawings, and sculptures to be shipped to museums in the Northern Hemisphere and saturate the galleries.

All year, I was delighted to find his work on display. Like millions of other people, I admire Picasso's art. Arguably, he contributed to ten different artistic movements throughout his career. Sure, Synthetic Cubism was one of them, but he also experimented in Surrealism, in Cubist sculpture, in linocuts. Picasso's work has a surety of form that is still enticing, that calls to you from across the room in a big museum. He was so bold in his willingness to break rules, to create tension on the canvas, that even today some of his work is viscerally upsetting.

At the Los Angeles County Museum of Art, I spent half an hour in a room with three small Picassos, completely infatuated with them. One of them moved me almost to tears. In it the background is deep black; in the foreground, a woman weeps. The painting is from 1937, from Picasso's Cubist era. The woman's mouth is an inflamed, ugly lime green. Her neck, a triangle, has three semicircular wrinkles recorded for all eternity. Her eyes are shaped like teardrops, and her actual tears are drawn like pendant earrings, hanging from the corners of her eyes in straight lines. In front of half of her face is a white kind of hand-shaped blob scribbled in with lines that look like graphite. Her hair is red. Standing in front of this painting, I felt the agony in the woman's face, the ugly clench of her jaw reminiscent of awful times in my own past. I found myself frowning, mirroring the way her stubby fingers sat on her chest.

Weeping Woman with a Handkerchief is one in a series of paintings Picasso created after the bombing of Guernica, Spain, during the Spanish Civil War. *Guernica*, the mammoth black-and-white Cubist rendering of the bombing, is far more famous, but the weeping women enchant me in their consistency. Whenever an artist paints the same thing over and over again, their infatuation is evident, but so is their growth. You can see the way their understanding of the subject shifts over time in the same way you can see the progress from a sketch to a final painting. Picasso was haunted by the weeping women. From May to October 1937, he created a dozen drawings and four oil paintings of them.

He painted the weeping women from studies of Dora Maar, whom he was romantically involved with for nine years, while he was still also involved with Marie-Thérèse Walter, the mother of his child. While with both of them, he was legally married to Olga Khokhlova, a Russian ballet dancer.

Picasso is a hard artist to love as a woman, as a feminist, as a person who cares about power and the abuse of it. He was famously a misogynist and a womanizer. He physically abused his wife. He disowned some of his children. He talked shit about his closest friends. Those are all facts.

For some, there is no room for nuance beyond those facts. Perhaps the best publicized and most derided American Picasso exhibition of 2023 was held at the Brooklyn Museum in New York. The exhibit had a guest curator: Australian comedian Hannah Gadsby, whose main qualifications were having an undergraduate degree in art history and making a few jokes about Picasso in their 2018 viral comedy special, *Nanette*. When *Nanette* was released, it received immense critical appreciation. It won a Peabody Award. It was endorsed by Kathy Griffin and Monica Lewinsky. In the set, Gadsby jokes, "Cubism...All the perspectives at once!...Any of those perspectives a woman's? No!...You just put a kaleidoscope filter on your cock."

As part of their set about what it means to make art in the world and how difficult it can be to survive as a comedian if you aren't willing to put up with the bad behavior of famous men, Gadsby picks a target, an easy one at that. This joke reduces the entirety of the Cubist movement (which included women like Natalia Goncharova and Tamara de Lempicka, among others) to only Picasso. But that's Gadsby's point. "I *hate him*," Gadsby seethes, "but you're not allowed to." The first time I watched *Nanette*, I almost yelled back at the screen. There are very few people who, at this juncture in history, would argue that Picasso *wasn't* an asshole. It's a common stance. Of all the famous modern artists, Picasso is maybe the one who is gossiped about the most.

"At this point, the charge that Picasso could be a tyrant to those around him—philandering, chauvinist, controlling, manipulative, abusive—is not even truly novel at the pop culture level," Ben Davis wrote on *Artnet* about the Gadsby show. Arianna Huffington's biography, *Picasso: Creator and Destroyer*, which argued (perhaps too strongly) that Picasso was an asshole, had been published thirty-five years earlier, in 1988.

What's interesting, though, is that the reason we know Picasso was an asshole at all is because of the codifying of gossip through memoir. We know about his snide remarks and underhanded digs because there was nothing that the artists of Paris in the 1930s and '40s loved to do more than talk shit about one another. We "know" the "truth" about Picasso, not because we saw him with our own eyes and heard him with our own ears and made a value judgment but because we have consumed stories about him that we find believable and honest.

The seminal text that established Picasso's private life, that brought all of his dirty laundry out into the open, was the 1964 book *Life with Picasso*. Written by Françoise Gilot, who was in a relationship with Picasso for a decade starting in 1943, it is the gossipiest memoir I've ever read. *Life with Picasso* is a barn burner. It is a memoir so intimate and honest in its depiction of the private life of Picasso that it feels less like voyeurism and more like an embodiment of the writer's interactions with him.

Memoir is the art of codifying gossip. Gossip, at its best, can be used to grab back power that has not been given to you, and there are few greater forms for that practice than memoir. It is the art of honing a single perspective until it feels like the only one. But part of how we verify gossip and remain skeptical of it is by consuming as many perspectives on a situation as possible. The truth of any story is never only one person's.

* * *

Picasso ran in circles with writers, but he did not write about himself. He dabbled in poetry that was bad enough that Alice B. Toklas wrote, "The trouble with Picasso was that he allowed himself to be flattered into believing he was a poet too." He wrote two Surrealist plays but no nonfiction. Few of his letters survived after his death. His life, then, was recorded by those who surrounded him: his fans and his many exes. It is an interesting flipping of the cliché "History is written by the victor." The life of Picasso, who was revered, beloved, and feared in his lifetime, was written by the women he used and left behind.

Life with Picasso does not cover Picasso's whole life because it is not his story. It covers Gilot's life during the decade they were together. While it is technically a memoir, it is at its core a biography. The majority of the book has almost nothing to do with their relationship; it is a meticulously recounted version of Picasso's interactions with his friends and enemies and dealers and fans. It begins with Gilot, as a young woman in Paris, encountering Picasso at a restaurant with her hot friend. They are introduced by a mutual friend as essentially the brains and the beauty, Gilot being the brains. She was a painter in her own right and very quickly was inducted into the kind of pseudo salon that Picasso ran from his apartment during the Second World War. She would ride her bike across the city, arrive at his home, and allow him to whisk her off into private rooms to show her his paintings, objects he had collected, or anything else. She realized that he was interested in her after she spent a couple of weeks away.

"I passed through one of those crises young people sometimes experience in the process of growing up," she wrote. "Picasso wasn't the cause of it; it had been coming on for some time before I met him. It was a kind of mental stocktaking brought on by the conflict between the life I had led up until then and the vision I had of the kind of life I should be leading." She was twenty-one years old. He had a wife and two girlfriends. At the time they met, he was sixty-one years old and one of the most famous living painters.

With our 2023 gaze, it is immediately easy to pinpoint how a forty-year age difference and an insurmountable difference in career levels raise a slew of red flags. Often (though not always), a large age gap creates a power imbalance that allows for abuse. And though later in their relationship that would be the case, Gilot's chronicling of their early days together is filled with longing and idealism. In one of her first sexual experiences with Picasso, she wrote that he had undressed her in the middle of his bedroom to see if "your body corresponds to the mental idea I have of it." She abided but, naked and being observed, felt embarrassed. "He must have sensed that and realized I was still, in a measure, undecided and had no real desire, because he began to reassure me." Even writing after the collapse of their relationship decades later, Gilot's primary memory was that "he was very gentle, and that is the impression that remains with me to this day—his extraordinary gentleness." Elsewhere, she had recounted Picasso saying, "For me, there are only two kinds of women— goddesses and doormats." At that moment, she was a goddess.

Though she was much younger than him, she was an adult. And though he was more powerful than her, more famous than her, and certainly better connected than her in the career that she hoped to fulfill, Gilot doesn't seem naive in her idealization of the relationship early on. "When I left that day, I knew that whatever came to pass—however wonderful or painful, or both mixed together—it would be tremendously important."

This, to me, is the crux of Gilot's book: that she was a willing participant in all that came to pass. She had a form of agency that Picasso's other mistresses never seemed to have. She was, in fact, the only one of his women who managed to leave him on her own terms.

The book spills all sorts of secrets, many of them salacious and plenty of them pure gossip in that Gilot relayed experiences she was told about by other people. She wrote about Picasso's complicated relationship with Henri Matisse and his shit talk about his fellow

Surrealists. In one scene, in which they visited Matisse, she relayed every nice thing he had said to his friend inside his house followed by every nasty one he had said about him the minute the door was closed behind them.

Already, by the time Gilot arrived, gossip about Matisse and Picasso's relationship swirled around the art world. "Matisse had never heard of Picasso and Picasso had never met Matisse," Gertrude Stein wrote in her autobiography from the perspective of her girlfriend Alice B. Toklas. The two artists, she said, were "friends but they were enemies." *The Autobiography of Alice B. Toklas* is another memoir that became the defining truth for a half dozen Parisian artists upon its publication. Artists were so angry about it that in 1935, six people (among them Georges Braque and Matisse) published a pamphlet titled *Testimony Against Gertrude Stein*. "There is a unanimity of opinion that [Stein] had no understanding of what was really happening around her, that the mutation of ideas beneath the surface of the more obvious contacts and clashes of personalities during that period escaped her entirely," the intro reads.

The pamphlet is one of the pettiest publications I've ever read in my life. The artists go page by page refuting details from Stein's book. Matisse clarified that he did not purchase a Paul Cézanne painting with a tent and bathers on it. He purchased one with women bathers and trees but no tent on it. He stated that a lunch they shared had been in a different region than Stein had said. Georges Braque insisted that he had not painted Marie Laurencin's portrait. André Salmon protested that Guillaume Apollinaire did not sing a song like she said he did. The whole pamphlet has an air of people who were too early to know about the Streisand effect, yelling "I'm not owned" into the abyss. None of their clarifications are damning enough to overturn the meaning behind the anecdotes in the book. And *The Autobiography of Alice B. Toklas* is now considered a great work of English literature.

Gilot, too, challenged Stein's portrayals. "I thought it was interesting that the critics like to make out as if [Picasso and Matisse] were almost enemies. They were rivals in art, yes, but they were friends in life. Matisse was 12 years older and had a kind of parental attitude towards Pablo—I was always amused by this—as if Picasso were the bad boy, and Matisse the nice parent," she told *Harper's Bazaar* in 2019.

What's interesting is that both Stein and Gilot became chroniclers of their environments such that they created gossip for the general public by codifying the beliefs of a select few. In this way, through the publication of this book, Gilot became after Picasso's death in 1973 the main source of information on his life. And she pulled no punches: in the book and afterward. She wrote that he had employed a "standard technique of using people like ninepins, of hitting one person with the ball in order to make another fall down." Her portrait of him is relentless. She writes that he "took the cigarette he was smoking and touched it to my right cheek and held it there. He must have expected me to pull away, but I was determined not to give him the satisfaction."

Within the swirling layers of the gossip in this book, there is the canonical gossip that existed about Picasso before Gilot's arrival (his many women, his late nights, his coterie of painters). And then there is the gossip she described within her relationship with him: the whispers of his colleagues and friends every time he pulled her away into another room, his desire to quiet rumors by taking her to strange parts of the city, away from where they might be seen. Near the end of their relationship (and the end of the book), Gilot said that she had "asked Pablo to let me go to the mountains for three months. He refused. And since he talked about our separation with everyone and it was now the chief nourishment of all the gossips, it became inevitable."

By nourishing the gossips, Picasso hoped, perhaps, to keep Gilot with him, to trap her inside their marriage forever. But gossip is a form of power, and Gilot knew that. She knew that the viewpoint of gossip determines your perspective of the situation. If we gossip as a way of making sense of the world and gossip is a form of storytelling, this perspective is critical.

"As young women, we were taught to keep silent," Gilot told Ruth La Ferla in the *New York Times* in January 2022, just seventeen months before her death at age 101. "We were taught early that taking second place is easier than first. You tell yourself that's all right, but it's not all right. It is important that we learn to express ourselves, to say what it is that we like, that we want." In writing *Life with Picasso*, she found a way to become the mouthpiece of the gossip that swirled about them and around her and thus reclaim its power.

Like Stein's writing, many people were unhappy about Gilot's. There was widespread outrage after her book was published. Forty French intellectuals and artists signed a petition to suppress it. Picasso was one of their icons, and they wanted to protect him. Picasso himself filed three unsuccessful lawsuits against the book. He attempted to sabotage Gilot's art career and remained estranged from their children.

The reviews of *Life with Picasso* were unabashedly in favor of Picasso and protecting his legacy. The *New York Times Book Review* written by Aline Saarinen begins "Kiss-and-tell books always make me uneasy. Written, invariably, After the Fall, their motives are usually spite or greed or self-justification. One feels squeamish enough at being a Peeping Tom, but peeping through a distorting lens—that's not sporting." It is extremely reductive and interesting to call the most comprehensive text we have on Picasso as a person and citizen of the art world a "kiss-and-tell" book, but I think Saarinen reveals something fundamental in the response to Gilot's work: she implies that the only reason for a person to tell their story is scandal and voyeurism. The assumption is that while many, many people would be interested in Picasso, none would be interested in Gilot.

John Richardson, a friend of Picasso's who later became his biographer, criticized Gilot in his review for exposing Picasso's life to the public, as if she had no right to do so. Carlton Lake, Gilot's coauthor of *Life with Picasso*, published a response to this criticism that included "[Gilot] has set forth ten crucial years of her life in the pattern of 'I was there; this is what happened to me.' Reviewers by the scores have saluted her for her effort. But Mr. Richardson—volunteer spokesman for the Inner Circle—intones: 'This breach of confidence is the more unconscionable, as Picasso loathes any public divulgence of his private views...' But this is Françoise Gilot's story, not Picasso's, not Mr. Richardson's, and I think we have to let her tell it as she sees it."

The "breach of confidence" is the cardinal sin: the gossiping, the fodder for gossip. Picasso could gossip about Gilot, the inner circle said, but Gilot could not gossip about Picasso. His perspective was the one that mattered. But when you read *Life with Picasso*, it is remarkable in its evenness. Gilot depicted Picasso as both a tyrant and a genius. He is brilliant, and he is unbelievably petty. He is emotionally abusive and gentle in his interactions. He burns her with a cigarette; he spends the holidays with their children. It is a portrait of a whole man, which is why others wanted to suppress it. It is much easier to exist in the world as an idol without flaws than as a man who has failed even once.

When, upon her memoir's reissue by New York Review Books Classics in 2019, Gilot was pushed about why she had written about Picasso instead of herself, she said, "I could write a book like that, but that would be with a different title. I'm quite capable of writing all those things. I've been writing poetry. I wrote other things. But, if I write about Picasso, it has to be about Picasso."

And it is. It is as clear a perspective of one of the most influential artists of the twentieth century as we ever got. We see him as she saw him: mean and loving, difficult and brilliant. She does not weaken her perspective of his genius on the canvas by injecting it with her experience of him as a lover. She is capable of holding both truths in her head at once, which is frankly remarkable. It is much easier to create a simple narrative, as Arianna Huffington did in her biography by borrowing anecdotes from *Life with Picasso* and chopping off the parts that were interesting or comedic or innovative so that only Picasso's many tyrantlike behaviors remained.

"Much biography shares its power to inspire comparison. Have I lived that way? Do I want to live that way? Could I make myself live that way if I wanted to?" Phyllis Rose wrote in *Parallel Lives*. Perhaps part of what makes *Life with Picasso* a good biography is that to read it as a person who cares about the people around them is to happily, emphatically, answer no. No, I could not live as Picasso did. No, I don't want to.

Life with Picasso was a bestseller. It was read by thousands of people. It was reissued a few years ago because people still care about Gilot's perspective.

We know from Gilot's memoir that Picasso was an asshole. And we know that gossip is often used to express what we find moral and immoral in society. The judgments of Picasso justifiably denounce misogyny and physical and emotional abuse and being a bad friend. But where does that leave us with all of the paintings and drawings and sculptures he made? Should we, as people in the world, allow the morality play of gossip to bleed into how we view a piece of art?

"You've got to learn to separate the man from the art," Gadsby says in *Nanette*. "Okay, let's give it a go. How about you take Picasso's name off his little paintings there and see how much his doodles are worth at auction? Fucking nothing!"

What is so complicated about Picasso is that it is not that simple. Life would be much easier if every artist who is openly known to be an asshole or an abuser or both also produced terrible work. But it just isn't true. If you take the names off Picasso's worst pieces, maybe they aren't worth much financially. That's how art for profit works after all. But that isn't how "worth" functions in art. In art, the worth of something is in its impact. And it's undeniable that Picasso's impact was almost infinite.

And while it is true that the work of women and people of color is often excluded from the canon of important art, it is also true that Picasso was incredibly impactful on some of the most important American women painting at the time. In her book *Ninth Street Women*, Mary Gabriel wrote that the women of the American Expressionist movement had viewed *Guernica* at the Museum of Modern Art in New York City. One of them, Lee Krasner, was so inspired by it that she'd had to leave the museum and take laps around the block before returning to gaze at it more. The inspiration she had taken from it was so great, Gabriel wrote, that she helped build an entire art movement, Abstract Expressionism, out of the inspiration from that one painting and the permission it gave them to break rules.

In the Brooklyn Museum exhibit that Gadsby curated, there were far fewer works by women Modernists than I expected going in. The goal of the exhibition did not seem to be to actually raise the profile or understanding of women's art so much as to take shots at Picasso's legacy. But by doing so without the context of a broader swath of work, viewers gained almost nothing. If the goal of any exhibition is to provide wonder or create thought, this one did neither, opting instead to stand firmly in a take several decades old. As Alex Greenberger wrote in *ARTnews*, "The supplement to this exhibition, available on the Bloomberg Connects app, includes an interview with one artist in this gallery, Harmony Hammond. Asked about her feelings on Picasso, she says, "Truth be told, I don't think about Picasso and his work. It would've been nice to have more artists who *were* thinking about Picasso, or whose work, at least, has something to do with him."

"*Nanette* and Hannah Gadsby are part of a growing movement that seeks to seal us into a public discourse of eternal and constantly re-enacted trauma, which paradoxically claims that the pain of reliving and revealing your trauma is the only way to ease it," Yasmin Nair wrote in *Evergreen Review*. "By collapsing *aesthetic judgement* with *moral evaluation* it would train its audience to judge art by how worthy the person behind it was, thereby losing sight of whether an artwork was independently compelling. This would, in turn, inhibit people's ability to see what *worked*, as art or as an argument, leading to isolation and fragmentation," wrote Ben Davis in *Artnet*.

In the manifesto signed by forty French intellectuals and artists and members of the art world to try to ban *Life with Picasso* in 1964, the painter Édouard Pignon wrote, "In Picasso, there is no divorce between the man and the painter. It's of no use exalting the painter if one destroys the man…Picasso's way of painting is a source of morality in itself." Pignon's argument, then, is that you do not get the emotional volatility of Picasso's paintings without the emotionally volatile man. Pignon meant it as a defense of Picasso's behavior, but it is true that you cannot separate one from the other fully. You don't need to. Part of what makes art interesting and exciting to engage with is that tension between what the artist is trying to say and what they achieved on the page.

None of the art exhibitions that featured Picasso that I visited in 2023 revered him as a good person. There is a difference between being a good person and being a good artist. Most curators emphasize that. Only the Gadsby exhibition asked its viewers to take a hard moral stance. Picasso was *bad*, the exhibition seemed to say, and therefore his work is worthless. This kind of moral policing based on gossip wants art to be something it cannot be.

"Art is not meant to please," Gilot told *Harper's Bazaar* in 2019.

"It is about trying to get to the truth of something." And in her work, both on canvas and on the page, Gilot tried to do that. Not to create a version of Picasso that is morally clear, or to build out a narrative that will destroy him, but to sharpen our understanding of both his brutality and his brilliance.

Art and gossip both function as lenses to help us see the truth in the world. In the same way that we cannot take Picasso's self-made legacy as truth, we cannot take Gilot's story as our only truth, either. To do so is to deny that it is complicated to be a person in the world. In memoir we find an interesting combination of both: the narrative itself is art and gossip. The perspective is singular.

I cannot separate Picasso's paintings of Dora Maar from the stories about how badly he treated her. "Consuming a piece of art is two biographies meeting: the biography of the artist that might disrupt the viewing of the art; the biography of the audience member that might shape the viewing of the art. This occurs in every case," Claire Dederer wrote in *Monsters: A Fan's Dilemma*. "This tension—between what I've been through as a woman and the fact that I want to experience the freedom and beauty and grandeur and strangeness of great art—this is at the heart of the matter. It's not a philosophical query; it's an emotional one."

The Weeping Women series is upsetting both viscerally and emotionally when you know about their relationship. It enhances the viewing experience, for me at least. Like Dederer, I identify far more with the woman weeping than with the hallowed genius painting her. Maar's pain on the canvas feels real. It feels honest. It is so close to you that the emotion can transfer into your body. Her pain, often caused by Picasso, is preserved by him for us to feel almost a century later. And it's beautiful. It is strange and upsetting and absolutely beautiful.

Maar's own painted works were unrecognized until after her death. My favorite painting she ever made, *La Conversation*, is rarely exhibited. It is privately owned, and I have never seen it in person. Most recently, in 2019, it was in a major Maar retrospective displayed at the Tate Modern in London. In the painting, two women sit inside a red room. One of them, a blonde, sits at a table facing the viewer. She is well lit, beautiful despite her Cubist proportion distortions. The other faces away from the viewer. Only her back is visible, and her body is cast in shadow. The painting is meant to represent Maar's interactions with Picasso's other girlfriend, Marie-Thérèse Walter.

It is only by looking at that painting and the Weeping Women series, reading Gilot's book, and seeing Maar's paintings that I can begin to understand who all of these people were. "I believe we could paint a better world if we learned to see it from all perspectives, as many perspectives as we possibly could," Gadsby said about Picasso in *Nanette*. Somewhat ironically, a quote often attributed to Picasso says the same thing: "Who sees the human face correctly: the photographer, the mirror, or the painter?" Each provides its own perspective. Each is right. All are true. Except for the Picasso quote, which he may or may not have said.

In this way gossip about artists should enhance our understanding of how they worked and why. It should allow us to criticize the work they have left behind more thoroughly and accurately. The goal of gossip about strangers is not to try people according to their secondhand deeds; it is to increase our own understanding of the world, to allow us to find enchantment and discovery in places we didn't expect it.

When my now wife and I were in college, we once splurged for a date night at Red Lobster. We ended up not speaking to each other the entire date because in the booth behind me, there was another couple loudly discussing their divorce. The husband could not understand why his wife was leaving him, and she screamed at him a litany of reasons: he never did anything around the house, and his mother was awful from the first day they met... the list went on and on!

Our poor waitress was very stressed about our experience, but we were thoroughly entertained. Ten years later, it's still one of our favorite dates and we will still stop conversations to listen in on juicy gossip.

Things Half Heard

There were eight Kelseys in my middle school grade. It was a Texas public middle school, so the grade had almost three hundred people in it, but still. Six of the Kelseys, including me, were Kelsey M's. Three of us played volleyball. The curse of having a trendy name is that you never get to use it. Until I transferred to a magnet high school, I mostly went by my last name. McKinney was plastered on the back of all my jerseys, ironed onto the T-shirts we wore in gym class. The girl who ran laps was McKinney, and so was the girl who did drills. McKinney was the one in class who needed to stop talking and the one who got straight As. But that didn't stop me from turning when someone said "Kelsey," didn't keep me from eavesdropping if I heard someone say my name. And people were always saying my name—our name, really.

One day, I was in the locker room after volleyball practice. The locker room was damp from the condensation of sweat and smelled of dozens of girls who had just run miles in the Texas summer. On top of that salty, putrid smell of puberty sat the floating cloud of Britney

Spears's Fantasy perfume. I always had a headache in there, partly from the smell and partly because there are few places as stressful as a locker room when you are stuck in the quicksand of puberty. There were so many social cues to abide by. There are only two bad things a girl could be, and I didn't want to be either of them. I didn't want to change in the bathroom stalls, because that was what prudes did. But I also didn't want to be naked in front of my peers, which at the time everyone considered slutty. So I became a master at putting an underwire bra on underneath a sports bra, a Renaissance woman of snaking an undershirt out through the sleeve of a jersey, a magician whose greatest trick was modesty.

I was one of the last girls in the locker room that day. I was going to softball practice afterward, and that magic trick is much more difficult to perform because you need to wear sliding shorts underneath your regular shorts and high socks and a different sports bra. I was standing, facing the lockers, when I overheard whispering on the other side. It was a Kelsey they were talking about. Was it me? I stayed quiet.

The Kelsey they were talking about was a tease and a prude and a baby. I felt nauseous. I *was* a tease and a prude and a baby! I knew it! At that time in my life, I was kissing many girls who played on sports teams with me, while maintaining a slew of what I would later learn are beards: boys I "dated." I had dozens of "boyfriends" over the course of a couple of years, all of whom I avoided. In a place where the only sexuality acknowledged was hetero, I was a prude *and* a tease. But the fact that those accusations were true didn't stop it from stinging.

I don't know whether those girls were even talking about me at all. When we hear pieces of a conversation, our brains fill in the gaps. In 2015, research by O2 found that 84 percent of people eavesdrop on public transportation. We are more easily distracted by conversations we can hear only part of, according to researchers. For example, someone having a phone conversation on a train is more distracting than two people talking to each other. Only getting half of the conversation means innately our brain will try to make sense of it, to fill in the gaps. We use our own reason to determine what we think to be the truth, and then we act on that.

Nowhere is this behavior of eavesdropping poorly and then making decisions about what you heard confidently more common in popular culture than in the classic romantic comedy format. A common trope in rom-coms is "the misunderstanding." The main couple of the story, we the viewers know, is supposed to be together. They love each other! They are predestined—by god or the moon or whatever else—to kiss on the mouth. And for a second, they know that: the arc of the universe bends toward love. Until suddenly, one of them misunderstands the other. Often, the big misunderstanding is caused by one person overhearing another incorrectly, jumping to a (wrong) conclusion, and rather than confronting the other person directly, proceeding as if that is the only truth.

In *Anyone but You*, the 2023 romantic comedy based on the William Shakespeare play *Much Ado About Nothing*, Bea (Sydney Sweeney) falls for Ben (Glen Powell) after he pretends to be her husband in order to get her access to a customers-only bathroom at a coffee shop. They have a whirlwind day. Ben takes her back to his apartment, makes her a grilled cheese sandwich, tells her about his dead mom. They are both so beautiful it is almost painful to watch them interact. They fall asleep in their jeans on the couch, as wholesome (if as uncomfortable) as it gets.

The next morning, Bea gets up early and leaves. This does not make any sense. She had a great night and had no reason to need an escape, and she realizes this within a few blocks. But somehow, by the time she returns, Ben's best friend is already there, trying to convince him that he is in love with her. Ben, who is mad, I guess, that she left early, retorts, "I couldn't get her out of here fast enough. This girl's a disaster. She's a nothing." Bea, of course, is standing in the doorway to hear this line crystal clear. What she doesn't know, but that we the viewer can see, is that he's lying, hurt because she left early.

Anyone but You has more plot holes and weird dialogue than any movie I've seen in the last decade. The characters are flat. Their decisions make no sense. Even this interaction isn't mean enough to believably create the hour and a half of petty warfare Bea and Ben aim at each other in the lead-up to her sister's wedding. This misunderstanding, though, is the inciting incident for the entire plot. The reason it doesn't work is that a good "big misunderstanding" usually shows how the content that the listener overhears pokes at some personal wound of the eavesdropper.

In one of my favorite romantic comedies, *Notting Hill* (1999), for example, Anna (Julia Roberts) blames Will (Hugh Grant) for his roommate tipping off the paparazzi to her location. Even though he didn't do it, he is guilty by association. Then when he goes to visit her to apologize, he overhears her telling her costar that he is "just some guy from the past." This is Will's greatest fear: that the famous movie star he loves might think so dismissively of him. The misunderstanding comes not only from the actual content overheard, but from the biases and fears the character overhearing brings to that conversation.

If my life were a rom-com, the overhearing in the locker room would have been a perfect inciting incident because even if it had been a massive misunderstanding and they were talking about another of the many Kelseys, the pain of believing that someone could think that about me was just as real as them actually thinking it. In mishearing, we find another truth, one that tells us about ourselves more than about the world we live in.

And I should know, really, because I mishear so much.

* * *

The silence inside the booth was always laden with potential disaster. It enveloped you, lay sticky on the skin like humidity. The door was always heavy, hard for the technician to pull behind her, and adorned with soft, lumpy padding that gobbled up any remnants of sound that could exist in there, taking every noise until you were left with nothing at all. There was somewhere to sit, but unlike in a recording booth, the chair was not designed for comfort. No one was supposed to be in this booth for long, its chair not for utility but for shame. Or at least that's how it felt. Sit here. Let your legs fall asleep like they had at the desk in elementary school. And embody the dread of knowing that you are going to fail.

I remember the first hearing test I failed. Failure was a new feeling. I was a precocious smart aleck of a child, always raising my hand first in class, always annoying adults by demanding they let me stay and listen to their conversations instead of going off to play. Adults, I learned, could be impressed with children, and I wanted them to be impressed with me. There was no greater success than getting an adult to raise eyebrows and ask my parents, "She's how old?" I wasn't just precocious; I could spell precocious. And so when I was sent to take my first hearing test in second grade, I never considered that I would not ace it. Tests were something I was good at.

The audiologist was kind. They almost always are. Once I was situated in the booth that I didn't know yet to fear, she walked me through what would happen. Hearing tests usually consist of both beeps and words. You, the patient, sit in the uncomfortable chair and put on headphones, and the audiologist plays sound frequencies: low bass tones in the 50-to-60 Hz zone and high-pitched tones beginning at 10,000 Hz and higher. A person with normal hearing can hear between 250 and 8,000 Hz. The headphones make a beep, and (depending on the office) you raise your hand or press a button in response. The audiologist sits outside the booth, but you can see them through the window, not dissimilar to the ones found in the recording booths that you see in documentaries about pop stars making their albums. The audiologist wears a headset identical to the ones fast-food workers wear in drive-throughs and they can talk to you through your headphones. They make notes. You cannot see the notes. The notes are for the doctor.

I don't remember the beep portion of the first hearing test I took. I did not know then that anything was wrong, and so my brain did not retain the memory. But the second section, the verbal portion, I remember. I can't not remember it.

The audiologist was a young Black woman with box braids that I thought were so beautiful. She had taught me before the test how to spell *audiologist*, so I loved her. In my headphones, her voice was soft. Gentle. I didn't notice that anything was wrong during the beep portion, but she must have. She must have watched me, an eight-year-old child, gangly, with hair made white by the sun, swing my legs while the beeps played in the right headphone and my hands stayed still in my lap. Her tone, when she explained the next section, gave me warning. Through the glass, she held eye contact with me, but her gaze had gone softer. Was it pity or compassion? It can be so hard to tell the difference in someone you don't know.

I focused harder on her, confused. I was alone in the room. My mother sat outside in the hallway. For the first time, I wondered why she wasn't allowed into the booth with me, because I wanted her there. Nothing makes you look for your mom more than a fear that creeps in and doesn't show signs of leaving. The audiologist asked if I was ready to continue, and I told her I was. In the verbal portion of a hearing test, the audiologist says a word, and you repeat it back to them. If they say "fire truck," you say "fire truck." If they say "date," you say "date." Usually, during this section, they also play some kind of staticky background noise. The goal is to see how well you can separate speech from background noise.

At first everything was fine. She said "cowboy." I said "cowboy." I was doing great. Until the noise shifted. Now my left ear was filled with the humming thickness of brown noise. On the other side of the window, the audiologist held the manila folder in front of her mouth so that I couldn't read her lips. Her eyebrows moved. Her forehead moved. I knew that her lips were moving, but I heard nothing. "I can't hear you," I said, and she nodded, made a note, and clicked her voice over to my left ear. "Okay!" she said in the fake upbeat voice that adults love to use to convince children that they must continue something terrible. "Just a few more." Her eyebrows indicated the words she must have been saying, but still I heard nothing.

To be betrayed by your body is a universal horror, but I was too young to know that, so it felt like a personal failing. Why couldn't I hear? Why didn't my ear work? And worst of all, why hadn't I realized it earlier? It felt like noticing, after a long day of interacting with people, that the whole time, a piece of spinach has been stuck in your teeth. It was a bodily betrayal, sure, but in my chest, I felt the spread of embarrassment. Even there, in the room, the audiologist wouldn't tell me. "Is it broken?" I asked. Her voice clicked back over. "Don't worry," she said. "The doctor will take care of everything."

Later, I would watch *Little Miss Sunshine* and cry when the older brother realized he was color-blind and his dreams of becoming a fighter pilot would never come true. I was too little to have a long-held career dream shattered, but I knew in that moment that a hundred doors of opportunity had slammed shut, the future irrevocably changed by the present. The fact that I now spend a significant portion of my career working in audio is one of life's great ironies.

I don't remember coming out of the booth or hearing finally from the doctor that all of the hearing in my right ear was gone. I don't remember what my mother said to me, either. What I remember

215

is how dumb I felt for not realizing it was missing earlier. My own body. How had I not known? I should have known.

For months before that hearing test, I had been in pain. My right ear was always infected. The doctor would diagnose me. There would be days filled with the hissing terror of eardrops and a course of antibiotics, and the ear infection would go away for a little bit. But it always returned. Sometimes still, I have nightmares about the antibiotic shots I was given during that time that went into the top of my thighs, straight into the femoral artery. Occasionally, a phantom pain emerges deep inside my head and I rush to the ear, nose, and throat doctor's office, where they check and assure me that everything is fine.

But for a little while, things weren't fine. The doctor pulled my mother into the hallway to talk to her after the hearing test, and then they came back in. A scope was put into my ear. Because my ear canals twist toward the back of my head, there was nothing to see on the screen for a minute, only the dark red of my ear canal illuminated by the light on the end of the scope. But then, around a corner, there it was.

The eardrum is a thin concave flap of skin. In theory it is lovely: an oval with a grayish blue color like a transparent dolphin or an animated bubble. In a healthy ear, nothing can be seen behind the eardrum, besides maybe the tippy top of one of the hearing bones. The eardrum is a wall. It helps us hear, sure, but it also keeps water out and with our eustachian tubes helps stabilize the pressure in our middle ears. But my eardrum was gone. There was no wall there, no shiny beautiful taut piece of skin. Instead, there was something else lurking.

It was a cholesteatoma, a word the nurses promptly taught me to spell as a way to demystify it, entertain me, or both. Its name, they told me, was a misnomer. In 1838, the German anatomist Johannes Müller named it *cholesteatoma*, which essentially means "cholesterol tumor." This, scientists now know, is incorrect. *Toma* means "tumor," but it is not a tumor. *Cholestea* would mean that it contains fat or cholesterol crystals, which it does not. It is instead a growing mass of skin, a cyst made of skin. In medical drawings, it is often represented as a blurry little blob as if even in the journals of medicine, it cannot quite be pinned down. One early record of a cholesteatoma comes from the French anatomist and pathologist Jean Cruveilhier, who described it as a pearly tumor. And it did look like a pearl way back there in my ear, shiny and white and evil.

The only cure for cholesteatomas is surgery. In childhood, they are aggressive. Cholesteatomas don't eat, really; they erode things. They grow slowly, bleeding outward like spilled ink, like the banks of a river, consuming things in their path and making them their own. First, maybe, just a patch of skin cells, then some wax. But there is so little room in the ear canal, so little space to expand. Things must be eroded. Eardrums. Little bones. The wall of the canal itself. It is not malignant, which in medicine means that it can still destroy you, just in a less ominous way.

After diagnosing the cholesteatoma in my ear, the doctors were in a rush, which is never a good sign. And because they were in a rush and there were no available operating rooms at the children's hospital, we had to go to the adult hospital, where I was doted on like a princess and given a teddy bear, and after that given only bad news. I went under for what should have been a three-hour surgery. My medical records say I was in there for eight.

Sometimes I run a finger over the bumped scar tissue behind my ear and feel the raised spaces where the stitches used to be. The half-circle scar runs perfectly from my jawline behind my ear up to where the helix meets the side of my head. I imagine that when they did the surgery, my ear must have been flopped forward toward my face. Did it touch my eye? Or did it sit softly on the peak of my cheekbone, waiting patiently to be sewn back into its proper place?

I wonder if they could have taken it off entirely, set it on ice like an oyster to wait.

Inside my ear, the doctors found the cholesteatoma they knew was there, but the damage it had wrought was catastrophic. It had eroded everything, consumed the inside of my ear like the hungry, hungry caterpillar: my eardrum, my bones, part of my ear canal, part of my skull. It was on my brain when they pulled it out. Six more months and it would have won.

It is jarring to survive something that tried to kill you. Life feels like borrowed time, as if you cheated the system, and one day, the system will find out. There's a kind of mysticism that lives in survival. Your days are always numbered from birth. But how many are there? As I grew up, I became obsessed with the idea that maybe I shouldn't have survived, that maybe I was meant to have been consumed. In my twenties, I traveled to the French Quarter in New Orleans and got my palm read by as many women as would read it. Many of them would not take my money. One glance at my palm, and these women, who have seen so many palms, blanched and sent me on my way. Eventually, I was able to trade someone a twenty-dollar bill to tell me why. My life line, near my wrist, has a very clear break in it. It was hard to read, uncertain. "This could [have been] very bad," she told me. "It could have been life threatening." Some of the women turning me away might have been unqualified to reckon with it, but more likely, they were concerned that I might have been a ghost, she said. A broken life line.

I did not tell the palm reader about my ear, about the brain abscess, about the tumor that wasn't a tumor that had tried to destroy me. Because it hadn't. I (or rather the doctors) had destroyed it. My life had continued, does continue still. The consequence of that success is that I remain fully deaf in my right ear, a simple, worthwhile trade. The doctors tried, over several more surgeries, to save my hearing: implanting monkey bones and synthetic bones and reconstructing my eardrum. My body rejected all of them. Deafness, as disability advocates often joke, is the disability that comes for us all. Nearly 20 percent of the world's population lives with hearing loss. More than a quarter of adults over the age of sixty are affected by disabling hearing loss. I just got there a little early.

* * *

You would think that because I am fully deaf in my right ear, I would be more skeptical of the things I hear. But I never have been. I love to listen, even if I'm not very good at it. I listen everywhere all the time. My ears are always pointed toward whoever has the most dramatic tone. When I walk on the street with my dog, I don't want headphones. I want the world. I want to hear what hostesses are saying about people they need to seat as I walk by. I want to catch snippets of a phone conversation not meant for me. My favorite political scandal of all time is Watergate. It makes perfect sense to me that having the full power of the president, you would use it to record the conversations happening around you. A woman at the airport recently said to a friend, "A walnut killed him." Imagine missing that drama because you were listening to something else! I can't help it. There is something so delicious, so pleasurable, about eavesdropping.

During my freshman year of college, my roommate and I became overly invested in our next-door neighbor. We did not meet her, incredibly, the whole year that we lived in that dorm with its paper-thin walls, but we heard so, so much about her. She and her boyfriend had screaming fights constantly; never violent that we heard, but always ridiculous. They fought about what he wore and where they ate and what Arctic Monkeys song was best. My roommate and I (we had little else in common) transcribed their fights into emails that we sent back and forth to each other.

Something big would happen, and, gasping in the dining hall, I would read to my friends the things my roommate had sent to me. In that moment, eavesdropping had transformed into gossip. Maybe even in the transcribing it became gossip, since one of us wasn't there to hear it firsthand. But once it was verbalized, it was free as wildfire. It didn't matter that this information had been gathered through a literal wall. No one questioned it. All gossip needs evidence, and hearing is one of our best evidence collection methods.

But none of our senses are actually capturing the whole of reality. Biologically, an eye doctor can ask you to read some letters and pick *a* or *b*, and determine whether your vision is good. But the act of seeing in a memory sense is a bit more complicated. Those of us with decent vision or corrective lenses of some sort can see. We can read a street sign. We can notice a cool pair of pants on someone at a bar. The problem isn't the ability of our eyes; it's our brain.

My freshman year sociology professor, Dr. Robert Crosnoe, tried to soothe us with psychology. We were all eighteen and filled with the kind of self-consciousness that unformed freshmen all reek of: that our peers might observe us and judge us and make assumptions about us. And so, he assured us that no one saw us the way we saw us. Not in the metaphorical sense that we are harder on the person we see in the mirror than any stranger might be, but in the literal sense. Your eyes, he told us, cheat any way they can. If our brain registered every single minute thing that our eyes take in, we would be overloaded with information and unable to exist in the world. Just looking at a counter and seeing a crumb would derail us from something much more important. So our brain doesn't see things it doesn't need to see. It takes shortcuts. It assumes it knows what is on the coffee table, and so it doesn't register the remote in front of us even when we are looking for it.

Or, as Dr. Crosnoe told us, other people's brains don't see your actual face. They see the composite of your face that already exists in their memory. So, unless the pimple you have is directly in the center line of your face and the size of Mount Kilimanjaro, no one is going to notice it but you. So how then can we have confidence in the things we observe in the world? The things that stand out to us as observers or eavesdroppers or town criers aren't even necessarily the most prominent things to notice. Maybe they aren't even there at all, or maybe we corrupt their existences with our brains into something unreal.

David Eagleman, a neuroscientist from Stanford University, explained in his book *Incognito* that eyes are not high-resolution digital cameras; they do not "see" the same way your phone records. The brain processes only small parts of what we see: what we deem important. And there's no better example of this than "the invisible gorilla" experiment: a selective attention experiment created by Christopher Chabris and Daniel Simons. When they began conducting the experiment around 1999, their results were stunning. Participants were asked to watch a short video. In the video, six people (three in white shirts and three in black shirts) moved around one another while passing a ball. Participants were told to keep a silent count of the number of passes made by people in the white shirts. At the end of the video, they were asked how many passes the white-shirted people had made. The correct answer was somewhere in the thirties. It could be thirty-four or thirty-five. It doesn't really matter because that wasn't the test.

They were then asked something else: Had they noticed a gorilla? No, the participants said. If a person in a gorilla suit had strolled into the middle of the game, faced the camera, and then left, spanning a total of five seconds, researchers asked, would you have seen it? Almost everyone said yes, of course they would have noticed that. It's a gorilla! But when Chabris and Simons did the experiment at Harvard, they found that half of the people who watched the video missed the gorilla entirely. It might as well have been invisible.

The gorilla in the video enters from stage left, stands in the middle while the ball is passed, beats its chest, and then leaves. "Your moment-to-moment expectations, more than the visual distinctiveness of the object, determine what you see—and what you miss," Chabris and Simons wrote in 2010 in *The Invisible Gorilla: And Other Ways Our Intuitions Deceive Us*. Because our brains are focused on the ball and the people wearing white, we do not notice another figure in black, even though they are ridiculously dressed as a gorilla. Even though we watched the whole scene, we didn't see what was important at all.

That's part of why eyewitness accounts are notoriously untrustworthy. The Innocence Project, a nonprofit group that attempts to get innocent people's unlawful convictions reversed, says, "Eyewitness misidentification contributes to an overwhelming majority of wrongful convictions that have been overturned by post-conviction DNA testing." In the aftermath of a rape of a nine-year-old girl in 1984, five eyewitnesses said that they had seen Kirk Bloodworth with the victim that day. He was sentenced to death and served nine years in prison before DNA evidence proved him innocent.

"We have all had cases where there is physical and scientific evidence which demonstrates that an adverse eyewitness is wrong. Our first attack is to look for some motive or memory loss, and, if that fails, to try clever cross examination to establish that the witness's attention was not on the critical part of the scene at the critical moment," Larry Booth wrote in *Plaintiff* magazine in 2011. "We are missing the big picture. Eyewitness testimony is unreliable because of the science of how we see."

Our perception of the events we experience firsthand with our eyes is already skewed when we obtain it, and the same is true for our ears. Like our sight, our hearing is overruled by the brain every chance it gets. Our ears (or, more accurately, most of *your* ears) have the ability to filter out sound. That's why in a crowded restaurant, you can focus on the person across from you and hear what they say better than the person at the table to your left. Your brain is filtering out the stuff that doesn't matter.

But the brain's ability to interfere with what we hear is even more stark. The McGurk effect is an audio illusion that proves that our ears do the same thing as our eyes do: they take in correct, comprehensive information, and then our brain corrupts it. In a popular demonstration of the McGurk effect, you watch a video of a man saying "Bah" over and over again like a little lamb. You close your eyes, you hear "Bah." You open your eyes, you hear "Bah." Great. That makes sense. But then the video is replaced so that the man's lips say "Gah" or "Nah" or "Dah." The audio doesn't change. The audio is still saying "Bah bah bah." When you close your eyes, you hear "Bah bah bah," just like you should. But when you open them (even though you know better), your brain hears "Gah" or "Nah" or "Dah."

The biggest problem with being deaf in one ear isn't difficulty hearing; it's echolocation. The way our brains determine where a sound is coming from is based on the input from both of our ears. For me, every sound comes from one side. Sound lives on the left. Not being able to echolocate means that someone calling you off a fly ball could be behind you or to your right, and you can't know which. It means that a girl yelling "Me!" or "Here!" to receive a set volleyball could be in any direction. It means that when you lose your mom in the grocery store, you cannot find her voice. But even for people with perfect hearing, your brain can interfere with your ability to echolocate correctly.

Psychologist Diana Deutsch, an emeritus professor at the University of California, San Diego, made an audio illusion in which an oboe plays from one speaker and a synthesized sine wave glissando (a slide between two notes) plays from the other. The sounds switch rapidly back and forth from speaker to speaker. But that's not what listeners hear; they hear the glissando as a constant steady rise and fall in both ears. Only the oboe sound jumps back and forth. In 1997, Deutsch told *Science* magazine that "the illusions show us that there aren't hard-and-fast rules for how we hear things, as much as we would like there to be."

The thing that is so scary about these studies is that they don't feel true. Our instinct tells us to trust ourselves. Our intuition tells us that we should follow it. We know best because we have experienced it, and who are we supposed to trust if not ourselves? Other people? That's irrational. Chabris and Simons, in *The Invisible Gorilla*, cite Charles Darwin's observation that "ignorance more frequently begets confidence than does knowledge." Even when things are objectively true and apply to us, we ignore them. We don't believe that we are worse drivers when we text even though there is empirical data that using a phone while driving is as bad as driving drunk, because we feel confident while we do it.

I, of all people, should know better than to trust my own senses, but I don't. I overhear a snippet of a conversation with my one good ear, fill in the rest with my mind, and believe fully that what I have heard is true. This is part of gossiping, that unearned confidence.

* * *

When I tell the story about overhearing the girls in the locker room talking about me, I tell it confidently. I don't second-guess the details. The memory is as raw and real as it was when I sat feeling nauseous on the other side of those red lockers. But memory is a fickle beast. Checking my middle school yearbook, there were only seven Kelseys, not the eight I remembered, but there were also two Chelseas. How could I have known, then, with my one good ear and inability to see the girls talking, that those girls even said Kelsey? What do I do with that uncertainty?

In 2010, Elizabeth F. Loftus, a memory researcher and psychologist at the University of California, Irvine, told *Scientific American* that the act of remembering is "more akin to putting puzzle pieces together than retrieving a video recording." Our memories (be they vague and dry or emotional and precise) are often wrong. *Review of General Psychology* called Loftus the most influential female psychologist of the twentieth century. Previously, psychologists believed that our memories maintained a literal interpretation of events, and Loftus worked her whole career to disprove that. Her life's work (more than twenty books and more than six hundred papers) argues over and over again that our memories are not fixed and immutable but malleable. Rachel Aviv's excellent profile of Loftus in the *New Yorker* carefully tied her research and her insistence that memory is untrustworthy to Loftus's own memories of her depressed mother's presumed suicide that she doesn't want to confront. What we believe about what we remember is as much a part of our memory as the images themselves.

And sometimes what we believe we remember isn't just wrong; it's a complete fabrication. Oliver Sacks, the renowned neurologist, wrote in his 2001 memoir, *Uncle Tungsten: Memories of a Chemical Boyhood*, a detailed account of an evening during a Nazi bombing of London. He remembered "vicious hissing and sputtering" and "jets of molten metal." Or at least he said he did. After the book was published, he learned that he hadn't been there when that event happened; he'd learned about it from a letter from his brother, and his brain had reimagined it as his own. We can create a "memory" out of a story we hear over and over again and not even know it.

Mishearing. Misremembering. Misseeing. Mistakes. What's unsettling is the knowledge that we are ourselves untrustworthy at every level. In rom-coms, the mishearing is always corrected. The truth always prevails. The lead bows before the romantic interest, confesses their true feelings, makes sure that those mistakes don't continue. Sometimes in real life, that kind of confrontation with another truth exists as well. Many times, I have recounted a gossip story to a group of people only to be corrected. Someone else remembers it differently or heard an account that was closer to the source account. It is always kind of funny when this happens: someone who heard the story secondhand correcting a story told thirdhand feels so petty.

The point of the story about my locker room eavesdropping stands whether there were seven Kelseys or eight in my middle school class because the story isn't about the details but about the feeling. The point wasn't whether they were talking about me or not, but that it *felt* like they were. When we gossip, we have to acknowledge that the truths we are attempting to convey are in the meanings we take from moments, the way hearing something felt in the body, the fallout from an event.

Because even if I misheard them entirely, the feeling I had in my body was real. Or at least, I remember it that way.

A year ago I was told by a friend that another friend had claimed I was "too much." This effectively ruined our friendship, especially after I confronted this person and they didn't take responsibility. I learned this month that the person who told me the other person said it might've been the one to say it in the first place.

There is no recovering the friendship, and soon we will all be traveling around the world together for ten days.

Tell It Slant

Recently, I went to dinner at an old red sauce, members-only social club in South Philadelphia. We ate buckets of bread and a bowl of Caesar salad the size of a basketball. As the olive oil–washed martinis gave way to espresso martinis, we began talking about a woman we all kind of knew who lies all the time. This animated, exciting conversation and the safety of being in a space that literally forbids the use of cell phones and the taking of photos allowed me to reference offhandedly one of my favorite gossip stories. I dropped the names of the people involved casually, expecting my friends to know the tale already. It had spread in our social circles like wildfire a little less than a decade before. But one of my friend's faces remained blank. I prompted her a little more, but she didn't know it.

There are few greater feelings than getting to tell a story that you know will hit every time. If you tell a story enough times, you learn when to pause, how to wait for a question to be asked, and how to respond to that question so that it will lead to your exciting and memorable climactic conclusion. The joy of getting to share this kind of gossip with someone you like is the verbal equivalent of buying someone the present they've always wanted for half off. I felt the excitement on an atomic level, a vibration that made me sit up straighter and pitch myself toward her. Though maybe the espresso martini had something to do with that as well. But it really is one of my favorite gossip stories of all time. I told this story in an SUV somewhere in northern California while on tour with the podcast. I told it at a dinner party last year. I told it while on a hike in the Catskills. It's a story with infinite moments to shine, because I love it so much.

I told my friend in the dark restaurant the real version, with all the names and details. Obviously, I cannot do that here, but while the names and identifying details are changed, the spirit is the same.

> In the past, there were two painters. One of them was famous for beautiful, florid work. Her paintings were looked at by women, shared by women, beloved by women. They were depictions of what it meant to be a daughter and a person and in love. She was a painter's painter, in that many of the people who loved her work either painted or wanted to paint themselves. That's not to say her paintings didn't sell, but they did not sell as well as her husband's. Her husband had achieved a moderate amount of public notoriety. Replicas of his paintings were in households across America. One of his paintings was even getting international recognition, being shipped around the world to be shown in galleries.
>
> Each painter was famous, but their coupling raised both of their profiles. They were married. They lived together on the West Coast in a giant sprawling house. They painted each day in their individual studios, each waiting until a piece was done to show it to

the other. A piece of lore that they each repeated in many interviews is that many of their paintings contained the same motifs and shapes because of their shared life. Both paintings contained a red circle because the rug in their dining room was a red circle, for example. Or both paintings were dark in a week when all the light bulbs in their home had burnt out and both were too busy to replace them. This kind of couple, with their mythos and publicity and sap, is always popular in any creative field because people envy them. To be envied is to be talked about, and to be talked about is good PR for any artist. This went on for years. The couple had a few kids.

Then, one day, the opportunity of a lifetime presented itself to, of course, the man. A pop star (famous but not the most famous) had seen one of his paintings that he had made to advocate for a great moral cause. She had become inspired by it. She wanted to adapt it into an album, and she wanted him to help her with the visuals: album cover, music videos, the works. This was a huge career moment for him, but it was not entirely unheard of. Every once in a while, a Hollywood A-lister plucks a regular artist out from their normal life and offers them a better one. He wasn't the first this had happened to. But he was the first to blow up his opportunity so swiftly and thoroughly.

You see, a few months after his collaboration with the pop star was announced, rumors that they were sleeping together began to circulate. The rumors would have been good for him had he been single. But he was married, and the pop star was married to a producer (who was much hotter and much more successful than the artist), so the rumors were passed with a hushed tone of concern. The problem with being a creative couple whose power is derived from envy is that if one of you ever fucks up, it all comes tumbling down. And here was the fuck-up: cheating. The rumor spread like wildfire for a few days. I heard it from several different sources.

Then another rumor arrived: he had been kicked out of the house.

But it wasn't true. The facts trickled out slowly over the course of days. His wife hadn't kicked him out. He had left of his own accord: told her he was having an affair, called off their marriage, and moved out, just like that.

Except that version of the story was wrong, too.

The truth was: he had told his wife that he was having an affair with the pop star, that they were in love, and he had moved out of their enviable, fancy, well-lit home. This information came firsthand from the wife, so it was what she believed to be true. But of course, he had lied. Because the truth was, he wasn't having an affair at all. He was flirting. Every day, he went to work with the pop star, and they had somewhere between a cordial relationship and a flirty one, and he had interpreted that as a signal that they should be together.

The truth was much worse for him. The truth was that fresh off of ending his marriage, he appeared before the pop star and told her that he had broken it off, that they could finally be together, and she had...no idea what he was talking about. She had only ever viewed their relationship as well within the boundaries of coworkers' camaraderie. It is a story of a failure to communicate. Surely, we can imagine that if this man had told the famous woman how he felt explicitly instead of trying to communicate through gestures and subtlety, she could have corrected him and perhaps saved his marriage. But he didn't, and so in one day he went from thinking that he had both a beautiful and talented wife and a beautiful and talented and famous girlfriend to having neither one.

I love this story because it was kept quiet by their PR professionals—quiet enough that most Americans have no idea it happened. But because people whisper and because the industries of these two people are notoriously gossipy, the story spread too quickly for a PR campaign to squash it. The publicists tried, of course, with articles and placed blind items and very careful coordination of when the two interacted. But within those stories, if you knew what to look for, you could see the truth peeking through between the words: the shame and the embarrassment, and the unbelievable cockiness to assume that a star would leave her husband to be with you without ever having had a conversation about it.

"I don't call it gossip," a character in Laurie Colwin's 1978 novel *Happy All the Time* says, "I call it 'emotional speculation.'" That's our job here: to speculate. Why would he do this? we ask. Can you imagine how stunned the pop star must have been?

It is such a joy to tell this story; to relish the man's failure but also discuss the way that fame can corrupt your perception of yourself to the point that you think that you have a shot at dating a pop star just because she likes your work. And every time I tell it, I remember that part of why we gossip is that gossiping is fun.

Telling this story and watching people hear it for the first time feels like seeing a couple making out in the park on the first warm day. It feels like the scream that emerges from your mouth on the way down the roller-coaster hill. It is play.

"Play is serious. Play is absolute. Play is the complete absorption in something that doesn't matter to the external world, but which matters completely to you. It's an immersion in your own interests that becomes a feeling in itself, a potent emotion. Play is a disappearance into the space of our choosing, invisible to those outside the game. It is the pursuit of pure flow, a sandbox mind in which we can test new thoughts, new selves. It's a form of symbolic living, a way to transpose one reality onto another and to mine it for meaning," Katherine May wrote in *Enchantment: Awakening Wonder in an Anxious Age*. When we gossip, we are playing, allowing ourselves a little bit of fun, as a treat. A study published in the *Journal of Personality and Social Psychology* in 2012 found that when subjects actively gossiped about an unfair person or situation, it soothed them and kept their heart rate down.

Still, it's hard to pinpoint exactly why gossip feels so good to us. "To explain what's rewarding in gossip, like efforts to elucidate what's funny in a joke, risks destroying what the explanation purports to clarify," Patricia Meyer Spacks wrote. "Gossips look in each other's eyes, listen to each other's voices amuse, amend, and instruct each other. Their magic is wise and pious: worthy of non-ironic praise."

And it does feel like magic, like a balm. Partly it is the magic of the mundane, but gossip is also a fairy tale we tell ourselves, a moment in which we are happy to suspend disbelief in favor of awe.

* * *

Is this story about the painter true? I think so. But like all stories of perspective, it is impossible to know what's true. The version of the story I know makes one party (the man) look exceptionally bad. Is it possible that by the time I heard this story, it had already been corrupted as it passed through the grapevine? Maybe. For all I know, they were having an affair all along, and had discussed these decisions, and then, when he left his wife formally, the pop star panicked and back-tracked. It's possible, though everything else I have heard about this man leads me to believe that these actions would be fully in line with his character, so if it is a PR scheme, it's an incredibly good one.

What I know for sure is that it isn't a lie. In "On Lying," St. Augustine wrote that a liar "takes delight in lying, rejoicing in the falsehood itself." When you lie about other people consciously, that's slander (or, if it is written, libel). Part of any slander or libel case in the United States is to prove intentionality. You have to mean to lie to be a liar. I know this story isn't a lie. It isn't a complete fabrication. I know this because I have gotten within one degree of separation from the story, and it holds up.

I also know that it's possible that parts of the story are bullshit. In *On Bullshit*, the philosopher Harry G. Frankfurt wrote, "The bullshitter is faking things. But this does not mean that he necessarily gets them wrong." A liar, he argues, is less dangerous than a bullshitter, because sometimes pieces of what the bullshitter tells you are true. A liar is conscious of the truth and actively chooses to work against it. But a bullshitter ignores any distinction between true and false. Frankfurt continued. "For the bullshitter, however, all these bets are off…He does not reject the authority of the truth, as the liar does, and oppose himself to it. He pays no attention to it at all. By virtue of this, bullshit is a greater enemy of truth than lies are."

In some ways, my story about the man and his famous crush is bullshit. When I tell it, I add a detail that I know about the man and his wife, about their relationship, to imply that they were happy together in some way. I know this information from reading profiles about them, but it is not actually related to the story itself. The details of their shared life only serve to intensify the devastation of the listener when realizing that the woman's life was destroyed because her husband believed he could leave her for a star. But I don't know the couple. They might have been miserable. Do I care particularly if the details from the profiles that I add to my version of the story are true? Not really. For all I know, the couple lied to the journalist who printed them in the first place, and now I rehash the story wholesale without a care in the world.

"Gossip is again the inverse of bullshit: it cares deeply about what is and is not true, but one's investment in the gossip is not diminished by its possible fictionality," Sophus Helle, a translator of *The Epic of Gilgamesh*, told me in an email. That's the distinction that is complicated. When we expand a gossip story (add an extra detail, imagine a feeling that might accompany it, adjust the timeline to make it a little bit sexier), we do not do so to lie or even to bullshit. We aren't actively ignoring the truth and trying to subvert it; we are trying to get closer to the truth through our telling, despite the limited information we began with.

Part of the fun of gossiping is to wonder which parts are true, to hold a story up to the light and try to see the cracks in it. "There are no facts, only interpretations," Friedrich Nietzsche once said. Facts, like gravity and the earth being round, exist. But when it comes to interpersonal relationships, maybe they don't. Maybe it's all just about viewpoint and opinion and perception. But then how do we decide which parts are true? Does it matter?

Gossip allows us to decide for ourselves.

Emily Dickinson wrote:

Tell all the truth but tell it slant—
Success in Circuit lies
Too bright for our infirm Delight
The Truth's superb surprise
As Lightning to the Children eased
With explanation kind
The Truth must dazzle gradually
Or every man be blind—

Dickinson's truth is lightning, something that can be bright, "too bright," and a powerful force of nature. But her metaphors are mixed. Truth as lightning, truth as dazzling gradually. Truth as something scary, truth as delight. In "'Tell All the Truth but Tell It Slant—': Dickinson's Poetics of Indirection in Contemporary Poetry," Farnoosh Fathi argued that Dickinson used "multiple and ambiguous meanings of tropes to afford, rather than to preclude, the articulation of complex ideas and feelings more richly told slant." It is as if Dickinson was not in pursuit of a definitive answer about what truth is as much as she was interested in the space around truth and how we perceive it.

Still, this question of truth within the gossip we receive and around the concept of gossip hovers. It haunts us. We want to reach the center, where everything is confirmed, all the ends are tied up, and we no longer have to sit in the discomfort of not knowing. Durga Chew-Bose wrote in *Too Much and Not the Mood*, "Rarely does a subject disturb me as much as when it slopes my ability to discern what is real and what isn't. Likely because I fear—more alarmingly quick as the years pass—the fine line between being conscious and becoming jaded." I do not gossip to sit in the discomfort of the unknown. I gossip for the thrill, for the revelation in it. I wanted to become conscious of how it worked so that I could relish it more. I've spent years now trying to get closer to a definitive answer of what gossip is and what to think about it, but the path is windy, and the years are passing, and I am still unable to determine exactly what is real.

* * *

When I began this seeking, my personal bias was that gossip was an unfairly maligned part of our experience in the world that needed to be redeemed. In *Second Place*, Rachel Cusk wrote, "And given that life as it goes on works to reinforce our personal bias more and more in order to allow us to accept the limitations of our fate, the artist must stay especially alert so as to avoid those temptations and hear the call of truth when it comes…Most people prefer to take care of themselves before they take care of truth, and then wonder where their talent has disappeared off to." There was a version of this book that I thought I might be able to write at the beginning that would neatly tie up here in this conclusion with the bias I entered with. But the more I read and thought, the more I took gossip submissions for the podcast, told them to the world, and watched the way listeners responded to them, the more I realized what gossip actually is: a way of searching for truth.

"Truth is, in its nature, multiple and contradictory, part of the flux of history, untrappable in language. The only real road to truth is through doubt and tolerance," Janet Malcolm wrote in *The Silent Woman: Sylvia Plath and Ted Hughes*. Doubt causes you to question which parts of a story you believe and forces you to tolerate the knowledge that you'll never fully, truly know.

The story about the painter has been anonymized. I've changed as much as I felt necessary to keep it from being traceable, while making it recognizable to people already in the know. The careers have been changed; so have the emotional beats. Moments that feel important might not be important at all. I know that this is infuriating. You want to know who it was. Of course you do. If gossip is a way to search for truth, you might argue that the distortion of the story corrupts the use of gossip at all.

But those aren't the kinds of truths that matter in gossip. The truths that matter are bigger and stranger and more interesting than whatever job the man who left his wife without actually obtaining a mistress had. There is no veracity or certainty in gossip, just as there is no full truth and no full and complete knowledge of ourselves. To gossip is just to live, to be a person, for better or for worse. It feels important to know whether the stories we are telling ourselves and one another are true in the same way it feels important to know whether or not the mirrors in a fitting room are distorted, an image has been edited, or a facial filter has been used in a video. The interest is in ourselves.

In 1948, the *Saturday Evening Post* put a Norman Rockwell painting on the cover. The painting was done from studies of his neighbors in Arlington, Vermont. In the painting, pairs of people talk to each other, on the phone or in person. They laugh. They point. They put their hands up to their faces. The painting is called *The Gossips*, and theoretically, Rockwell painted people in the act of gossiping. Thousands of people wrote in to the *Saturday Evening Post* after the cover ran, wanting to know what the gossip was, but Rockwell never revealed it. When I look at it, I wonder if there was ever any actual gossip at the center of the painting at all. The painting's success is not in its depiction of gossipers but in the feeling it creates in the viewer: call it envy or FOMO or nosiness. "The gossips" Rockwell referred to in the title might as well have been all of us begging to know what they were talking about in Arlington, Vermont.

"Strong minds discuss ideas, average minds discuss events, weak minds discuss people," Socrates or Eleanor Roosevelt or whoever said. But the ancient Greeks also said that all philosophical commandments can be reduced to a simple goal: "Know yourself." And what I know, about myself at least, is that gossip isn't a tool so much as it is a reflection. The way we gossip, who we gossip about, and how we respond to these stories show us the person we are. They help us understand where we fit in the greater scheme of trying to be a person in the world. The truth we are searching so desperately for is self-knowledge.

In every thought and mindset and comparison, we reveal who we are. The way I gossip is different from the way you gossip, because we are each our own person, trying to learn separate things about ourselves and our place in the world.

That, of course, is also only my perspective. There is no universal truth in these pages or in the world. "It could never be resolved, not so long as the aim was to establish the truth, for there was no single truth anymore, that was the point. There was no shared vision, a shared reality even. Each of them saw things now solely from his own perspective; there was only one point of view," Rachel Cusk wrote in *Outline*.

At the end of all of this thinking and worrying and wondering about what roles gossip can play in our society and how to understand this broad amorphous entity that we all engage in, I've come to realize that perhaps the greatest purpose of gossip is helping us understand our own perspective.

When we hear a salacious story, we put ourselves in that situation. We try to decipher what angles the original players might have missed that we can avoid. The theory of mind that allows us to imagine these things is what makes us fundamentally human, and within that humanity is a search, a desire to understand who we really are and who we really could be. Through all this gossiping, I've realized that what I am actually looking for when I gossip is pleasure—and community. I'm trying to find truths about myself reflected in people I admire. It's less important that I know about someone's failed affair with a pop star than it is that I understand why that story is so amusing to me personally.

"To understand just one life, you have to swallow the world," the narrator of Salman Rushdie's *Midnight's Children* says. That is maybe what gossip is to me: the swallowing of the world, not whole but one bite at a time. We cannot know ourselves truly, madly, or deeply without gossip as a way to contextualize our space within the world. We gossip not only because we can but because we have to. Without the self-awareness gained by gossiping, we would become husks of ourselves, so uninterested in the world around us that we become separated from it entirely.

But then again, you didn't hear any of this from me.

Acknowledgments

Like all good gossip, a book is molded by so many people before it reaches you. I am the one whose name goes on the cover, but the building of this book took a grapevine. I am so grateful not to work in isolation, to be challenged and pushed and prodded, to be given gossip as a little treat, and to have the absolute honor of sharing gossip with all of you.

Thank you to Dana Murphy, who listened to the three-minute voice memo I sent on a random Saturday and believed this could be a book. Thank you for worshipping conjoined Cheez-Its with me, learning to love baseball for me, and always knowing I could do this, even when I wasn't so sure. I am so lucky to have found you.

To my brilliant editor, Maddie Caldwell: thank you for drinking beers, always talking on the phone, and telling me the first draft of this book wasn't good enough. You were right. It's so much better because of you. And thank you to Morgan Spehar for all of your enthusiasm and for dealing with my emails.

Thank you to everyone at Grand Central Publishing: Carolyn Kurek, Eric Arroyo, Marie Mundaca, Dana Li, Rebecca Holland, Jimmy Franco, Lauren Sum, Tiffany Porcelli, Leena Oropez. This book was fact-checked by Daniel Ajootian, who saved my ass so many times. Ashley Gelman, thank you for taking the first head-shot I've ever loved. Also thank you to my amazing champions in the UK: Florence Rees, Alexandra Mulholland, Shyam Kuma, and Alpana Sajip.

None of this ever would have happened without the *Normal Gossip* podcast. Alex Sujong Laughlin, my angel, my Scorpio queen, my cocreator, you not only taught me how to be a podcast host, but you made the whole thing shine from start to finish. Jasper Wang and Justin Ellis and Tom Ley, thank you for yelling at me when I tweeted out my good idea and convincing me not to bail on it when I panicked a hundred times. There is nothing I've done that I'm more proud of than helping to found the company we all share. Thank you to the entire Defector staff. I love all of you so much. Eat shit forever. Thank you to Jae Towle Viera. Thank you to everyone who came on the show, and everyone who listened. Thank you the most to everyone who forced their friends to listen. I love y'all. To Rach-elle Hampton, I know you'll be great.

Thank you to everyone who submitted gossip blurbs to use between the chapters of this book. I love them.

To my Tree Paines. Brittani Hilles and Amelia Possanza at Lav-ender Public Relations, I would die for you. Thank you to Kristina Moore and the rest of the team at UTA. Thank you to Mills Enter-tainment for teaching me to be on stage.

Perhaps most important, thank you to my community. Thank you, Aleks Chan, Lauren L'amie, and Sarah-Grace Sweeney; I'd never survive without the three of you. Megan Greenwell, it's an honor to be bullied by you. Chrissy Mullan, it is an honor to always have you fix my commas and to evangelize to each other. Olivia Nuzzi, thank you for telling me all of this would be worth it when I was panicking before the first episode came out.

I wrote this book in my free time, which was already limited. Thank you also to all my friends who put up with all my nonsense

Acknowledgments

and sent me infinite voice memos, and forgave me for disappearing for three years to do all of this: Hannah Grouch-Begley, Jessica Zetzman, Bethany Hayes, Fred Tally-Foos, Molly Hensley-Clancy, Dayna Evans, Molly Fitzpatrick, Jess Goodman, Kelly Fine, Laura Wright, Maya Rhodan, Lucy Junker, Kyle Perry, Mike Quigley, Tahirah Hairston, Alison Hollander, Gaby Simundson and Andrew Rutledge, Karl and Tressie Daum, Danielle Henderson, Sam Irby, Amanda Montell, Lyz Lenz, Kalyn Kahler, Lindsey Adler, Emma Baccalleri, Caroline Moss, Isle McElroy, Danya Kukafka, Alex Tanner, Sasha Fletcher, Margaret Eby, Casey Johnson, Liz Groethe, Evans Mullan, Meleana Shim, Beth Hetzler, Caroline Moss, Hannah Giorgis, Claire Fallon, Emma Gray, Lindy West, Hanif Abbdurraqib, Josh Gondleman, Maris Kreizman, Tuck Woodstock, Kristin Arnett, Blythe Roberson, Kalyn Kahler, Alexa Ura, and everyone whose texts I have forgotten to return.

Thank you to the bearers of my mental health: Wellbutrin, every soundtrack made by Trent Reznor, Buccee's Strawberry Sour Belts, my therapist Ariel, G-Strength, and the Philadelphia Phillies. I would die without all of you. Britney Spears, thank you for surviving 2007.

Thank you to my family: my parents, Brent and Tracy, my aunt and uncle Jill and Shane Sentz. My perfect sister, Shelby, please don't be mad I haven't dedicated a book to you yet.

And to Trey Dondrea: you're the best thing to ever happen to me—for everything, for ever. I love you.

Notes

A Note on Gossip

2   **At its most basic:** "Gossip," Merriam-Webster, https://www.merriam
-webster.com/dictionary/gossip.

2   **Even in scientific research:** Terence D. Dores Cruz et al., "An Integra-
tive Definition and Framework to Study Gossip," *Group & Organization
Management* 46, no. 2 (April 2021): 252–85, https://doi.org/10.1177
/1059601121992887.

2   **Aaron Ben-Ze'ev wrote:** Aaron Ben-Ze'ev, "The Vindication of Gossip,"
in *Good Gossip*, ed. Robert F. Goodman and Aaron Ben-Ze'ev (Lawrence:
University Press of Kansas, 1994).

2   **Robin Dunbar argued:** Robin Dunbar, *Grooming, Gossip and the Evolution of Language* (Cambridge, MA: Harvard University Press, 2002).

3   **Erik Hoel…argues:** Erik Hoel, "The Gossip Trap," The Intrinsic Perspective, September 6, 2022, https://www.theintrinsicperspective.com/p
/the-gossip-trap.

3   **somewhere between 12,000 and 5000 BCE:** Elizabeth Pollard, *Worlds
Together, Worlds Apart* (New York: W. W. Norton, 2016).

4   **the moral philosophical "Trolley Problem":** Philippa Foot, *The Problem
of Abortion and the Doctrine of Double Effect* (Oxford, UK: Oxford University Press, 1978).

What Makes Us Human

9   **write you a play:** Peter Marks, "What's Next, AI Writing an Off-
Broadway Musical? It Already Has," *Washington Post*, November 1, 2016,
https://www.washingtonpost.com/entertainment/theater/2023/11/01
/ai-chatgpt-musical-civilians-artificial/.

9   **bring your favorite comedian back:** Chris Williams, "AI George Carlin
Just Dropped a Comedy Special. The Estate Isn't Too Happy About
That," Above the Law, January 26, 2024, abovethelaw.com/2024/01/ai
-george-carlin-just-dropped-a-comedy-special-the-estate-isnt-too
-happy-about-that/.

9   **Scarlett Johansson:** Kate Knibbs, "What Scarlett Johansson v. OpenAI
Could Look Like in Court," *Wired*, May 22, 2024, https://www.wired
.com/story/scarlett-johansson-v-openai-could-look-like-in-court/.

10   **Goldman Sachs published:** "Generative AI Could Raise Global GDP by 7%," Goldman Sachs, April 5, 2023, https://www.goldmansachs.com /intelligence/pages/generative-ai-could-raise-global-gdp-by-7-percent .html.

10   **anthropologists have argued:** Robin Dunbar, *Grooming, Gossip and the Evolution of Language* (Cambridge, MA: Harvard University Press, 2002).

11   **dates back to around 2100 BCE:** Gilgamesh, *The Epic of Gilgamesh: An English Version with an Introduction*, trans. N. K. Sandars (London: Penguin Books, 1972).

11   **over more than five hundred years:** Jon Stewart, *The Emergence of Subjectivity in the Ancient and Medieval World: An Interpretation of Western Civilization* (Oxford, UK: Oxford University Press, 2020).

12   **pass the bar exam:** *GPT-4 Technical Report*, March 27, 2023, cdn.openai .com/papers/gpt-4.pdf.

14   **"If we could suppose":** Søren Kierkegaard, *The Present Age*, trans. Alexander Dru (New York: Harper Torchbooks, 1962), 72.

14   **John Berendt:** John Berendt, *Midnight in the Garden of Good and Evil: A Savannah Story* (New York: Vintage Books, 2023).

15   **developed the ability to speak:** "The 1.6 Million-Year-Old Discovery That Changes What We Know About Human Evolution," *Independent*, March 24, 2024.

16   **Phyllis Rose:** Phyllis Rose, *Parallel Lives: Five Victorian Marriages* (New York: Vintage, 1994).

17   **Emily Dickinson:** Emily Dickinson, "Tell All the Truth but Tell It Slant—(1263)," Poetry Foundation, https://www.poetryfoundation.org /poems/56824/tell-all-the-truth-but-tell-it-slant-1263.

17   **Fritz Heider and Marianne Simmel:** Fritz Heider and Marianne Simmel, "An Experimental Study of Apparent Behavior," *American Journal of Psychology* 57, no. 2 (April 1944): 243–59, https://www.jstor.org /stable/1416950.

18   **any animal is capable:** Jane C. Hu, "These Animals Use Personal Names, but Never Gossip," Nautilus, November 9, 2015, nautil.us/these-animals -use-personal-names-but-never-gossip-235681/.

18   **moʻolelo:** "Moʻolelo (Stories)," National Park Service, https://www.nps .gov/havo/learn/historyculture/moolelo.htm.

18   **told for generations:** Matthew Wills, "How Do We Know That Epic Poems Were Recited from Memory?," JSTOR Daily, February 28, 2020, daily.jstor.org/how-do-we-know-that-epic-poems-were-recited-from -memory/.

19   **Milman Parry:** "Milman Parry Collection of Oral Literature," Harvard Library, library.harvard.edu/collections/milman-parry-collection-oral -literature.

Notes

19   *The Singer of Tales*: Albert Bates Lord and David F. Elmer, *The Singer of Tales*, 3rd ed., ed. David F. Elmer (Cambridge, MA: Harvard University Press, 2019).

21   **Judge Beryl A. Howell:** *Stephen Thaler v. Shira Perlmutter*, August 18, 2023, https://www.copyright.gov/ai/docs/district-court-decision-affirming-refusal-of-registration.pdf.

22   **Walter Benjamin:** Walter Benjamin, "The Work of Art in the Age of Mechanical Reproduction," trans. Harry Zohn (Adansonia Press, 2018).

22   **404 Media:** Jason Koebler, "Facebook's AI Told Parents Group It Has a Gifted, Disabled Child," 404 Media, April 17, 2024, https://www.404media.co/facebooks-ai-told-parents-group-it-has-a-disabled-child/.

23   **Karl Ove Knausgaard:** Lydia Kiesling, "Being Reckless: An Interview with Karl Ove Knausgaard," *Paris Review*, January 13, 2021, https://www.theparisreview.org/blog/2021/01/13/being-reckless-an-interview-with-karl-ove-knausgaard/.

23   **Maggie Nelson:** Maggie Nelson, "Art Song," in *On Freedom: Four Songs of Care and Constraint* (Minneapolis: Graywolf Press, 2022), 167.

23   **"You read":** James Baldwin, *Conversations with James Baldwin*, ed. Fred R. Standley and Louis H. Pratt (Jackson: University Press of Mississippi, 1996).

24   **Hannah Baer:** Hannah Baer, "Projective Reality," *Artforum*, September 26, 2023, https://www.artforum.com/features/hannah-baer-on-mythologies-of-intelligence-252734/.

24   **The Qur'an existed:** Betsy Williams, "The Third Caliph: Uthman Ibn Affan," The Metropolitan Museum of Art, April 5, 2012, https://www.metmuseum.org/exhibitions/listings/2012/byzantium-and-islam/blog/characters/posts/uthman#:~:text=Uthman ibn Affan's reign.

Thou Shalt Not Gossip

29   **thorn shoved:** 2 Corinthians 12, The Bible (London: Ensign/Chrysalis, 1989).

32   **Proverbs:** Proverbs 16:28, The Bible (London: Ensign/Chrysalis, 1989).

32   **Book of Romans:** Romans 1:30–32, The Bible (London: Ensign/Chrysalis, 1989).

33   **eight are about gossip:** Original data gathered from the King James Version of the Bible.

33   **The Buddha:** "The Fourth Precept: Abstain from False and Harmful Speech," Tricycle, January 25, 2021, https://tricycle.org/beginners/buddhism/fourth-precept/.

33   **Imam Ja'far al-Sadiq:** "Hating Gossip," Al-Islam.org, https://www.al-islam.org/living-right-way-jawad-tehrani/hating-gossip.

33   **Torah injunction:** Uzi Weingarten, "Cursed Is One Who Does Not

247

Uphold the Words of This Torah?," The Torah.com, https://www.thetorah
.com/article/cursed-is-one-who-does-not-uphold-the-words-of-this
-torah.

33 **Pheme:** "Pheme & Ossa," The Theoi Project, www.theoi.com/Daimon
/Pheme.html.

34 **Emily Wilson:** Homer, *The Odyssey*, trans. Emily Wilson (New York:
W. W. Norton, 2018).

34 *The Book of Margery Kempe*: Margery Kempe, *The Book of Margery
Kempe: A Modern Version by W. Butler Bowdon* (Oxford, UK: Oxford University Press, 1954), https://ia902903.us.archive.org/14/items/in.ernet
.dli.2015.186348/2015.186348.The-Book-Of-Margery-Kempe.pdf.

35 **A meta-analysis:** Megan L. Robbins and Alexander Karan, "Who
Gossips and How in Everyday Life?," *Social Psychological and Personality
Science* 11, no. 2 (March 2020): 185–95, https://doi.org/10.1177
/1948550619837000.

39 *lashon hara:* "Lashon Hara (Evil Speech)," My Jewish Learning, August
4, 2023, https://www.myjewishlearning.com/article/gossip-rumors-and
-lashon-hara-evil-speech/.

39 **in Islam a distinction:** "The Summary of ^Abdullah Al-Harariyy," Association of Islamic Charitable Projects, https://www.aicp.org/index.php
/islamic-information/text/english/99-ensuring-the-personal-obligatory
-knowledge-of-the-religion.

40 **Billy Graham:** "What's the Harm in Gossiping?," Billy Graham Evange-
listic Association, November 2, 2016, https://billygraham.org/answer
/gossiping-is-dangerous-and-wrong-in-gods-eyes/.

40 **Dave Ramsey:** Ramsey, "Gossip Is Poison to Your Team," Ramsey Solu-
tions, September 27, 2023, https://www.ramseysolutions.com/business
/gossip-is-poison-to-your-team.

41 *Christianity Today* **reported in 2021:** Kate Shellnutt, "Why Defining
Gossip Matters in the Church's Response to Abuse," Christianity Today,
April 20, 2021, https://www.christianitytoday.com/ct/2021/may-june
/gossip-bible-definition-response-abuse-criticism.html.

41 **Matthew Mitchell:** "Don't Misuse 'Resisting Gossip,'" Hot Orthodoxy,
January 2019, https://matt-mitchell.blogspot.com/2019/01/dont-misuse
-resisting-gossip.html.

41 **Bill Hybels:** Emily McFarlan Miller, "Bill Hybels Independent Investigation Finds Allegations Against Willow Creek Founder Credible,"
Washington Post, March 1, 2019, https://www.washingtonpost.com
/religion/2019/03/01/independent-report-finds-allegations-against
-willow-creek-founder-bill-hybels-are-credible/.

41 **Emily Joy Allison:** Becca Andrews, "As a Teen, Emily Joy Was Abused
by a Church Youth Leader. Now She's Leading a Movement to Change

Evangelical America," *Mother Jones*, May 25, 2018, https://www.mother
jones.com/criminal-justice/2018/05/evangelical-church-metoo
-movement-abuse/.

42   **Paige Patterson:** Liam Adams, "Southern Baptist Seminary Admitted
Registered Sex Offender During High-Profile Leader's Tenure," *Tennes-sean*, June 3, 2022, https://www.tennessean.com/story/news
/religion/2022/06/03/southwestern-baptist-theological-seminary
-admitted-sex-offender-under-paige-patterson-tenure/7492609001/.

42   **Beth Moore:** Beth Moore, "A Letter to My Brothers," The LPM Blog,
May 31, 2018, https://blog.lproof.org/2018/05/a-letter-to-my-brothers
.html.

44   **Marianne Bjelland Kartzow:** Lectio Difficilior, https://www.lectio
.unibe.ch/10_1/kartzow2.html.

The Burn Book

50   *Mean Girls*: *Mean Girls*, Paramount Pictures, 2004.

51   **Henri Tajfel and John Turner:** Saul Mcleod, "Social Identity Theory
in Psychology (Tajfel & Turner, 1979)," Simply Psychology, October 5,
2023, https://www.simplypsychology.org/social-identity-theory.html.

51   **A 1944 *Life* magazine article:** Ben Cosgrove, "Teenagers: A 1944 Photo
Essay on a New American Phenomenon," *Time*, September 28, 2013,
https://time.com/3639041/the-invention-of-teenagers-life-and-the
-triumph-of-youth-culture/.

52   **the ability to engage:** Herbert H. Clark, *Using Language* (Cambridge,
UK: Cambridge University Press, 1996).

52   **A study of five teenage girls:** Jackie Guendouzi, "Social Functions of
Gossip in Adolescent Girl's Talk," *Discourse Studies* 22, no. 6 (December
2020): 678–96.

52   *god-sibb*: Esther Eidinow, "Identifying Gossip," in *Envy, Poison, and
Death: Women on Trial in Classical Athens* (Oxford, UK: Oxford University
Press, 2016), 171–79, https://library.oapen.org/bitstream/handle/20
.500.12657/39478/9780199562602.pdf?sequence=1&isAllowed=y171–79.

52   **A wood-block print:** "Tittle-Tattle; Or, the Several Branches of Gossip-ping," The British Museum, https://www.britishmuseum.org/collection
/object/P_1973-U-216.

53   **1611 French-to-English dictionary:** Randle Cotgrave, *A Dictionarie of
the French and English Tongues* (London: Georg Olms Verlag, 1970).

53   **the brank:** William Andrews, *Punishments in the Olden Time: Being an
Historical Account of the Ducking Stool, Brank, Pillory, Stocks, Drunkard's
Cloak, Whipping Post, Riding the Stang, etc.* (London: W. Stewart &
Co., 1881), HathiTrust, https://babel.hathitrust.org/cgi/pt?id=uc1
.aa0008935629&seq=38&q1=gossip%27s%2Bbridle.

Notes

53 **a person named Chester:** Walter Besant, *Mediæval London*, vol. 1 (London: Adam & Charles Black, 1906), 356–57.

54 **"male gossip":** "Almost every Alehouse has a Convention every Evening of these Kind of Male Gossips, of all Occupations," *Derby Mercury*, 1767.

54 **Jane West:** Jane West, *A Gossip's Story, and a Legendary Tale*, Vol. 2 (London: Longman and Rees, 1799).

54 **Louise Collins:** Louise Collins, "Gossip: A Feminist Defense," in *Good Gossip*, ed. Robert F. Goodman and Aaron Ben-Ze'ev (Lawrence: University Press of Kansas, 1994), 14–106.

55 *All About Love:* bell hooks, *All About Love: New Visions* (New York: William Morrow, 2022).

55 **Rosalind Wiseman's book:** Rosalind Wiseman, *Queen Bees & Wannabes: Helping Your Daughter Survive Cliques, Gossip, Boys, and the New Realities of Girl World* (New York: Harmony, 2022).

57 **Thomas Hine:** Thomas Hine, *The Rise and Fall of the American Teenager: A New History of the American Adolescent Experience* (New York: Perennial, 2006).

58 **Dwight Macdonald wrote in the *New Yorker*:** Dwight Macdonald, "A Caste, a Culture, a Market—II," *New Yorker*, November 21, 1958, https://www.newyorker.com/magazine/1958/11/29/inventing-the-american-teenager.

59 **David Resnick:** David Resnick, "Life in an Unjust Community: A Hollywood View of High School Moral Life," *Journal of Moral Education* 37, no. 1 (2008): 99–113, https://doi.org/10.1080/03057240701803718.

60 **Thomas F. Green:** Thomas F. Green, *Voices: The Educational Formation of Conscience* (Notre Dame, IN: University of Notre Dame Press, 2001).

61 **To re-release *Mean Girls*:** *Mean Girls*, Paramount Pictures, 2024.

62 **In Agatha Christie's:** Agatha Christie, *The Murder at the Vicarage* (New York: Signet, 2000).

63 **University of California, Berkeley:** Matthew Feinberg et al., "The Virtues of Gossip: Reputational Information Sharing as Prosocial Behavior," *Journal of Personality and Social Psychology* 102, no. 5 (May 2012): 1015–30.

63 **Evette Dionne:** Clayman Institute, *Whisper Networks: On the Feminist Function of Rumor*, YouTube, November 14, 2019, https://www.youtube.com/watch?v=LoUwWMgkOTE.

64 **Jacqueline Rose:** Jacqueline Rose, *On Violence and On Violence Against Women* (New York: Farrar, Straus and Giroux, 2021).

65 **Lacy Crawford:** Lacy Crawford, *Notes on a Silencing: A Memoir* (New York: Back Bay Books, 2021).

66 **A thematic analysis:** Erin Rennie, "'What a Lying Slut': The (Re)production of Rape Myths in Online Misogyny Towards Women Disclosing

Their Experiences of Rape Through the #MeToo Movement," *Journal of Gender-Based Violence* 7, no. 2 (June 2023): 204–19.

67   **Lois Shepherd:** Lois Shepherd, "The Danger of the 'He Said, She Said' Expression," The Hill, October 12, 2018, https://thehill.com /opinion/judiciary/411157-the-danger-of-the-he-said-she-said -expression/.

67   **Eric Pooley:** Eric Pooley, "Kiss but Don't Tell," *Time*, March 23, 1998, https://content.time.com/time/subscriber/article/0,33009,988009-2,00 .html.

70   **Chanel Miller:** Chanel Miller, *Know My Name: A Memoir* (New York: Penguin Books, 2020).

70   **resolved in a jury trial:** Katharine Webster, "Why Do So Few Rape Cases End in Arrest?," UMass Lowell, April 17, 2019, https://www.uml .edu/news/stories/2019/sexual_assault_research.aspx.

70   **cases were dropped:** Jan Ransom, "'Nobody Believed Me': How Rape Cases Get Dropped," *New York Times*, July 18, 2021, https://www .nytimes.com/2021/07/18/nyregion/manhattan-da-rape-cases-dropped .html.

71   **Sarah Jeong:** Sarah Jeong, "When Whisper Networks Let Us Down," The Verge, February 21, 2018, https://www.theverge.com/2018/2/21 /17035552/sexual-assault-harassment-whisper-network-reporting -failure-marquis-boire.

71   **Jenna Wortham:** Jenna Wortham et al., "The Reckoning: Women and Power in the Workplace," *New York Times*, December 13, 2017, https: //www.nytimes.com/interactive/2017/12/13/magazine/the-reckoning -women-and-power-in-the-workplace.html.

73   **Jia Tolentino's book:** Jia Tolentino, *Trick Mirror: Reflections on Self-Delusion* (New York: Random House, 2020).

Anon Plz

77   *Gossip Girl*: *Gossip Girl*, The CW, 2007.

79   **Joy Montgomery:** Joy Montgomery, "The 'Gossip Girl' Reboot Has Nothing on the Original Series," *British Vogue*, May 17, 2023, https: //www.vogue.co.uk/arts-and-lifestyle/article/gossip-girl-reboot -cancelled.

79   **Joshua Safran:** Marlow Stern, "'Gossip Girl' Creator: Why We Revealed Gossip Girl's Identity," *The Daily Beast*, July 8, 2021, https://www.the dailybeast.com/gossip-girl-creator-joshua-safran-on-why-he-revealed -gossip-girls-identity.

81   *Money Diaries*: R29 Team, "Money Diaries," Refinery29, https://www .refinery29.com/en-us/money-diary.

81   **a July 2018 entry:** "A Week in New York City on $25/Hour and $1k

Monthly Allowance," Refinery29, July 15, 2018, https://www.refinery29
.com/en-us/money-diary-new-york-city-marketing-intern-income.

82 **Carrie Battan:** Carrie Battan, "Money Diaries, Where Millennial Women
Go to Judge One Another's Spending Habits," *New Yorker*, November 16,
2017, https://www.newyorker.com/culture/rabbit-holes/money-diaries
-where-millennial-women-go-to-judge-one-anothers-spending
-habits.

82 *The Incest Diary*: Anonymous, *The Incest Diary* (London: Bloomsbury
Publishing, 2018).

84 *Town Tattle*: Sarah Churchwell, "'The Scandal Detectives': Town Topics
and F. Scott Fitzgerald, 1916–23," *F. Scott Fitzgerald Review* 18 (December 2020): 1–47, https://doi.org/10.5325/fscotfitzrevi.18.1.0001.

84 *Town Topics*: Katrin Horn, "The Public Gossip of *Town Topics: The Journal of Society* (1885–1937)," *European Journal of American Studies* 15, no. 4
(2020), https://doi.org/10.4000/ejas.16423.

85 **President Roosevelt is quoted:** "Alice Roosevelt Longworth," National
Park Service, https://www.nps.gov/people/alice-roosevelt-longworth.htm.

85 **sued for an extortion scheme:** Evangeline Holland, "Colonel Mann
and Town Topics," Edwardian Promenade, August 22, 2011, https://
www.edwardianpromenade.com/scandal/colonel-mann-and-town
-topics/.

86 **Blind Item Rehash:** "January 2021," Blind Item Rehash, http://www
.agcwebpages.com/BLINDITEMS/2021/JANUARY.html.

86 **court documents were filed:** Bethy Squires, "Crazy Days and Nights
Blogger Enty Reportedly Revealed in Lawsuit," Vulture, February 7,
2024, https://www.vulture.com/article/crazy-days-and-nights-blogger
-enty-revealed.html.

87 **told *Vanity Fair*:** Maureen O'Connor, "The Joy and Agony of Being
@deuxmoi, Instagram's Accidental Gossip Queen," *Vanity Fair*, February 4,
2021, https://www.vanityfair.com/style/2021/02/deuxmoi-instagrams
-accidental-celebrity-gossip-queen.

88 **Maryann Ayim:** Maryann Ayim, "Knowledge Through the Grapevine,"
in *Good Gossip*, ed. Robert F. Goodman and Aaron Ben-Ze'ev (Lawrence:
University Press of Kansas, 1994), 93.

88 **propagation of infectious disease:** Rachid Guerraoui et al., "On the
Inherent Anonymity of Gossiping," arXiv, August 4, 2023, https://doi.org
/https://arxiv.org/pdf/2308.02477.

89 **told Vice in 2020:** Amelia Tait, "Some of Reddit's Wildest Relationship
Stories Are Lies. I'd Know—I Wrote Them," Vice, July 13, 2020, https:
//www.vice.com/en/article/4ay4vn/reddit-relationships-fake-stories
-authors.

89 **Cartoons Hate Her:** Cartoons Hate Her, *The Troll Handbook: 100s of*

Accounts, 100s of Bans, 100s of Posts, One Bored Girl, independently published.

90   **Eleanor Gordon-Smith:** Elle Hunt, "AITA? How a Reddit Forum Posed the Defining Question of Our Age," *Guardian*, October 22, 2020, https://www.theguardian.com/technology/2020/oct/22/aita-how-a -reddit-forum-posed-the-defining-question-of-our-age.

90   **In a meta-analysis:** Nathan Walter and Riva Tukachinsky, "A Meta-Analytic Examination of the Continued Influence of Misinformation in the Face of Correction: How Powerful Is It, Why Does It Happen, and How to Stop It?," *Communication Research* 47, no. 2 (March 2020): 155–77, https://journals.sagepub.com/doi/abs/10.1177/00936502198 54600.

92   **a petition asking Instagram:** "Teachers and Parents Demand Instagram Stop Enabling Bullying of Kids and Educators on Anonymous School 'Confessions' Accounts," American Federation of Teachers, October 7, 2022, https://www.aft.org/press-release/teachers-and-parents-demand -instagram-stop-enabling-bullying-kids-and-educators.

92   **Emily Weinstein and Carrie James:** Emily Weinstein and Carrie James, *Behind Their Screens: What Teens Are Facing (and Adults Are Missing)* (Cambridge, MA: MIT Press, 2022).

92   **Libs of TikTok:** Doree Lewak, "From Mask-Shaming to Bad Teachers, Mystery Woman Exposes 'Lefty Lunacy' on 'Libs of TikTok,'" *New York Post*, February 3, 2022, https://nypost.com/2022/02/02/the-mystery -woman-behind-the-viral-libs-of-tik-tok-account/.

93   **Taylor Lorenz:** Taylor Lorenz, "Meet the Woman Behind Libs of TikTok, Secretly Fueling the Right's Outrage Machine," *Washington Post*, April 19, 2022, https://www.washingtonpost.com/technology/2022 /04/19/libs-of-tiktok-right-wing-media/.

93   **Charlie Markbreiter:** Charlie Markbreiter, *Gossip Girl Fanfic Novella* (Berkeley, CA: Kenning Editions, 2022).

94   **Claudia Picado:** Claudia Picado, "The 'Gossip Girl' Reboot Never Lived Up to the Original Show," Collider, January 28, 2023, https://collider .com/gossip-girl-reboot-cancelled/.

95   **Ferrante's true identity:** Claudio Gatti, "Ecco la vera identità di Elena Ferrante," *Il Sole 24 Ore*, October 2, 2016, https://www.ilsole24ore.com /art/ecco-vera-identita-elena-ferrante-ADEqsgUB.

96   **Alexandra Schwartz:** Alexandra Schwartz, "The 'Unmasking' of Elena Ferrante," *New Yorker*, October 3, 2016, https://www.newyorker.com /culture/cultural-comment/the-unmasking-of-elena-ferrante.

96   **Ferrante quotes Italo Calvino:** Elena Ferrante, *Frantumaglia*, trans. Ann Goldstein (New York: Europa Editions, 2016).

96   **real physiological responses:** Lauri Nummenmaa, "Psychology and

Neurobiology of Horror Movies," PsyArXiv, March 4, 2021, https://osf .io/preprints/psyarxiv/b8tgs.

97   *Anatomy of a Fall*: *Anatomy of a Fall*, Le Pacte, 2023.

Leave Britney Alone

103   **Spears wrote:** Britney Spears, *The Woman in Me* (New York: Gallery Books, 2023).

103   *Framing Britney Spears*: "Framing Britney Spears," *New York Times*, November 2, 2021, https://www.nytimes.com/article/framing-britney -spears.html.

103   **Kentwood, Louisiana:** Fusion Staff, "Finding the American Dream in Britney Spears' Hometown," Splinter, August 4, 2016, https://www .splinter.com/finding-the-american-dream-in-britney-spears-hometown -1793860896.

105   **This exact room:** Steven Daly, "Britney Spears, Teen Queen," *Rolling Stone*, December 5, 2023, https://www.rollingstone.com/music/music -news/britney-spears-teen-queen-rolling-stones-1999-cover-story -254871/.

106   **would tell *British GQ*:** "A Conversation with Britney Spears," *British GQ*, November 2003.

107   *Mercury News*: Associated Press, "Court Places Britney Spears Under Temporary Conservatorship of Her Father," *Mercury News*, August 14, 2016, https://www.mercurynews.com/2008/02/01/court-places-britney -spears-under-temporary-conservatorship-of-her-father/.

107   **Jansen Fitzgerald:** *People* Staff, "Britney Spears Hospitalized for 'an Evaluation,'" *People*, January 4, 2008, https://people.com/celebrity /britney-spears-hospitalized-for-an-evaluation/.

108   **The "halo effect":** Jacqueline L. Longe, ed., *The Gale Encyclopedia of Psychology*, 3rd ed., vol. 1 (Farmington Hills, MI: Gale Group, 2016), 507–9.

109   **both celebrities:** Anna Silman, "Lorde Finally Speaks Out About Those Jack Antonoff Dating Rumors," *The Cut*, February 23, 2018, https://www .thecut.com/2018/02/lorde-speaks-out-about-those-jack-antonoff -dating-rumors.html.

109   **provoked to deny them:** Lisa Ryan, "Jack Antonoff Says the Lorde Rumors Are 'Dumb Heteronormative Gossip,'" *The Cut*, January 17, 2018, https://www.thecut.com/2018/01/jack-antonoff-lorde-rumors-lena -dunham-split.html.

109   **They played three songs:** Ostin Torre, *Lorde with Jack Antonoff— New York/Hard Feelings/Liability—Barclays Center NY—4/4/2018*, YouTube, April 5, 2018, https://www.youtube.com/watch?v=1yN6ws AByCE.

Notes

110 **Mariah Smith said:** Mariah Smith and Lindsey Weber, "So, What Happened Between Lorde and Jack Antonoff at Her Show Last Night?," *The Cut*, April 5, 2018, https://www.thecut.com/2018/04/what-happened -with-jack-antonoff-at-lordes-show-last-night.html.

110 **Emily Ratajkowski:** Emily Ratajkowski, *My Body* (New York: Metropolitan Books, 2021).

110 **Jonathan Leder:** Highsnobiety, "Jonathan Leder Reveals Details of His Emily Ratajkowski Shoot (NSFW)," Highsnobiety, February 8, 2017, https://www.highsnobiety.com/p/jonathan-leder-emily-ratajkowski -nude-interview/.

112 **"Celebrity Attitude Scale":** Lynn E. McCutcheon, Ágnes Zsila, and Zsolt Demetrovics, "Celebrity Worship and Cognitive Skills Revisited: Applying Cattell's Two-Factor Theory of Intelligence in a Cross-Sectional Study," *BMC Psychology*, November 8, 2021, https://bmcpsychology .biomedcentral.com/articles/10.1186/s40359-021-00679-3.

112 **John Maltby and his coauthors:** John Maltby, James Houran, and Lynn E. McCutcheon, "A Clinical Interpretation of Attitudes and Behaviors Associated with Celebrity Worship," *Journal of Nervous and Mental Disease* 191, no. 1 (2003): 25–29, https://doi.org/10.1097/00005053 -200301000-00005.

113 **Kineta H. Hung:** Kineta Hung, "Celebrity and Influencer in a Fan Economy: Unfolding the Fans' Roles in Enhancing Endorsement Effects," in *Multidisciplinary Perspectives on Media Fandom*, ed. Robert Andrew Dunn, 323–40 (Hershey, PA: IGI Global, 2020), https://doi .org/10.4018/978-1-7998-3323-9.ch018.

113 **Drew Barrymore left:** Maureen Lee Lenker, "Drew Barrymore's Alleged Stalker Arrested for Seeking Out Emma Watson," *Entertainment Weekly*, September 14, 2023, https://ew.com/celebrity/drew-barrymore-stalker -arrested-again-allegedly-nyfw-emma-watson/.

113 **a man was arrested:** Associated Press, "Man Accused of Stalking After Arrests near Taylor Swift's Home Held Without Bail for Violating Protective Order," NBC News, January 26, 2024, https://www.nbcnews .com/news/us-news/man-accused-stalking-taylor-swift-held-bail -violating-protective-order-rcna135845.

114 **Donald Horton and R. Richard Wohl:** Donald Horton and R. Richard Wohl, "Mass Communication and Para-Social Interaction: Observations on Intimacy at a Distance," *Psychiatry* 19, no. 3 (1956): 215–29, https: //doi.org/10.1080/00332747.1956.11023049.

114 **listening with headphones:** Daniela Schlütz and Imke Hedder, "Aural Parasocial Relations: Host–Listener Relationships in Podcasts," *Journal of Radio & Audio Media* 29, no. 2 (2022): 457–74, https://doi.org/10.1080 /19376529.2020.1870467.

115 **Emmeline Clein:** Emmeline Clein, "A Celebrity Lesbian Romance Changed My Life. (Even If It Never Happened.)," *New York Times*, July 18, 2023, https://www.nytimes.com/2023/07/18/magazine/celebrity-lesbian-fan-fiction.html.

116 **Anna Marks:** Anna Marks, "Look What We Made Taylor Swift Do," *New York Times*, January 4, 2024, https://www.nytimes.com/2024/01/04/opinion/taylor-swift-queer.html.

117 *Broadway Brevities & Society Gossip:* Brevities, https://www.queermusicheritage.com/gayephemera5.html.

118 **Jeannette Walls:** Jeannette Walls, *Dish: The Inside Story on the World of Gossip* (New York: William Morrow, 2000).

119 **dancing in celebration:** Walls, *Dish*, 66–69.

120 **Alana Hope Levinson:** Alana Hope Levinson, "Why We Can't Leave Britney Spears Alone," *GQ*, October 27, 2023, https://www.gq.com/story/why-we-cant-leave-britney-spears-alone.

120 **discredit and harass her:** Janet Maslin, "Star and Victim," *New York Times*, July 12, 1981, https://www.nytimes.com/1981/07/12/books/star-and-victim.html.

120 *Newsweek* **named her directly:** "May 28, 1970, Page 19–the Courier-News at Newspapers.Com," *Historical Newspapers from 1700s-2000s–Newspapers .Com*, Newspapers.com, https://www.newspapers.com/image/222417604/.

120 **to arrest and prosecute her:** Erica Gonzales, "*The United States vs. Billie Holiday*: What Really Happened," *Harper's Bazaar*, https://www.harpersbazaar.com/culture/film-tv/a35639408/united-states-billie-holiday-true-story/.

121 **Later, it was revealed:** "Crash Driver Was over Alcohol Limit," BBC, https://www.bbc.co.uk/news/special/politics97/diana/driver.html.

122 **Cara Cunningham:** Sharon Pruitt-Young, "Chris Crocker, 'Leave Britney Alone' Video Creator, Reflects on What's Changed," NPR, June 27, 2021, https://www.npr.org/2021/06/27/1010355669/chris-crocker-leave-britney-alone-video-creator-reflects-on-whats-changed.

122 **In the now famous video:** madringking1119, *Leave Britney Alone (Complete)*, YouTube, August 11, 2011, https://www.youtube.com/watch?v=WqSTXuJeTks&ab_channel=madringking1119.

122 **Mark Stevens:** Mark Stevens, "Britney Spears's Meltdown—Why She Shaved Her Head," *New York*, February 23, 2007, https://nymag.com/news/intelligencer/features/28528/.

122 **Anna Holmes:** Anna Holmes, "In Defense of the Badly-Behaved Britney Spears," Jezebel, https://jezebel.com/in-defense-of-the-badly-behaved-britney-spears-290011. This url is archived at https://web.archive.org/.

123 **told *Vanity Fair*:** Maureen O'Connor, "The Joy and Agony of Being @deuxmoi, Instagram's Accidental Gossip Queen," *Vanity Fair*, February 4,

2021, https://www.vanityfair.com/style/2021/02/deuxmoi-instagrams
-accidental-celebrity-gossip-queen.

123 **told Rachel Sylvester in** *Cosmopolitan*: "There's a Dark Side to the
Online Gossip Mill. I Would Know—I'm the Brains Behind Deuxmoi,"
Cosmopolitan, https://www.cosmopolitan.com/entertainment/celebs
/a43620663/deux-moi-identity-dark-side/.

124 **Ronald de Sousa:** Aaron Ben-Ze'ev, "A Vindication of Gossip," *Good
Gossip*, ed. Robert F. Goodman and Aaron Ben-Ze'ev (Lawrence: University Press of Kansas, 1994), 15.

124 **Ruth Graham:** Ruth Graham, "One of *Us*: 'Stars—They're Just like Us'
and the Future of Always-'on' Celebrity Coverage," Slate, September 22,
2016, https://slate.com/human-interest/2016/09/the-invention-of-us
-weeklys-stars-theyre-just-like-us-feature.html.

125 **she had checked into:** Safeeyah Kazi, "Britney Spears Has Canceled Her
Shows Indefinitely to Spend Time with Her Father After He 'Almost
Died,'" Business Insider, January 5, 2019, https://www.businessinsider.com
/britney-spears-cancels-shows-indefinitely-father-almost-died-2019-1.

126 **Lyz Lenz:** Lyz Lenz, "Can Britney Spears Ever Truly Be Free?," Men Yell at
Me, November 1, 2023, https://lyz.substack.com/home/post/p-138492597.

127 **Amanda Montell:** Amanda Montell, *The Age of Magical Overthinking*
(New York: Simon & Schuster, 2024).

The Plight of West Elm Caleb

131 **a PR director tweeted:** Ed Pilkington, "Justine Sacco, PR Executive
Fired over Racist Tweet, 'Ashamed,'" *Guardian*, December 22, 2013,
https://www.theguardian.com/world/2013/dec/22/pr-exec-fired-racist
-tweet-aids-africa-apology.

131 **flipping off the camera:** Pete D'Amato, "Non-Profit Worker Who Provoked Fury with Disrespectful Arlington Photo Tells How She Lost Her
Job, Can't Date and Now Lives in Fear," *Daily Mail*, February 22, 2015,
https://www.dailymail.co.uk/news/article-2964489/I-really-obsessed
-reading-Woman-fired-photo-giving-middle-finger-Arlington-National
-Cemetery-says-finally-Google-without-fear.html.

132 **a girl who dressed as:** Jon Ronson, "'Overnight, Everything I Loved Was
Gone': The Internet Shaming of Lindsey Stone," *Guardian*, February 21,
2015, https://www.theguardian.com/technology/2015/feb/21/internet
-shaming-lindsey-stone-jon-ronson.

132 **a media man:** Sarah Brieco, "Gawker: The Internet Bully," *Columbia Journalism Review*, October 24, 2014, https://www.cjr.org/the_kicker
/gawker_bullying.php.

132 **"everything is copy":** "In 'Everything Is Copy,' Nora Ephron's Son Tries
Her Philosophy," NPR, March 31, 2016, https://www.npr.org/2016

/03/31/472534582/in-everything-is-copy-nora-ephrons-son-tries-her
-philosophy.

133   **we are neotenous creatures:** "Neoteny," ScienceDirect, https:
//www.sciencedirect.com/topics/agricultural-and-biological-sciences
/neoteny.

134   **could not beat her:** Mehmet Somel et al., "Transcriptional Neoteny in
the Human Brain," *Proceedings of the National Academy of Sciences of the
United States of America* 106, no. 14 (April 7, 2009): 5743–48, https://doi
.org/10.1073/pnas.0900544106.

134   **We are inherently more curious:** Chip Walter, "Childhood Made Humans Invincible," Slate, January 29, 2013, https://slate.com/technology
/2013/01/evolution-of-childhood-prolonged-development-helped-homo
-sapiens-succeed.html.

134   **Kurt Vonnegut:** Ben Frawley, *We Are Here on Earth to Fart Around, Kurt
Vonnegut (2004),* YouTube, September 12, 2019, https://www.youtube
.com/watch?v=nxpITF8fswE.

134   **Our brains reward us:** Daniel J. Levitin, "Why the Modern World Is
Bad for Your Brain," *Guardian,* January 18, 2015, https://www.theguard
ian.com/science/2015/jan/18/modern-world-bad-for-brain
-daniel-j-levitin-organized-mind-information-overload.

134   **It is in our biology to snoop:** J. R. Thorpe, "This Is the Biological Reason
You Love to Snoop on Social Media," Bustle, August 22, 2017, https:
//www.bustle.com/p/why-do-we-love-to-snoop-on-social-media-it
-might-be-in-our-biology-77482.

135   **Jon Ronson:** Jon Ronson, "How One Stupid Tweet Blew up Justine
Sacco's Life," *New York Times,* February 12, 2015, https://www.nytimes
.com/2015/02/15/magazine/how-one-stupid-tweet-ruined-justine
-saccos-life.html.

136   **could watch the inmates:** Christian Fuchs, "New Media, Web 2.0 and
Surveillance," *Sociology Compass* 5, no. 2 (February 2011): 134–47, https:
//doi.org/10.1111/j.1751-9020.2010.00354.x.

138   **The rules of "Are We Dating the Same Guy?" groups:** Emily Bloch,
"Chicago Man Sues over 'Are We Dating the Same Guy' Posts About
Him," *Philadelphia Inquirer,* January 10 2024, https://www.inquirer.com
/news/nation-world/are-we-dating-the-same-guy-lawsuit-awdtsg
-chicago-man-20240110.html.

138   **the TikTok algorithm:** Louise Matsakis, "The Sneaky Way TikTok
Is Connecting You to Real-Life Friends," *Wired,* November 12, 2021,
https://www.wired.com/story/tiktok-friends-contacts-people-you-may
-know/.

139   **Patricia Meyer Spacks:** Patricia Meyer Spacks, *Gossip* (New York: Knopf,
1985), 18.

Notes

139 **Brittany Spanos:** Brittany Spanos, "The Internet Uproar Around West Elm Caleb Is Out of Control," *Rolling Stone*, January 21, 2022, https://www.rollingstone.com/culture/culture-news/caleb-west-elm-dating-saga-1288386/.

139 **"Couch Guy":** Robert McCoy, "I'm the TikTok Couch Guy. Here's What It Was Like Being Investigated on the Internet," Slate, December 6, 2021, https://slate.com/technology/2021/12/tiktok-couch-guy-internet-sleuths.html.

140 **Jon Ronson wrote in his 2015 book:** Jon Ronson, *So You've Been Publicly Shamed* (New York: Penguin Publishing Group, 2015).

140 **Kellie Yancy:** J'Nae Phillips, "TikTok Is Making Gossip Public, but Is That Ethical?" *Teen Vogue*, October 18, 2023, www.teenvogue.com/story/tiktok-is-making-gossip-public-but-is-that-ethical.

141 **CT Jones:** CT Jones, "They Gossiped at Brunch. Now There's a Mob after Them," *Rolling Stone*, September 22, 2023, www.rolling stone.com/culture/culture-features/gossip-tiktoks-drama-overheard-1234829552/.

142 **Michel Foucault:** Michel Foucault, *Discipline and Punish: The Birth of the Prison* (London: Tavistock, 1977).

142 **The Stasi:** Jim Willis, *Daily Life Behind the Iron Curtain* (Santa Barbara, CA: ABC-CLIO, 2014).

142 **Germany now has:** Charlotte Bailey, "The Lingering Trauma of Stasi Surveillance," *Atlantic*, November 9, 2019, https://www.theatlantic.com/international/archive/2019/11/lingering-trauma-east-german-police-state/601669/.

Knowledge Is Power

148 **What Heather is accusing Monica of:** Reality TV Fan, *The Epic Bermuda Triangle Dinner from Hell, Pt. 1 (Season 4, Episode 16)*, YouTube, January 3, 2024, https://www.youtube.com/watch?v=CMTgatRr12w&ab_channel=RealityTVFan.

148 **Two million people:** BreAnna Bell, "The Shocking Finale of 'The Real Housewives of Salt Lake City' Hits 2 Million Viewers (Exclusive)," *Variety*, January 9, 2024, https://variety.com/2024/tv/news/the-real-housewives-salt-lake-city-season-4-finale-ratings-1235867014/.

148 **Jennifer Lawrence:** Meredith Blake, "How Monica Garcia Made 'The Real Housewives of Salt Lake City' Unhinged, Unmissable TV," *Los Angeles Times*, January 23, 2024, https://www.latimes.com/entertainment-arts/tv/story/2024-01-23/monica-garcia-season-4-real-housewives-of-salt-lake-city.

150 **Danielle J. Lindemann:** Danielle J. Lindemann, *True Story: What Reality TV Says About Us* (New York: Picador, 2023).

259

150   **more people were applying:** Mark Andrejevic, *Reality TV: The Work of Being Watched* (Lanham, MD: Rowman & Littlefield, 2010).

150   **In their seminal study:** Steven Reiss and James Wiltz, "Why People Watch Reality TV," *Media Psychology* 6, no. 4 (2004): 363–78, https://doi .org/10.1207/s1532785xmep0604_3.

150   **another study has found:** Michal Hershman Shitrit and Jonathan Cohen, "Why Do We Enjoy Reality Shows: Is It Really All About Humiliation and Gloating?," *Journal of Media Psychology* 30, no. 2 (April 2018): 1–8, https://doi.org/10.1027/1864-1105/a000186.

151   **Mark Burnett:** *Mediaweek*, February 14, 2000, https://worldradiohistory .com/Archive-Mediaweek/2000/Mediaweek-2000-02-14.pdf.

152   **Erving Goffman:** Erving Goffman, *The Presentation of Self in Everyday Life* (New York: Anchor Books, 1959).

152   **according to a study:** Melissa S. Kearney and Phillip B. Levine, "Media Influences on Social Outcomes: The Impact of MTV's 16 and Pregnant on Teen Childbearing," National Bureau of Economic Research, August 2015, https://www.nber.org/system/files/working_papers/w19795/w19795.pdf.

152   **Joyce Chen:** Joyce Chen, "*The Bachelorette*'s Mike Johnson Is an Expert Tattler—& It's Why Bachelor Nation Already Adores Him," Refinery29, June 11, 2019, https://www.refinery29.com/en-us/2019/06/235042 /mike-johnson-from-the-bachelorette-fan-favorite.

153   **declares that she wants to:** Emma Gray, "'The Bachelorette' Episode 5: Emily Maynard Goes 'West Virginia Hood Rat Backwoods,'" HuffPost, December 6, 2017, https://www.huffpost.com/entry/the-bachelorette -episode-5-emily-maynard-west-virginia-back-woods-hood-rat -backwoods_b_1588568.

155   **A perfect play of this kind:** "You Get What You Give," *Survivor*, season 37, episode 8, 2018.

156   **researchers Matthew Feinberg, Robb Willer, Jennifer Steller, and Dacher Keltner:** Matthew Feinberg et al., "The Virtues of Gossip: Reputational Information Sharing as Prosocial Behavior," *Journal of Personality and Social Psychology* 102, no. 5 (May 2012): 1015–30, https:// doi.org/10.1037/a0026650.

159   **Émile Durkheim:** Émile Durkheim, "The Rules of Sociological Method (1895)," https://durkheim.uchicago.edu/Summaries/rules.html.

160   **Irving Janis:** Irving Lester Janis, *Groupthink: Psychological Studies of Policy Decisions and Fiascoes* (Boston: Wadsworth, 2013).

161   **Erin O'Mara Kunz:** Erin M. O'Mara Kunz, Jennifer L. Howell, and Nicole Beasley, "Surviving Racism and Sexism: What Votes in the Television Program *Survivor* Reveal About Discrimination," *Psychological Science* 34, no. 6 (June 2023): 726–35, https://doi.org/10.1177/0956 7976231165665.

163   **Mariah Smith:** Mariah Smith, "Keeping Up with the Kontinuity Errors," *The Cut*, https://www.thecut.com/tags/keeping-up-with-the-kontinuity -errors/.

164   **Morgan Baila:** Morgan Baila, "Fan or Not, the Kardashians Have You Trapped in Their Scandalous Web," Refinery29, March 11, 2019, https: //www.refinery29.com/en-us/2019/03/226331/kardashian-drama-scandal -fake-kuwtk-ratings-publicity.

164   **cheating on his girlfriend:** "Tom Sandoval & Ariana Madix Call It Quits ... Allegations He Cheated with Costar Raquel Leviss," *TMZ*, March 8, 2023, https://www.tmz.com/2023/03/03/tom-sandoval-ariana -madix-breakup-split-cheating-raquel-leviss/.

165   **fights on set:** Hannah Selinger, "Every Detail of the *Vanderpump Rules* #scandoval Drama in Chronological Order," Vulture, May 25, 2023, https://www.vulture.com/article/vanderpump-rules-affair-timeline -scandoval.html.

165   **Barbara Herrnstein Smith:** Barbara Herrnstein Smith, *On the Margins of Discourse: The Relation of Literature to Language* (Chicago: University of Chicago Press, 1983), 85.

The Truth About Urban Legends

170   **called it in to *Normal Gossip*:** "Pole Dancing, Book Clubs, and Gay Men's Chorus: Your Niche Gossip," *Normal Gossip*, season 2, episode 10.

171   **a woman became stuck:** "Woman Trapped in Window Trying to Retrieve Poo After Tinder Date," BBC, https://www.bbc.com/news/uk -england-bristol-41167296.

175   **many of the children did not:** Taylor Pettaway, "The Ghost Tracks: 82 Years Ago Tuesday, One of San Antonio's Most Famous Ghost Stories Was Born," MySA, December 2, 2020, https://www.mysanantonio.com /news/local/slideshow/The-Ghost-Tracks-82-years-ago-today-one-of -San-213626.php.

176   **Andrea Kitta:** Kelsey McKinney, "Spreading Fear: How 'the Licked Hand' and Other Scary Stories Move around the Country," Thrillist, October 12, 2017, https://www.thrillist.com/entertainment/nation/humans -can-lick-too-how-urban-legends-spread.

176   **Oscar Washburn:** "Alton, Texas and the Haunted Goatman's Bridge," Legends of America, https://www.legendsofamerica.com/tx-alton/.

177   **Jan Harold Brunvand:** Jan Harold Brunvand, *The Vanishing Hitchhiker: American Urban Legends and Their Meanings* (New York: Norton, 2003).

177   **Nicholas DiFonzo and Prashant Bordia:** Nicholas DiFonzo and Prashant Bordia, "Rumor, Gossip and Urban Legends," *Diogenes* 54, no. 1 (February 2007): 19–35, https://doi.org/10.1177/0392192107073433.

178   **George Washington:** "'I Can't Tell a Lie, Pa,' George Washington and

the Cherry Tree Myth," George Washington's Mount Vernon, https: //www.mountvernon.org/george-washington/facts/myths/george -washington-and-the-cherry-tree-myth.

179 **already had a wife:** "The Roman Empire in the First Century: Cleopatra & Egypt," PBS, https://www.pbs.org/empires/romans/empire/cleopatra .html#.

179 **Gail Collins:** Gail Collins, *Scorpion Tongues: The Irresistible History of Gossip in American Politics* (New York: Harcourt, Brace, 1999).

179 **William Henry Harrison:** Jane McHugh and Philip A. Mackowiak, "What Really Killed William Henry Harrison?," *New York Times*, March 31, 2014, https://www.nytimes.com/2014/04/01/science/what-really -killed-william-henry-harrison.html.

180 **as cheaply as possible:** Louise Hall: "Trump Administration Includes Nearly $400m to Remodel West Wing in Coronavirus Relief Bill," *Independent*, August 3, 2020, https://www.independent.co.uk/news/world /americas/trump-administration-white-house-remodel-coronavirus -relief-bill-oval-office-a9652146.html.

181 **Emily Heil:** Emily Heil, "That 'Hillary Clinton Threw a Lamp/Book/Bible' Story Has Been Circulating for Ages," *Washington Post*, April 9, 2015, https://www.washingtonpost.com/news/reliable-source/wp/2015/04/09 /that-hillary-clinton-threw-a-lampbookbible-story-has-been-circulating -for-ages/.

182 **David Coady:** David Coady, "Rumour Has It," *International Journal of Applied Philosophy* 20, no. 1 (Spring 2006): 41–53.

182 **a digital photocopy:** Jess Henig, "Born in the U.S.A.," FactCheck.org, April 27, 2011, https://www.factcheck.org/2008/08/born-in-the-usa/.

184 **Anna Merlan:** Anna Merlan, *Republic of Lies: American Conspiracy Theorists and Their Surprising Rise to Power* (New York: Arrow Books, 2020).

184 **had been replaced by a body double:** Kate Bennett, "No, Melania Trump Does Not Have a Body Double," CNN, October 19, 2017, https://www .cnn.com/2017/10/19/politics/melania-trump-body-double-false/index .html.

184 **in the photo:** Kate Taylor, "Melania Trump Has a Secret Service Agent Who Looks Strikingly Similar to Her—and It's Fueling a Wild Conspiracy Theory," Business Insider, October 18, 2017, https://www.business insider.com/melania-trump-secret-service-agent-body-double-conspiracy -2017-10.

185 **more than 30,500 false or misleading claims:** Glenn Kessler et al., "A Term of Untruths: The Longer Trump Was President, the More Frequently He Made False or Misleading Claims," *Washington Post*, January 23, 2021, https://www.washingtonpost.com/politics/interactive/2021 /timeline-trump-claims-as-president/.

Notes

186 **Alex Abad-Santos:** Alex Abad-Santos, "The 'Fake Melania' Conspiracy Theory, Explained," *Vox*, October 20, 2017, https://www.vox.com /culture/2017/10/20/16503870/fake-melania-conspiracy-theory -explained.

186 **A 2015 psychological study:** Lisa K. Fazio et al., "Knowledge Does Not Protect Against Illusory Truth," *Journal of Experimental Psychology: General* 144, no. 5 (October 2015): 993–1002, https://doi.org/10.1037 /xge0000098.

187 **Frank Rich:** Frank Rich, "Whose Hillary?," *New York Times*, June 13, 1993, https://www.nytimes.com/1993/06/13/magazine/endpaper-public -stages-whose-hillary.html?searchResultPosition=1.

187 **In a 1996 interview:** Caleb Rojas Castillo, *Hillary Clinton Interview with Barbara Walters, 20/20 (1996, Remastered)*, YouTube, January 12, 2023, https://www.youtube.com/watch?v=eD-drSU2amY&ab_channel=Caleb RojasCastillo.

My Life with Picasso

192 **a dozen drawings and four oil paintings:** *Picasso and the Weeping Women: The Years of Marie-Thérèse Walter & Dora Maar*, exhibition catalog, Los Angeles County Museum of Art, 2023, 61.

193 **He physically abused his wife:** Françoise Gilot and Carlton Lake, *Life with Picasso* (New York: Flammarion, 1986).

193 **He disowned some of his children:** Kim Willsher, "The Picasso Mystery," *Guardian*, December 3, 2010, https://www.theguardian.com/artanddesign /2010/dec/04/picasso-unseen-works-mystery.

193 **Ben Davis:** Ben Davis, "The Brooklyn Museum's Much-Criticized 'It's Pablo-matic' Show Is Actually Weirdly at War with Itself over Hannah Gadsby's Art History," *Artnet*, June 19, 2023, https://news.artnet.com /art-world-archives/hannah-gadsby-brooklyn-museum-its-pablomatic -2322389.

194 **Arianna Huffington's biography:** Arianna Stassinopoulos Huffington, *Picasso: Creator and Destroyer* (New York: Simon & Schuster, 1988).

195 **Alice B. Toklas:** Jeffrey Meyers, "Picasso and Hemingway: A Dud Poem and a Live Grenade," *Michigan Quarterly Review* 45, no. 3 (Summer 2006): 422–28.

197 **the intro reads:** Georges Braque et al., *Testimony Against Gertrude Stein* (The Hague: Servire Press, 1935).

199 **told Ruth La Ferla:** Ruth La Ferla, "Françoise Gilot: 'It Girl' at 100," *New York Times*, January 19, 2022, https://www.nytimes.com/2022/01 /19/style/francoise-gilot-it-girl.html.

199 **Aline Saarinen:** Aline Saarinen, "Aspects of the Artist; Life with Picasso. By Françoise Gilot and Carlton Lake," *New York Times*, November 8,

1964, https://timesmachine.nytimes.com/timesmachine/1964/11/08
/97283073.html?pageNumber=138.

202 **Alex Greenberger:** Alex Greenberger, "Hannah Gadsby's Disastrous
'Pablo-matic' Show at the Brooklyn Museum Has Some 'Pablo-ms' of Its
Own," *ARTnews*, June 1, 2023, https://www.artnews.com/art-news
/reviews/hannah-gadsby-its-pablo-matic-brooklyn-museum-review
-1234670115/.

203 **Yasmin Nair:** Yasmin Nair, "No, No, *Nanette*: Hannah Gadsby, Trauma,
and Comedy as Emotional Manipulation," *Evergreen Review*, https:
//evergreenreview.com/read/your-laughter-is-my-trauma/.

203 **Ben Davis:** Ben Davis, "How the Many Dilemmas of Hannah Gadsby's
Anti-Picasso Show Feed Our Contemporary Cultural Doom Loop,"
Artnet, July 25, 2023, https://news.artnet.com/art-world-archives
/hannah-gadsby-brooklyn-museum-pablomatic-2322392.

203 **Édouard Pignon:** Édouard Pignon, "Portrait de Francoise Gilot," 1962,
https://www.artnet.com/artists/%C3%A9douard-pignon/portrait-de
-francoise-gilot-3UsWTZLakDxmAm-W5iuvCQ2.

204 **Gilot told *Harper's Bazaar*:** "French Artist Françoise Gilot Dies Aged
101," *Harper's Bazaar*, June 7, 2023, https://www.harpersbazaar.com/uk
/culture/bazaar-art/a44115062/francoise-gilot-dies/.

204 **Claire Dederer:** Claire Dederer, *Monsters: A Fan's Dilemma* (New York:
Knopf, 2023).

Things Half Heard

210 **research by O2:** James Phillips, "84% of Us Eavesdrop on Other People's
Conversations, Survey Reveals," *Independent*, February 13, 2015, https:
//www.independent.co.uk/travel/news-and-advice/84-of-us-eavesdrop
-on-other-people-s-conversations-survey-reveals-10044327.html.

213 **the audiologist plays sound frequencies:** "Hearing (Audiometry) Test,"
Mayfield Brain & Spine, https://mayfieldclinic.com/pe-hearing.htm.

215 **The goal is to see:** Carla K. Johnson, "Have You Tried Pink Noise for
Sleep? Here's What to Know," AP, May 20 2024, https://apnews.com
/article/pink-brown-white-noise-sleep-focus-concentration-f5f24dad1
effb09c1cf8b607bd22ebc7.

216 **Johannes Müller:** Cristina Laza and Eugenia Enciu, "Giant Congenital
Cholesteatoma of the Temporal Bone," *Global Journal of Otolaryngology*
18, no. 5 (2019): 555998, https://doi.org/10.19080/GJO.2019.18.555998.

219 **lives with hearing loss:** "Deafness and Hearing Loss," World Health
Organization, https://www.who.int/health-topics/hearing-loss.

219 **More than a quarter of adults:** "Deafness and Hearing Loss," World
Health Organization.

221 **Christopher Chabris and Daniel Simons:** Christopher Chabris and

Daniel Simons, *The Invisible Gorilla,* http://www.theinvisiblegorilla.com /gorilla_experiment.html.

221 **their results were stunning:** Daniel J. Simons and Christopher F. Chabris, "Gorillas in Our Midst: Sustained Inattentional Blindness for Dynamic Events," *Perception* 28, no. 9 (September 1999): 1059–74, https: //doi.org/10.1068/p281059.

222 **unlawful convictions:** The National Registry of Exonerations, https: //www.law.umich.edu/special/exoneration/Pages/detaillist.aspx.

222 **Larry Booth:** "About," *Plaintiff,* https://plaintiffmagazine.com/about.

223 **The McGurk effect:** *Try This Bizarre Audio Illusion!* 👁 🄟 😲— *BBC,* YouTube, November 10, 2010, https://www.youtube.com/watch?v =G-lN8vWm3m0&t=92s.

223 **Diana Deutsch:** *Science* Staff, "Sounds of Deception," *Science,* February 20, 1997, https://www.sciencemag.org/news/1997/02/sounds -deception.

225 **Elizabeth F. Loftus:** Hal Arkowitz and Scott O. Lilienfeld, "Why Science Tells Us Not to Rely on Eyewitness Accounts," *Scientific American,* January 1, 2010, https://www.scientificamerican.com/article/do-the-eyes -have-it/.

225 **Rachel Aviv's excellent profile:** Rachel Aviv, "How Elizabeth Loftus Changed the Meaning of Memory," *New Yorker,* March 29, 2021, https: //www.newyorker.com/magazine/2021/04/05/how-elizabeth-loftus -changed-the-meaning-of-memory.

Tell It Slant

233 **Laurie Colwin's 1978 novel:** Laurie Colwin, *Happy All the Time* (London: Weidenfeld & Nicolson, 2021).

233 **Katherine May:** Katherine May, *Enchantment: Awakening Wonder in an Anxious Age* (New York: Riverhead Books, 2023).

233 **A study published:** Matthew Feinberg et al., "The Virtues of Gossip: Reputational Information Sharing as Prosocial Behavior," *Journal of Personality and Social Psychology* 102, no. 5 (May 2012):1015–30, https://doi .org/10.1037/a0026650.

234 **St. Augustine:** Jim Holt, "Say Anything," *New Yorker,* August 14, 2005, https://www.newyorker.com/magazine/2005/08/22/say-anything.

234 **Harry G. Frankfurt:** Harry G. Frankfurt, *On Bullshit* (Princeton, NJ: Princeton University Press, 2005).

236 **Farnoosh Fathi:** Farnoosh Fathi, "'Tell All the Truth but Tell It Slant–': Dickinson's Poetics of Indirection in Contemporary Poetry," *Emily Dickinson Journal* 17, no. 2 (2008): 77–99, https://doi.org/10.1353/edj.0.0184.

236 **Durga Chew-Bose:** Durga Chew-Bose, *Too Much and Not the Mood: Essays* (New York: Farrar, Straus and Giroux, 2017).

Notes

237 **In *Second Place*, Rachel Cusk:** Rachel Cusk, *Second Place* (London: Faber & Faber, 2022).

237 **Janet Malcolm:** Janet Malcolm, *The Silent Woman: Sylvia Plath and Ted Hughes* (London: Granta, 2020).

238 **Norman Rockwell:** Rich Bradway, "Norman Rockwell Museum Welcomes Back Norman Rockwell's 'The Gossips,'" Norman Rockwell Museum, March 1, 2017, https://www.nrm.org/2014/02/norman -rockwell-museum-welcomes-back-norman-rockwells-the-gossips/.

239 **Socrates:** Plato, "Protagoras," January 16, 2013, https://www.gutenberg .org/cache/epub/1591/pg1591-images.html.

239 **Rachel Cusk wrote in *Outline*:** Rachel Cusk, *Outline: A Novel* (London: Faber & Faber, 2018).

240 **the narrator:** Salman Rushdie, *Midnight's Children* (New York: Knopf, 1977), 18.

Index

267

Index

Index

First Amendment, 117
Fitzgerald, F. Scott, 84
Fitzgerald, Jansen, 107
Flo Rida, 64
Foucault, Michel, 142
Fox News, 92
Framing Britney Spears (documentary), 103, 122, 123, 126
Frankfurt, Harry G., 235–36
Frantumaglia, 96
#FreeBritney, 126–27
French Revolution, 187
Fuchs, Christian, 136

Gabriel, Mary, 202
Gadsby, Hannah, 193–94, 201, 202–3, 205
Garcia, Monica, 147–49, 157
Gates, Phyllis, 119
Gatti, Claudio, 95–96
Gawker, 83
Gay, Heather, 147–49, 157
Gaylors, 115–16
Gehringer, Fay, 105
gender differences, 5, 40, 42, 52–55, 58
Gerwig, Greta, 72–73
Gevinson, Tavi, 94
Gilot, Françoise, 194 195–201, 203–4
glissando illusion, 223–24
Goatman's Bridge, 176–77
god-sibb, 52–53
Goffman, Erving, 152
Goncharova, Natalia, 193
good gossip, 47, 88
Good Gossip (Sousa), 124
Gordon-Smith, Eleanor, 90
Gosling, Ryan, 72
gossip
    functions of, 11
    origin of term, 52–53
    overview of, 1–5
    use of term, 2, 39, 54
Gossip (Spacks), 139, 234

"Gossip: A Feminist Defense" (Collins), 54–55
Gossip Girl (TV series), 52, 77–80, 88, 91–92, 93–95, 97
gossip magazines, 84–86, 117–18
Gossips, The (Rockwell), 239
Gossip's Story, A (West), 54
"Gossip Trap, The" (Hoel), 3–5
Graham, Billy, 40
Graham, Ruth, 124
Grant, Hugh, 212
Gray, Nancy, 118
Great Gatsby, The (Fitzgerald), 84
Green, Thomas F., 60
Greenberger, Alex, 202
Griffin, Kathy, 193
grooming, 2–3
Grooming, Gossip and the Evolution of Language (Dunbar), 2–3, 4, 15–16, 17, 24–25, 108–9
groupthink, 160
Guernica (Picasso), 192, 202

Haber, Joyce, 120
halo effect, 108
Hamm, Jon, 62, 70
Hammond, Harmony, 202–3
Happy All the Time (Colwin), 233
Harlow, Jean, 118
Harrison, William Henry, 180
Hassan, Adrian, 153
Hatch, Richard, 154
hate speech, 2, 33
Heard, Amber, 70, 123
hearing tests, 213–16
Heidegger, Martin, 54
Heider, Fritz, 17
Helle, Sophus, 11, 19–20, 236
Henningen, John, 156
"he said, she said," 65, 66–68, 156
heuristics, 220–21
Hill, Anita, 67–68
Hilton, Perez, 86
Hine, Thomas, 57–58

270

Index

Index

Index

Index

About the Author

Kelsey McKinney is a reporter and writer who lives in Philadelphia. She is the host of *Normal Gossip* and a co-owner of and features writer at the website Defector. She has worked as a staff writer at Deadspin, Fusion, and *Vox*, and her reporting and essays have appeared in the *New York Times*, *New York* magazine, *GQ*, *Vogue*, *Cosmopolitan*, *Vanity Fair*, and many others. Her first novel, *God Spare the Girls*, was published by William Morrow in the summer of 2021.